THE REAL MESSIAH

STEPHAN HULLER, a Canadian by birth, discovered that he is a direct descendant of Jacob Frank, an 18th-century Jewish messianic leader. Frankist Jews are known to have reconciled Christianity and Judaism as if they always belonged together. Stephan's discovery of his heritage inspired the research that he has conducted over twenty years and culminated in the writing of *The Real Messiah*.

After graduating with a degree in philosophy, he travelled the world and eventually started developing circus talents from Africa. His shows have toured America and he has ongoing African circus productions with Disney, Six Flags and various casinos in Las Vegas.

He is actively engaged with helping the Samaritan people of Israel, an ancient sect of Judaism which numbers about 700 people who currently live in Nablus and Tel Aviv.

THE REAL MESSIAH

The Throne of St Mark and the True Origins of Christianity

STEPHAN HULLER

WATKINS PUBLISHING

LONDON

This edition published in the UK 2009 by
Watkins Publishing, Sixth Floor, Castle House,
75–76 Wells Street, London WIT 3QH

1 3 5 7 9 10 8 6 4 2

Designed and typeset by Paul Saunders

Printed and bound in Great Britain

British Library Cataloguing-in-Publication Data Available

ISBN: 978-1-906787-01-1

www.watkinspublishing.co.uk

To my dearest mother Evelyne Frank for wanting me to grow up to be a writer.

To my beloved wife Lisa for putting up with the hidden financial consequences of that dream.

CONTENTS

List of Plates   xi

Acknowledgements   xii

Introduction   1

1. Marcus Agrippa and the Gospel of St Mark   5

2. Born in Interesting Times   14

3. The Survivor   22

4. An Enthronement   37

5. The Making of a Messiah   49

6. Allied to Monsters   59

7. The Messiah's War   67

8. Lifting the Veil of Veronica   75

9. Inside a Messiah   86

10. The Gospel Truth   94

11. The Super Gospel   104

12. The Hebrew Messiah   112

13. The Seeds of Gnosis   125

14. The Alexandrian Connection   132

15. The 'Mark' of Authenticity   140

16. Heretics and Gnostics   148

17. The Lost Past   157

18. St Mark's Throne   166

19. Decoding the Throne   176

20. Apocalypse Then   184

21. The Agrippa Code   192

22. Kidnapping a Tradition   203

    Concluding Thoughts   219

    Appendix A: The Resurrection occurred on March 25th   227

    Appendix B: Alexandrian Christianity and the Passion
    of 37 CE   231

    Appendix C: Agrippa as the Messiah of Daniel 9:26   237

    Appendix D: Further evidence of the 'real' intention
    of Jesus' ministry   240

    Endnotes   244

    Bibliography   253

    Index   262

LIST OF PLATES

Page 1. Full view of the Throne of St Mark. Courtesy of the Procuratoria of St Mark's Basilica.

Page 2. The top piece, crest or 'corona' of the throne. Courtesy of the Procuratoria of St Mark's Basilica.

Samaritan inscription on the front of the throne. Courtesy of the Procuratoria of St Mark's Basilica.

Page 3. The square Hebrew 'mirror writing' inscription. Courtesy of the Procuratoria of St Mark's Basilica.

A *tzitzit* (fringe). Illustration by Rodney Paull.

A *tallit* (prayer shawl). Courtesy of Richard T Nowitz/Corbis.

Page 4. The tamarisk on the backrest of the throne. The upper image indicates the number of fruit in each group, and the lower image shows these numbers translated into the Hebrew words 'the ninth vision'. Courtesy of the Procuratoria of St Mark's Basilica.

Page 5. The left side of the throne, showing the image of a bull. Courtesy of the Procuratoria of St Mark's Basilica.

Page 6. The right side of the throne, showing the image of a man. Courtesy of the Procuratoria of St Mark's Basilica.

Page 7. The back of the throne, showing the images of a lion and an eagle. Courtesy of the Procuratoria of St Mark's Basilica.

Page 8. The emergence of the palm tree into a rising sun. Courtesy of the Procuratoria of St Mark's Basilica.

Text illustrations (pages 212, 213 and 214) courtesy of Rodney Paull.

ACKNOWLEDGMENTS

Dr Rory Boid without whom this whole enterprise would have crashed and burned. Alan Butler, the best resource a guy with a crazy idea could ever hope for. Dr Bianchini and Nicola Benassi of the Basilica di San Marco for all their help and encouragement. Daniela Rosenberg, truly one of the nicest people I ever met in my life. My late father Dieter Huller for instilling in me a love books. Michael Mann for giving a chance to an unpublished author, and, of course, mister 345 himself, the one for whom all my life's efforts are directed …

From your childhood the light of truth
enlightened you, O Mark, and you loved the
labour of the Saviour Jesus

Traditional Orthodox prayer on April 25th, St Mark's feast day

INTRODUCTION

It is now over 20 years since I first began my research into the life and times of Marcus Julius Agrippa. I now know so much about this individual, his life and times that it sometimes comes as a shock to me to realize just how obscure he is, even to most historians of the period.

Nevertheless it is quite obvious that in his time Marcus Agrippa, the last and certainly the greatest of the Herodian kings of the Jews, was one of the most famous individuals in the known world. Not only was Marcus Agrippa the king of a significant domain, but he was also one of the most important allies that the Roman Empire would ever have in the Near and Middle East. His existence coincided with a pivotal period in Jewish history, coming right at the birth of Christianity, one of the world's most influential religions.

By the standards of any historian, Marcus Agrippa was no 'bit player' in history, but an important mover and shaker in the first century. However, what I came to discover is that he was very much more than a client king to the Roman Empire, and the last in the line of kings that the Jews themselves despised. In this book, I hope to prove beyond doubt that Marcus Julius Agrippa was *the* most important figure in developing Christianity. More than this, he was the acclaimed and almost universally accepted Messiah of the Jews, whose eventual presence in the world had been foretold for centuries.

This assertion, which must seem like blasphemy to many Christians, is not made lightly, and my research is based on the independent accounts of writers from the time. It is true that it has been necessary to strip away the indoctrination and developing dogma that became attached to Christianity in later years, but no such treatment was necessary in the case of many Roman or Jewish commentators – who were after all the people there at the time these events took place.

From the start of my research I was well aware that an acceptance of the major and rather shocking discoveries I had made were dependent on fairly obscure testimonies and upon an ability to 'read between the lines' of what the early Church Fathers had said. What I never expected was that an object would appear that, without any ambiguity what-soever, would give concrete evidence of my findings – an object that anyone in possession of an airline ticket to Italy can view for themselves.

The existence of the Throne of St Mark, still to be seen today in the city of Venice, introduces the world to a view of Christianity that will surprise a wealth of people and deeply shock many more. Its existence also introduces a previously unknown Jewish cipher that could turn out to expose many more facts regarding this most pivotal period of human history. This is the Agrippa Code, and it lies at the heart of what is perhaps the most surprising revelation that modern Christianity has had to face.

Over the last three decades or so, it has come to be realized that there is *something* at the heart of Christianity that is so startling and so damaging to the faith that the Catholic Church in particular has done everything it can to hide the truth from its devout followers. The general consensus has been that this is related in some way to a relationship between Jesus and one of his female followers, Mary Magdalene. The inference is that this liaison led to the birth of a child, the blood of whom passed into some of the most important royal families of Europe.

These theories have lain at the heart of a number of bestselling books and films, including the blockbuster *The Da Vinci Code* by Dan Brown. The leaders of the Roman Catholic Church have remained generally quiet about these theories, as I suppose one would expect them to do, though it now occurs to me that any worries they might have regarding Jesus and Mary Magdalene pale in significance in the light of my own discoveries. This book will turn everything you thought you knew about what Christianity actually is, how and where it developed and who its most pivotal characters are upside-down.

My findings show that Jesus could never have been the Messiah of ancient prophecy that most of his followers past and present believe him to have been. That he is thought of in this way is surprising since he did practically everything he could in his own lifetime to make it plain that he was not the Messiah. Even the many alterations that have been made to the gospel stories have failed to eradicate Jesus' indignation that anyone should think of him in this light.

The intended Messiah had to be a *king* – not simply in a spiritual sense but also in a political sense. His arrival would alter Judaism for ever. It would mean an abandonment of the Laws of Moses and a completely new Covenant with God that would be so all-encompassing that the very Temple of Jerusalem would be abolished and ultimately destroyed.

Thanks to a series of coincidences, and to his birth at a very strategic and important time in the history of Palestine, there was one child whose parentage and position seemed to fit him perfectly for the role of Messiah – who incidentally was fully expected to appear at this time. The individual in question was Marcus Julius Agrippa, and he was fully aware of the significance of his role in life.

By the time he was only eight or nine years of age, Marcus Agrippa believed himself to be, and was accepted as, the once and for all Messiah of the Jewish people – though he espoused a new religious covenant that was open to all, Jew and Gentile alike. He was anointed as such, not only in Palestine but far away in Egyptian Alexandria – undoubtedly on that very throne with its ciphered inscriptions that can now be seen in Venice. His position as Messiah had been proclaimed by Jesus himself during his own ministry, and Marcus Agrippa was present at Jesus' crucifixion. After a near-miraculous escape from custody himself, Marcus Agrippa went on to manipulate events in and around his own homeland for the next seven decades.

Agrippa's story is one of intrigue, incest, one of the most famous love affairs of its time, and a genius for power-play and influence that any dictator or monarch would have admired. Together with his sister/wife

Berenice, Marcus Agrippa went on to become the acclaimed Messiah of Jewish tradition. Berenice also enjoyed a long and tempestuous romantic liaison with none other than Titus, eventual emperor of Rome. And from the embers of the burning Temple in Jerusalem, a brand new religion was born.

The reasons why this story is not at all known today turn out to be as intriguing as the story itself. Changing times in Rome, continued instability in Palestine and a need for the new religion to vie with its competitors in the Roman world eventually marginalized Marcus Agrippa and elevated Jesus to a rank he never claimed and which he repeatedly shunned. Christianity as we know it today is a combination of garbled facts regarding the life of the real Jesus, the biography of Marcus Agrippa, and an overlay of Persian mysticism for good measure.

This book opens a door to the very start of Christianity – a door that can never again be closed. Unlike other books to which it might seem related, its findings are based on hard facts and historical realities, not slender conjectures. Twenty years of solid research have brought together a wealth of evidence that, to any fair-minded reader, will expose as lies and half-truths much of what we have been brought up to believe. The contents of the Agrippa Code will show that the world's most influential religion is based on a series of deliberately fostered misunderstandings and misinformation.

CHAPTER 1

MARCUS AGRIPPA AND THE GOSPEL OF ST MARK

In the twilight of Byzantine rule in Egypt, a simple but quite beautiful object was removed from Alexandria and taken to Constantinople for safety by order of the Byzantine emperor Heraclius. The object in question was an alabaster chair, said to be the legendary Throne of St Mark, the Christian apostle and gospel writer who, it was claimed, had once presided over the infant church in Egypt. This object must have represented the beating heart of the early Christian community of North Africa. It was so important that it had almost certainly been placed in a prominent position close to the High Altar of St Mark's Church in Boukolia, Alexandria, likely the old headquarters of the Egyptian Christian faith. Despite its significance, once it was taken away to Constantinople the throne was soon forgotten. It joined a long list of precious relics associated with St Mark that simply 'disappeared' in the period leading up to the Islamic conquests of the region.

We know very little about the throne once it left the African continent, which considering the chaos of the period is no surprise. Wild transformations to the political map of the Middle East were taking place almost on a daily basis during the seventh century CE. At one moment Persian armies were chasing Romans out of Egypt, and in the next instance Europeans were regaining control of the region and marching upon the gates of the Persian capital. Then, at the very moment when the Romans seemed to emerge triumphant, the whole balance of power became upset with the arrival of the Muslim horsemen from Arabia.

Where the throne went and what tumultuous events happened around it, we can never know. All we can be certain about is that, at some stage, it found its way from Constantinople to Venice in Italy. It was most likely already there by 828, when a brand new church was built to house the physical relics of St Mark, spirited out of Alexandria from under the noses of its Muslim rulers. The details of both the throne and the relics are sketchy and, perhaps because in both cases theft was involved, only legends remain. What is probably true is that St Mark's skeletal relics were smuggled out of Alexandria in barrels filled with pork. However how the throne was stolen and shipped to Venice remains a mystery.

As we shall see, Venice had very good reasons for adopting St Mark as its patron saint and, theft or not, there can be little doubt that the Venetians rescued the throne from historical oblivion. At the very least, scholars are in possession of something from the early Alexandrian Church that they can study. Few if any academics doubt the throne's antiquity. Most place it at least as old as other surviving Egyptian 'martyr thrones' – that is, to a period no later than the fourth century CE. Nevertheless a paper by Dr Rory Boid of the Centre for Religion and Theology at Monash University in Melbourne, Australia, has pushed that date much further back in time.

I had the good fortune to come across St Mark's Throne when I was on vacation in Italy some years ago. I had long since given up working on a graduate paper on the origins of St Mark when I finally came to visit the Basilica San Marco, the church built for St Mark's relics in Venice. Of course I was interested in the church and its treasures, though I never really took any of the European claims regarding various patron saints all that seriously. I was actually quite prejudiced against any Christian tradition that had a European origin. To my way of thinking at the time, the Catholic Church and its version of the Christian story probably had little to do with the reality of Jesus and his Palestinian followers.

So it was that I wandered into the museum thinking I would have an interesting though probably not especially illuminating afternoon.

However, what I came away with was nothing short of a powerful life-changing experience. Within a few minutes of looking at St Mark's Throne the hairs on the back of my neck stood on end. I may not have known much about the Christian Church in Europe at that time, but it did seem to me that this particular object was something very special. The throne has had the misfortune of being lumped together with countless other so-called Christian relics that the Venetians plundered from the Byzantine Empire. In the minds of most academics that studied these artefacts, there was little difference between the Throne of St Mark and, say, a piece of the True Cross.

Nevertheless I was left with the immediate impression that this alabaster chair was very different from everything else I saw in the Basilica that day. It isn't especially large – in fact, as we will presently see, it is actually a *miniature* throne. Its carvings are interesting but also fairly crude, and of course it has suffered somewhat from the ravages of time. But the reality is that the throne's claim to ancient antiquity depends almost entirely on an inscription in Hebrew found at the front of the seat. Not being experts in Hebrew, let alone having knowledge of the changes the language has gone through over the centuries, most historians and art critics who have looked at this inscription have been at a disadvantage. True, even the simplest English guidebooks in Venice acknowledge that there is 'a Hebrew inscription engraved in mirror-writing across part of the front of the seat', but what the guidebooks do not tell us is what these ancient Hebrew letters say when they are viewed the right way round.

In order to really understand what the inscription on St Mark's Throne is saying one would need to be conversant with the alphabet of a fringe community from Israel – an ancient people, but a group that now only numbers around 700 persons. As luck would have it, I happened to know a good deal about this culture because I had already traced a tradition of the 'writings of Mark' back to them. This small group, the last survivors of a once proud nation on the fringes of Judaism, are called 'the Samaritans', the same community referenced in the parable of the Good Samaritan in the Christian gospels.

The Samaritans believed, and still believe, that they are the true guardians of the original and ancient traditions of Israel. This is part of the reason why the Samaritan Hebrew alphabet looks so different from its modern Jewish counterpart. Whilst the Jews have updated their script in fairly recent times the Samaritans have been scrupulous about keeping theirs unchanged. Samaritan Hebrew looks almost deliberately archaic, as if to reinforce the conservative credentials of this most ancient of sects.

What really stood out for me as I contemplated the inscription on that day in Venice was the fact that I clearly recognized three Samaritan letters at the end of the Hebrew inscription. These were not in mirror writing but rather the correct way round. In reverse, these letters could also be read as part of the Hebrew script that everyone had recognized. Because of my past experience with Samaritan script, in a flash I knew who had created this cryptic sentence and what it was trying to tell a totally unsuspecting world.

My wife was with me that day and I pointed out to her that the Samaritan letters spelled a word or phrase roughly equivalent to '(the) year' or 'year one'. She could find no reference whatsoever to the Samaritan letters in our guidebook and I guessed that I had spotted something that had not been noticed before. The question was, how could I make the fact known to the world?

I contacted the office of Dr Biancini, the Director of the Basilica, and I asked him if anyone else had documented this detail regarding the throne. Dr Biancini told me he didn't think so, but he kindly sent me a series of photocopied articles about the throne. These were all in Italian so I couldn't read them at the time. Nevertheless I was so puzzled by my discovery that I contacted Benny Tsedaka, one of only a small number of Samaritans left in the world today and a man who also happens to be one of the leading authorities on the ancient culture of his people.

I e-mailed him a picture of the throne and in particular its inscription and, by the time I arrived home, he had already confirmed what I had originally suspected. The letters were definitely of Samaritan origin. With this confirmation I wanted to take matters one step further. I needed to make sense of my discovery and, if possible, to incorporate it into my existing theory about the origins of St Mark from a specifically Samaritan setting.

I had worked for so long without any concrete results on my theory about St Mark that I had resigned myself to never being able to express my ideas to other people in a meaningful way. I had long given up on the whole idea of ever writing a doctoral thesis on the subject and had turned my attention to other matters. Now, suddenly, quite out of the blue, fate had offered me a piece of tangible evidence that made sense of my long years of research.

This chance encounter became the basis of a long journey that led me out of Venice and back to my original passion, to uncover the origins of Christianity as a product of the life-experience of the first evangelist. In a nutshell, my idea was that St Mark's composition, as the first of the four gospels of the New Testament of the Bible, had been misunderstood by generations of scholars. During my years of research I had stumbled across a generally ignored passage from a virtually forgotten Christian manuscript, which said that the original Gospel of St Mark wasn't really about Jesus as much as it was about the author himself.[1] Mark had only used Jesus as a device to convey claims regarding his own status in Palestine and beyond.

Gradually I began to remember things I had lost touch with in those months and years after I had left the academic libraries of the university. Even though I could never have literally known about the Throne of St Mark before I saw it with my own two eyes, it seemed as if the author of St Mark's Gospel himself was talking to me through the inscription etched into its alabaster.

In those first few weeks I had only a tempting clue regarding the inscription on the throne. But clearly the full import of the message lay in all of the letters, and these represented words I still had to interpret. Fortunately the three Samaritan letters I could read gave me some clear suggestions.

By good fortune and years of past research I knew a great deal about the Samaritan people. I was aware that at one time the Samaritans dominated religious life in Israel. In fact, in the period that St Mark was supposed to have been active, soon after the crucifixion of Jesus, the community of Samaritans had recently emerged from a long, dark period and would soon enter what would be their last golden age.

Scholars estimate that in the first century CE the Samaritan community probably had over two million members across the Mediterranean region. Their largest community outside the Near East was located in Alexandria.[2] While few other people had ever suspected that St Mark was connected with the Samaritans, I had been convinced of the likelihood for years. While it is true that Samaritans don't appear anywhere in the text of St Mark's Gospel, ancient claims regarding their importance resurface in other sources. It is simply a matter of keeping one's eyes open, together with sourcing ancient manuscripts that are sometimes so unknown or obscure that even experts fail either to read them, or else they don't realize their importance.

I soon came to appreciate that the significance of the throne and its message could shake the Christian Church to its core. In all probability, the Venetians had at least guessed at its importance, though for them there was also great significance in accessing a form of Christianity that wasn't dependent on Rome. The relics of St Mark, together with the throne, went some way towards granting Venice theological immunity from the decrees of the Vatican and from the remnants of the old Roman Empire.

Everyone in antiquity understood that there wasn't simply one 'brand' of Christianity. There had originally been countless sects; each possessing its own gospel, claimed to be the 'true word of God'. The earlier we go back in time towards the first century, the more it becomes apparent that most of these early sects developed from Samaritan converts to Christianity.[3]

A little research quickly showed that the Hebrew and Samaritan letters carved onto the throne could not have been a medieval addition, and they also bore testimony to the throne's true age. The presence of the Samaritan letters completely rules out any chance of a later forgery. Any Christian artefact with Samaritan writing has to be extremely old because no Christian, across nearly 2,000 years, would have had any desire or even sufficient knowledge to connect themselves to the Samaritans. Even from a strictly Jewish perspective, the Samaritans were not only mistrusted by orthodox Jews, they were and still are the theological equivalents of lepers in the religious history of Israel. From a Jewish perspective, to construct even a simple phrase using letters associated with the Samaritans would be nothing short of a blatant declaration of one's heterodoxy.[4]

From a Christian point of view, it is likely that the only reason the inscription survived as long as it did is thanks to the fact that Samaritan scripts were and are almost totally unknown and unrecognized, even by experts. The dearth of academic papers on the subject of the Throne of St Mark proves this to be the case. After a long period of sustained Samaritan conversion to Christianity from the time of Jesus' ministry onwards, the developing Roman Church slammed the door on the Samaritan community.[5] A Christian writer says that, by the middle of the second century, 'almost all the Samaritans' had come over to a particular 'heretical' doctrine. The Church went on to declare effectively that Samaritans and their teachings should not be part of the general assembly of Christians.[6]

But it is almost certainly more complicated than a misunderstanding of ancient traditions and archaic forms of worship. There was something about this neo-Samaritan branch of Christianity that was seen to be dangerous to the greater Christian community. The Roman Church was jealous of its own practices and came to hate what it eventually saw as 'independent heretical traditions'. As a result it did everything it could to stamp them out.

If the Venetians of the ninth century CE had fully understood the meaning of the letters on the front of the throne, they would have realized the true origins of their new patron saint. The inscription stands as clear testimony that the apostle Mark, the man most scholars believe wrote the first gospel, was connected with this banned tradition and, as such, instead of being a Christian icon, was a heretic.

As I flew back home to America, I put the photographs I had obtained of St Mark's Throne on my lap and tried to absorb the true import of these discoveries. 'How,' I asked myself, 'did a "wandering disciple" of Jesus such as St Mark, supposedly sworn to a life of modesty and impoverishment, *ever end up being enthroned?*' There is clearly an underlying paradox about the two concepts. To be sure, we hear of other apostolic thrones in Catholic Christianity. Some appear relatively early, such as in the mid- to late-second century CE. Nevertheless this throne is, by all accounts, the earliest of them all – likely dating back to the life of St Mark himself. Apostolic thrones that appeared later were almost certainly copies of St Mark's Throne.

Thrones are created for kings, popes or archbishops, but such a concept seems to be well out of kilter with the humility and poverty that is usually suggested for the early Church Fathers.

Of course, some people might argue that the throne could have been made *after* St Mark passed away, perhaps in order to emphasize his rule in heaven, alongside the other apostles. However a careful examination of the inscription it carries negates this possibility.

There was absolutely no doubt that the Samaritan letters spell out the words 'the year'. My original hunch regarding the presence of Samaritan letters was confirmed by Dr Rory Boid. The term 'the year' in Jewish comprehension refers to the concept of the Jubilee, a messianic celebration that happens in the year immediately following a recurring period of 49 years. The cycle of Jubilees is calculated, in the minds of Jews, from the time of Creation, or from the entrance of the tribes of Israel into the 'Promised Land'. All that was required now was for me to determine which Jubilee year the inscription referred to.

On the surface at least, the dating should be quite easy. Tradition has it that St Mark had a very short period of ministry. The Jubilee would clearly have to be dated to the period between Jesus' crucifixion and the period of the Jewish War (*c.*66 CE). With such a limited scope, it necessarily implies that there could only have been one Samaritan Jubilee that would have fallen within the brief lifespan of St Mark.

Samaritans keep a detailed chronicle of all the events in their community since its inception. We can tell from this that the only 49th year that fits into the life of St Mark is that which occurred in 37 CE.[7] This means that the Jubilee referred to in the inscription necessarily occurred in 38 CE. As Dr Boid later confirmed, the Samaritan letters on the throne represent a proclamation announcing the reason for the throne's creation and the fact that it was used for the purpose for which it had been created – that is, an enthronement that took place upon it in that year.

As my story unfolds, I will offer the reader a fuller description of the throne. I shall explain how some of its figurative carvings have been deliberately altered to try to make what must always have seemed to be a fairly controversial object somehow fit into orthodox Christianity. I will also deal with one of the greatest puzzles regarding the throne: why is it so small it could be used only by a fairly young child? I will fit the throne in its rightful place historically speaking, as the true seat of a genuine king who was declared to be the promised Messiah of the Jewish faith. On the way I will demolish forever all conceptions that the form of Christianity we see across the world today is actually based on the true origins of the faith.

It can now be demonstrated that the Throne of St Mark is one of the most important historical artefacts ever to survive the turmoil of a turbulent history. Quite clearly, if the Church Fathers had ever realized how significant it actually is, we can be sure that it would not still be on display for anyone to see. Taken together with a veritable mountain of substantiating evidence that also exists from ancient documents, the throne allows me to tell, for the first time, the true story of early Christianity. It is a tale of intrigue, manipulation, tempestuous love and ultimate betrayal. It puts into perspective so much we all thought we understood about our beliefs, demonstrating how much the search for personal power has influenced humanity's relationship with God.

Our first port of call is to that very period of history in which the throne was made. We need to look at the world as it was in the period leading up to 38 CE, and ultimately at one person who will become increasingly important to our story. His name is Marcus Julius Agrippa and he owed his very survival to the caprices of a succession of mad emperors.

CHAPTER 2

BORN IN INTERESTING TIMES

On March 26th in the year 37 CE an old man lay gasping his last on the beautiful island of Capri. This was no ordinary passing because the dying man was none other than Tiberius, Caesar Augustus, emperor of Rome.[8] Few people would mourn the end of this particular emperor because, although Tiberius had started his long reign amidst great popularity and high expectations, he had eventually retired to his Capri palace, leaving all decisions regarding the empire to underlings. They ran both Rome and its empire for their own ends. The remote emperor took little interest in affairs of state after 26 CE and, for the remainder of his life, until 37 CE, he remained something of a recluse.

When the end of this particularly unpleasant man seemed imminent, it didn't take long for the vultures to circle. The one man who was most impatient for the last breath of Tiberius was the young Gaius Julius Caesar Augustus Germanicus – now better known by his nickname of 'Little Boots', which in Latin is Caligula.

Having disposed of anyone who might stand in his way, the 25-year-old Caligula was anxious to rule. It was even suggested by the historian Tacitus that Caligula or, more likely one of his allies, disgruntled that the emperor apparently died and then came back to life, smothered the old man with a pillow.

Far away to the east, another young man would no doubt have given a cheer had it been known that Tiberius was about to expire. This individual, Marcus Julius Agrippa, represents the central theme of this story. An understanding of his place amidst the machinations and power-play of Roman rule is central to all that follows.

Marcus Agrippa was born of a kingly line, though at the time of Tiberius' passing his prospects of kingship, or even survival, were not good. At the time he was, like so many other people, a pawn in the great chess game that Roman imperial power represented for millions across its vast empire. His home, the region of Judea, was certainly not central either to Roman aspirations or to wealth. Yet this one young man would indirectly be responsible for so much that now represents our history and the world we know today.

The Roman province of Judea (more properly *Iudæa*) represented a significant area of the Levant – that area of the Near East bordering the Mediterranean Sea and extending inland beyond the valley of the River Jordan – often referred to today as 'historic Palestine'. It also included the adjoining parts of what we now know as Syria. The Romans had laid claim to the area since 63 BCE, at the end of a protracted series of battles known as the Third Mithridatic War. At this time Rome had also won Syria and made it a province, though the creation of greater Iudæa did not take place until the year 6 CE. The Hasmonean Kingdom, which encompassed Judea, had become a client of the Roman Empire and had eventually been declared a province.

This comparatively small part of the globe may have been fought over more than most other locations around the world, and it was certainly no stranger to conflict long before the Roman Empire had even begun. As early as the late Bronze Age a specific ethnic group, originally probably of Kurdish origin, began to lay claim to areas of the Levant. It is argued by some historians that these people were not as unique as Bible accounts suggest, in that they differed very little, if at all, from the Canaanites surrounding them.

Old Testament accounts suggest that a loose confederacy of tribes, after spending a fairly long period as client peoples in Egypt, returned to the region and laid claim to large sections of the Levant which would eventually become the historic home of the Jewish nation. Eventually the region became a home for the Jews, who prospered at first under a succession of powerful kings. Amongst these was Solomon, who built the first Temple in his capital of Jerusalem around 970 BCE.

What set Solomon's people apart from their neighbours was their worship of a single, all-powerful deity. This religious preference would be a thorn in the side of the kingdom of Israel for centuries to come.

The United Kingdom of Israel was eventually beset with internal strife. This led, around 931 BCE, to a geographical division in which the north became known as Israel and the south Judah. These were two different kingdoms that not only warred with each other but were now also more susceptible to attacks from outside.

First, in 721 BCE, the northern kingdom of Israel was attacked and defeated by the Assyrians. For some time Judah held out against successive onslaughts, but it was finally captured by the Babylonians. In about 586 BCE Judah's capital, Jerusalem, was stormed by the forces of the Babylonian king Nebuchadnezzar and a large section of its population was carried off into slavery. At this time the first Temple in Jerusalem was destroyed.

Later, in 538 BCE, Cyrus, king of Persia, on overcoming Babylon, allowed the captives from Jerusalem to return to their former home, which many of them did. It was after this time that Jerusalem became a mighty city within its own great walls. The returning Jews never entirely forgot their Babylonian exile and, though a single deity remained essential to Jewish religion, exotic additions meant that religious belief and practice had altered substantially.

Around 332 BCE the region was conquered again, this time by the forces of Alexander the Great. Alexander was a Macedonian Greek, and Greek influence within the region began to show quite rapidly. However, since Alexander died young without an apparent heir, fighting to gain control of parts of his vast empire began almost immediately. In the case of the Levant the eventual successor was Ptolemy I. He had been one of Alexander's most trusted generals and immediately became *satrap* or ruler of Egypt. In 320 BCE Ptolemy captured the province of Judea, and the rule of the Egyptian Ptolemies began.

Eventually control of the region fell to another dynasty, the Syrian Seleucids, also successors to Alexander. In 169 BCE the Seleucid king,

Antiochus IV Epiphanes, outlawed Judaism and defiled the Jerusalem Temple. The scene was now set for an uprising that would, for a short while, set Israel free.

Under the general Judas Maccabaeus, an army was created that eventually triumphed over the forces of the Seleucid monarchs. After achieving liberation the region retained autonomy for about 100 years. During this time the Hasmonean kings were the ruling dynasty, having sprung from Simon, the Great High Priest. Despite Roman rule from 63 BCE, Hasmonean rule did not end until 37 BCE, at which time kingship of Jerusalem came to a man by the name of Herod.

Herod was the son of Antipater the Idumæan, a former aide and official to the last of the Hasmonean kings. When Roman rule became inevitable, Herod sided with Pompey the Great. Despite some problems when Pompey fell and Julius Caesar came to power in Rome, Antipater's son Herod was made chief minister of the province of Judea.

It is reported that, at the incredibly young age of 15, Herod was already the governor of Galilee.[9] However, his life was not without its problems and, after temporarily losing his power, the Romans reinstated Herod in 37 BCE. He went on to enjoy a reign of 34 years in total.

Herod the Great, the first of the Herodian kings, was not a particularly likeable or pleasant individual, even by the standards of ancient kingship. His position was not always secure and he was often beset with family intrigues and rivalry. His title 'the Great' is due mainly to the immense building programmes he inaugurated, not least of which was a rebuilding of the Temple in Jerusalem. Herod undertook this almost Herculean task in the hope that it would somehow ingratiate him with his subjects but, to many, it did not elevate him in the least. The basic problem was that, to most of the inhabitants of Jerusalem and the surrounding area, Herod was not a proper Jew.

Herod's father, Antipater, was an Idumæan, a people that had sprung from the Edomites who in turn, according to Biblical traditions, had descended from Esau. The Edomites had often fought against the Jewish nation and, at the fall of the First Temple, they had attacked Judah, defiling and looting the Temple – a crime for which many Jews would never forgive them. Eventually the Idumæans converted to

Judaism, but the most religiously inclined members of society in Judah never accepted their position as full brothers in faith. For this reason a large proportion of Herod the Great's subjects never considered him to be a Jew.

Despite his many failings, Herod the Great must surely have been a man of some personal charm. He managed to extricate himself from a number of tight corners in his relationship with Rome, with a mixture of fast talking and well-timed bribes. Octavian, later to become Augustus, the first true emperor of Rome, had as much right as anyone to dislike Herod, who had supported the assassins of his uncle Julius Caesar. Despite this, Herod had managed to bring Octavian round and eventually stood high in his favour.

In 4 BCE Herod the Great died. What followed was a protracted period of rebellion and fighting across the region, as successors vied for his throne and influence. The result was that Roman legions had to be brought in to stabilize the situation and thousands of people were killed in the disturbances as Jewish anger at the Roman presence constantly boiled over into armed insurrection. Ultimately Judea became a province of the Roman Empire.

The son of Herod the Great, Herod Antipas, was born sometime before 20 BCE and, at his father's death, he had been proclaimed ruler of Galilee and Perea. Seeking to ingratiate himself with the new Roman emperor Tiberius, Antipas built a fabulous capital on the western shores of the Sea of Galilee, which he named Tiberias. He was no more trusted as a true and devout Jew than his father had been, and things were made worse by the fact that it was claimed the new city had partly been built on an ancient Jewish burial ground. As far as orthodox Jews were concerned, this made the place unholy and unclean, so for many years large numbers of people refused to enter Tiberias.

Herod Antipas never attained the full status of kingship. Part of the reason he remained a mere tetrarch was that he was always offending the religious sensibilities of the Jews. No matter how hard Antipas tried to seduce his subjects by attempting to live a Jewish life, following its holy days and celebrations, he remained unpopular and proved himself to be little more than an outsider to their faith. It probably wouldn't have mattered what Herod Antipas had done to reassure the people under his rule because, as long as he remained a puppet of Rome, he was regarded as a failure, especially in the eyes of the most radical amongst the Jews.

As unpopular as Herod Antipas remained, he was successful insofar as he managed to retain his titles and holdings for four decades. But it is towards the end of his reign that the waters of history become murky. What is known is that, like many of his relatives, Herod Antipas found it difficult to live within his means, relying heavily on the practical and financial support of his Roman overlords. He had been fairly well supported by the emperor Tiberius, but when Tiberius died in 37 CE, Antipas seems to have made an immediate enemy of his successor, Caligula. For whatever reason, Herod Antipas was immediately stripped of his wealth and titles when Caligula became emperor of Rome.[10] Conflicting reports say that he was either summarily executed or banished to a remote part of the empire.[11]

The fate of the Roman world was now in the hands of Caligula, a 25-year-old man who, at first, ambitiously set out to correct many of the evils of the previous administration. He freed many people put under suspicion by Tiberius, recalling exiles and reimbursing those wronged by the imperial tax system. Caligula's popularity was immense – and it is with the accession of Caligula that we ultimately come to the chief character of our story. Among those liberated from their former imprisonment was a young Jewish prince named Marcus Julius Agrippa, of whom the new emperor seemed to have been inordinately fond.

Unfortunately it is at the very moment we want to get a clear image of Marcus Agrippa that our already murky picture of the period becomes almost unrecognizable. We face a dilemma in that there are two different historical opinions about Marcus Agrippa – but whoever he was Caligula quickly raised him in terms of both prestige and power. As Daniel Schwartz notes, the 2,000-year-old Jewish tradition knows of only one King Agrippa.

Any historical reconstruction exclusively based on these sources assumes that the same Marcus Agrippa who was liberated from prison in 37 CE went on to destroy the Jewish temple in 70.[12] This is completely out of step with the European tradition, based on the single authority of the writer Josephus and preserved by the Christian

Church, that there were two Marcus Agrippas – that is, a father and son of the same name.

Which tradition should we believe? In the end it is very difficult to be certain either way. How can we completely ignore a living tradition passed on from generation to generation in favour of an undoubtedly corrupt text? Flavius Josephus, upon whom much of our understanding of Palestine at this time depends, cannot be considered the most reliable of witnesses. For starters, he was formerly a Jewish rebel leader who eventually came over to the side of the Romans. For this reason alone his testimony is suspect. There are many different surviving versions of Josephus' history, any one of which may be authentic, but many of which have clearly been altered to suit the prevailing circumstances and needs of later generations.

Outside the traditions encouraged by the Catholic Church we can piece together an equally plausible argument in which Marcus Agrippa emerges as the son of Herod's eldest son Aristobulus and a woman named Salome.[13] As will become clear, he emerged into the pages of history in the right place and at the right time to transform Judea into something new and utterly dangerous. *Something* about his life must have been threatening enough to future generations of Roman rulers and to the Christian Church that they initiated a deliberate campaign to assault his place in history.

Indeed it is only in Josephus that we find it suggested there were two Marcus Agrippas. This is a preposterous idea in Jewish terms, since it is impossible amongst Jews for father and son to bear the same name.[14] Though Josephus is an invaluable guide as to many of the circumstances surrounding the Jews at this period, he could not have been considered an impartial historical source in his own time, and certainly not in the many alterations that have been made to his original works over the centuries.

According to this alternative hypothesis, by 37 CE the one and only Marcus Julius Agrippa was still a relatively small child, and he had survived a turbulent life before Caligula came to power to rescue him from probable obscurity. Marcus would become the most powerful ally of Rome in the oft-troubled region of Judea. But in his long life he would show himself to be much more than a simple acolyte to successive

Roman emperors. In the fullness of time, Marcus Julius Agrippa would become the last Jewish king and, to many thousands of his followers both then and subsequently, he would also be the promised Messiah. If we want to find the person for whom the alabaster throne in St Mark's Basilica in Venice was actually created, it is to Marcus Agrippa that we should look.

CHAPTER 3

THE SURVIVOR

Marcus Agrippa was born into some of the most turbulent times that Judea and even the Roman Empire ever knew. The confusion and danger of his earliest years reflect the disaffection in the Jewish homelands, destructive rivalries within his own family and the peculiarities of a dynasty of Roman emperors, most of whom would today be deemed clinically insane.

Putting aside the erroneous contrary claims of Josephus, according to all Jewish commentators Marcus Julius Agrippa was born around the year 29 CE. His parents were Aristobulus and Salome, the king and queen of the small Syrian principality of Chalcis, a region Marcus would one day himself inherit.[15] Aristobulus was a direct member of the Herodian family. He was most probably killed on the instruction of Herod Antipas in early 37 CE.[16]

Like all sons of client kings, Marcus would have spent much of his early life in Rome.[17] This was a deliberate policy of the empire, working on the assumption that the presence of these foreign princes in Rome would be likely to assure Rome of their parents' cooperation. At the same time, the children could be educated and indoctrinated into Roman ways.

Marcus Agrippa's problems, and ultimately his salvation, came as a result of a peculiar and very coincidental set of circumstances that took place when he was about eight years of age.[18] Having recently lost his

22

father, he had been living with his mother Salome and his sister Berenice in Rome. While the family was in Rome, the city fell under the spell and influence of Caligula, the emperor in waiting. Tiberius, away in Capri, was growing weaker by the moment, but he singularly refused to die. This inevitably led to rumours and counter-rumours regarding the succession. Rome was always filled with intrigue and it seems certain that there were suggestions that some of Caligula's supporters were planning to murder Tiberius and place Caligula, the darling of the Roman people, onto the imperial throne as soon as possible. Somehow Marcus and his family became embroiled in these plots, or at least they were considered to have been implicated. Discretion being the better part of valour, they left Rome and returned to Galilee, where the historical record shows them to have been around the time Tiberius finally died in 37 CE.

Marcus Agrippa was in prison in *Jerusalem* as Tiberius lay dying in Capri.[19] This state of affairs had nothing to do with any plotting that had taken place in Rome.[20] If this had been the case Marcus, and most likely his family, would have been housed in the dungeons of Rome, or else they would have gone the same way as most of Tiberius' enemies.[21] Marcus Agrippa's incarceration in Jerusalem was clearly connected with local events in Judea. Unfortunately there is no surviving testimony, except the later words of Marcus himself, to show why an eight-year-old boy was languishing in a prison cell at the same time that rule in Rome was passing from Tiberius to Caligula, though we can surmise from later events how this state of affairs had come about.

As always under Roman rule Judea was in a state of turmoil in 37 CE. The money extorted from the Jews by the empire crippled the local economy and brought great hardship to ordinary people, most of whom were already incensed at the thought of their homeland being under the heel of the Roman boot. Under normal circumstances the authorities would have been able to exercise their usual control over the populace but, at this particular time, there were other factors at work that brought the area closer and closer to armed insurrection.

The chief amongst these sprang from the almost fanatical interest the Jews had in numbers. As I observed earlier, in the calendar of the Samaritans the year 37 was the 49th year in the calendar cycle that was so important to the community. It was approaching the time of the Jubilee.[22] The Jubilee was by far the most important religious holiday in ancient Judaism; it embodied its original messianic spirit during the age of the Temple. The surviving Jewish faith has abandoned this once most sacred observance, explicitly commanded in the Laws of Moses. Undoubtedly this arose as a result of imperial pressure in the years immediately following the death of Agrippa.

Jubilees were significant because of the importance of the number seven in Jewish religion and tradition. It was at the end of every seventh year, itself a reflection of the seven days of the week, that Jews were expected to forgive the transgressions of their neighbours, settle debts or even forgive their debtors, and to carry out certain religious practices relating to the use of farmland. If seven years was an important time-period, how much more significant was seven times seven, or 49? As a result of ancient tradition and practices, the 50th year Jubilee itself was even more important than the 49th year. It embodied the concept of being 'one greater' than the holy number of 49.[23]

During the Jubilee, a time of great celebration, slaves were released (a fact that would have a great bearing on all that followed) and past debts had to be written off once and for all.

Since the most ancient of times, and during the various occupations of their homeland, the Jews had been looking for a Messiah – a mighty king sent by God to free them from captivity and establish a new Law throughout Judea and beyond. The Messiah's coming had been foretold by the prophets, most of whom had been specific about the fact that the deliverer would appear under very particular circumstances. It was certain that his arrival would coincide with a Jubilee[24] but, in a history that spanned many centuries, why would anyone think that the Jubilee year of 38 was the one forecast in the Old Testament? There are a number of possible explanations, but chief amongst them has to be the state of the sky at the time.

Most ancient peoples were sky-watchers. Almost all of them accepted that there were seven planetary 'watchers' hovering over this world – that is, the five traditional visible planets Mercury, Venus, Mars, Jupiter and Saturn, plus the two 'lights', the Sun and Moon. The ancients' need to keep track of the Sun and Moon in order to facilitate a good understanding of the calendar, mostly for agricultural purposes, was paramount to all farming communities. In the majority of cultures priesthoods developed whose major function was to track the heavenly bodies and regulate a civil calendar that always seemed to be getting out of step with the Sun's and Moon's position. It was inevitable that these sky-watchers would eventually turn their attention to the planets of the solar system and to the starry backdrop of the heavens. Actually it was vital because, unless the sky could be successfully split into known and recognizable segments, it would be impossible to track any heavenly body across the heavens.

This is how the zodiac constellations developed. These were groups of stars that straddled the ecliptic, the path that the Sun, Moon and planets seem to follow in the Earth's sky. Such groups of stars were given names and in most Western cultures there were twelve of them, reflecting threefold subdivisions of the four quarters of the year between the solstices and equinoxes, in the Sun's annual movement around the heavens as seen from Earth.

Humanity's understanding of planetary movement became more and more important and the ever-superstitious Jews were as susceptible as any race to the belief that the planets had a significant bearing on human affairs. In all ancient religions, the Sun, Moon and planets were associated with gods and goddesses and, although the Jews had abandoned polytheism in favour of a single deity, they had never totally forgotten their ancient pagan past. So even within the one-God concept of Judaism, the truly archaic practices of humanity showed through. In particular, as the work of Christopher Knight and Robert Lomas demonstrates, the Jews were fascinated by the interplay of the Sun and the planet Venus.[25]

Venus, at its 'great brilliance' when it is almost as far as it can get from the Sun, as seen in our sky, is the brightest object in the sky apart from the Sun and Moon. It alternates between rising before the Sun as a morning star and setting after the Sun as an evening star. According to Knight and Lomas, there were occasions during Venus' cyclic relationship with the Sun when it was seen as being crucially important to Jewish tradition.

On regular occasions Venus can be observed over a period of days to cross or conjunct with the Sun, changing from morning star to evening star or vice versa. Astronomically, this arises from the fact that Venus, inside the Earth's orbit, appears to swing back and forth, to the left and the right of the Sun, as it orbits around it. Such conjunctions, when it crosses in front of or behind the Sun, happen at various times in the year, but only rarely would it take place when both the Sun and Venus rose due east above the horizon at dawn. The Sun rises due east on two days each year, in late March and September, at the spring and autumn equinoxes respectively. So this involves the coincidence of an equinox with a conjunction of the Sun with Venus.

The chances of Venus conjuncting or crossing over the Sun at such times is low, only a 1-in-182 possibility for each transit of Venus across the Sun. Since such transits take place only every 300 days or so, the likelihood of the transit taking place on the day of the equinox is not at all high. But it wasn't the actual passing of Venus across the Sun that intrigued the Jews and many other cultures; rather it was those occasions when Venus was first seen to rise before the Sun as the morning star, before its light was overwhelmed by that of the Sun as it moved closer to it.

In the last few days before Venus crosses in front of the Sun, it rises just before dawn in the halo of the rising Sun. For a brief period the normal bright silver Venus appears blood red (because sunlight is shining at that time on the far side of Venus, as seen from Earth) and it was this phenomenon that seemed to have fascinated the Jewish priests. Knight and Lomas suggest that, when such an occurrence took place at the time of the equinox, the priests took it as a sign associated with kingship. In other cultures it represented the symbolic union between the gods and goddess, so that they could consummate their association ahead of the spring. Jewish fascination with the Sun and Venus may therefore have stemmed from a time before their monotheistic religion developed, or it could have been a legacy from the days of the Babylonian captivity.

Just a day or two before Tiberius died, on March 26th 37 CE, Venus rose just ahead of the Sun at the spring equinox. This must have seemed like a potent sign because, as Knight and Lomas point out, the event had been historically linked to the arrival of the promised Messiah.

That such an astronomical event also took place in a 49th year must have seemed like proof positive that the time of Jewish deliverance was at hand.[26]

Just to make sure that my suspicions regarding the Sun–Venus association were correct, I got in touch with my friend Alan Butler, a leading authority regarding ancient cosmology and its symbolism. He had cooperated with Knight and Lomas in their own research. Butler checked his astronomical programmes and was able to confirm that Venus did in fact rise just ahead of the Sun at the time of the spring equinox in 37 CE.

If the Jews knew about these important cosmological events, we can be certain that the Romans were also aware of them. It might not be too far-fetched to suggest that they were a motivating factor in the aged and sick Tiberius being dispatched on March 26th, so that he could die with the disappearing morning star, and his successor, Caligula, could be inaugurated under Venus as an evening star. More likely still, Caligula wanted his reign to start on, or close to, the time of the equinox, which was a powerful cornerstone of the year. It was associated with the beginning of spring and the rebirth of nature, as well as being the start of the calendar year. Thus, from the 'winter' of the old and despotic Tiberius' reign would come the 'spring' of the young hero Caligula.

But the Romans must also have realized that these events could easily spell the start of a major uprising in Judea. The governor of the region, Pontius Pilate, would have been on his guard. It is therefore not in the least surprising that a few contenders for the rank of Messiah appeared in Judea around this time, though there is one that stands out above the others. He was a man of Galilean ancestry known to us as Jesus. Even in the surviving Catholic gospel traditions at our disposal today, there are many utterances from Jesus' own mouth to demonstrate he *did not* claim to be the Messiah. One Christian sect in antiquity was associated with this position – the community of the 'Marcionites' or *Marqionai* in the original Aramaic, whose name is properly rendered in English as 'the followers of Mark'.[27] These ancient 'heretics' happen also to be consistently identified as being 'addicted' to astrology and sky-watching.

It is the Church Father Irenaeus, writing in the late second century, who gives us our first clue that this community that 'preferred' Mark's gospel emphasized that Jesus was not the Christ. His successors tell us that these same 'followers of Mark' cited seemingly familiar gospel passages with slightly amended punctuation, grammatical emphasis or missing words. The overall effect of these changes was that they reflected an understanding that Jesus denied he was the Messiah – he came as a herald for someone else.

Let me give you an example. When Jesus warned his disciples of the coming destruction of the Jewish Temple, he did so by emphasizing in our gospel texts that, 'Many will come in my name, claiming "I am Christ", and [they] will deceive many.'

We have learned to follow a distinctly Catholic reading of this material in which Jesus is understood to be declaring to his followers that only he was the true Christ of Israel. It uses these words in particular to emphasize that Jesus seemed to want us to avoid accepting anyone else's messianic claims after his crucifixion and resurrection.

Yet what the authorities *don't tell us* is that there was a slightly different reading of this same passage circulating in ancient times, and this happened to support the theological understanding of the 'followers of Mark' regarding Jesus as a herald for someone else. Let us note the differences in the earlier Markan tradition. The first clear difference was that the words 'in my name' did not appear there. This was clearly a Catholic interpretation. The next difference was that the original material was punctuated differently, without the presence of quotation marks – they didn't exist in antiquity.

As such, when all the dust settles, we see Jesus was understood in the Markan tradition to have simply declared to his followers that, 'Many will come claiming that I am Christ and [they] will deceive many.'

In other words, the followers of Mark understood the historical Jesus to have warned against those who would claim that he (Jesus) was the Messiah – the very position promoted by our surviving Catholic tradition.

The original followers of Mark understood the gospel to have been deliberately constructed in such a way that certain key words, which could be translated as 'the other' or 'another', 'little' or 'little one', 'child' and 'the Son' had special significance for the original gospel writer. These terms were – according to these original Markan authorities – developed as a part of a mystery religion that understood Jesus to have shielded his revelation of 'another Christ' from all but his truly initiated readers.

The gospel writer deliberately portrayed Jesus as either distancing himself from, or rejecting the claims of, some in his inner circle that he was the deliverer of Jewish prophecy. Rather than claiming to be the Messiah, Jesus declared himself to be the *herald* of the Messiah.[28] Jesus knew that the real Messiah would have to be a king – someone who enjoyed not only spiritual stature but also temporal power. The fact that successive generations of Christians have perverted the very Jewish concept of the Messiah in order to *make* Jesus fit the bill takes nothing away from what both ancient writers and the prophets of the Old Testament claimed for their prospective deliverer.[29] Few people at the time would have seen Jesus as a likely candidate, unless of course he had been able to surround himself with a suitable army, throw the Romans out of Judea and be proclaimed as the new king of Israel.

But no matter how hard one looks, there is very little evidence that this was ever Jesus' intention and, unless this was the case, he could not be the Messiah. Christians may protest that the Jesus of the scriptures we have at our disposal today was born of the House of David and in David's city of Bethlehem, but these facts alone would not have made a strong case for a *Jewish* Messiah, even if they are to be believed. On the other hand, as we shall demonstrate shortly, a near-universal chorus of ancient Jewish and Christian sages acknowledge Marcus Julius Agrippa, in some form or another, as the awaited Jewish Messiah. Indeed the understanding is woven deep within the fabric of our surviving historical information of the destruction of the Jewish Temple.

At the least one ancient historical text connects King Agrippa to the Passion. At the very moment his armies had surrounded Jerusalem in year 69, the oldest surviving manuscripts associated with the Jewish historian Josephus connect these events with matters described in the gospel. The author – or more than likely, a third or fourth century Christian editor adding new material to the original text – says that the decision on the part of Jews to free another man in place of Jesus 'sealed their fate' in the present age. He asks:

What were you thinking would happen, when with your own hands you put your salvation on the cross, with your own hands you extinguished your life, with your own voices you banished your supporter, with your own attacks you killed your helper, except that you also put your hands against yourself? You have what you sought, you have snatched away from yourself the patron of peace, you sought for the arbiter of life to be killed, for Barabbas to be released to you … Thus salvation departed from you, peace went away, calm left off, rebellion was given to you destruction was given. Recognize you that Barabbas is alive today, Jesus is dead.[30]

In other words, the decision to free 'Barabbas' and to execute Jesus has now come back to haunt the Jews. The text of 'Josephus' can be read as if the author was arguing that this 'Barabbas' eventually grew up to *cause* the cataclysmic end of Judaism.

So was Marcus Agrippa 'Barabbas'? I am not the first person to suggest that Agrippa was somehow connected with this name. Scholars as diverse as Paul Wendland, Alfred Loisy and S L Davies have all wrestled with the underlying relationship that resurfaces time and again from literary texts of the period. It will be enough for now to outline my argument that the gospel writer, as well as the entire tradition associated with him, knew who this 'Barabbas' was. 'Barabbas' was the author himself, Marcus Julius Agrippa.

It is my belief that the tradition took for granted a certain number of facts related to the period. It acknowledged that Jesus was preaching to large gatherings of people in Galilee as the 49th year approached.[31] They also knew that his historic ministry lasted only for that one year.[32] The gospel shows that Jesus was tremendously popular and worried the authorities on that account. Things came to a head when Jesus transferred his sphere of influence from Galilee and came to Jerusalem.

From the perspective of Pontius Pilate and those Jews who ran the Temple, who had somehow to rub along with the Romans, Jesus suddenly became a great threat. Having a troublemaker marching up and down the provinces was one thing, but when he came into Jerusalem itself and began to harangue the priests of Judaism it was a different matter altogether. Something had to be done, and it was arranged that

Jesus and his immediate followers should be surrounded and apprehended at night, when the throng had died down and it would not be
so dangerous to take him.

The gospel tells us that this incident took place in the Garden of
Gethsemane.[33] People have since claimed that Jesus' location was in the
environs of Jerusalem, but there is no proof to support this.[34] A rival
claim for the events of Jesus' arrest developed among Samaritan Christian sectarians, saying that it happened near to or on Mount Gerizim,
the holy mountain of the Samaritans.[35] There is also a very good reason
why it was subsequently covered up.

Indeed, when all the surviving evidence for the assignment of the
days, month and year of the Passion are brought together, they necessarily point to only one possibility: March 23rd–25th in the year 37.
These arguments are laid out in detail in Appendix A and B. With this
proper dating of the central event in Christianity, Marcus Agrippa can
effectively be placed in Jerusalem within a day of the recorded 'burial'
and 'resurrection' of the Christian Messiah.

It is my profound belief then that the oldest gospel tradition – that
associated with the aforementioned 'followers of Mark' – understood
that little Marcus Agrippa and his family were present with Jesus on
that first night of the Passion. There is very compelling evidence suggesting that this was an integral part of the original gospel claim in the
late first and early second centuries. It would follow that this tradition
must have understood that, at the time of Jesus, little Marcus Agrippa,
though doing his best to escape, was also taken into custody and
marched off by the authorities.

Some ancient traditions emphasize that Mark was indeed present as
an eyewitness of *all details*, including the trial and persecution of Jesus,
which made its way into his gospel. In other words, Mark did not use
any other source for his account of what happened during the Passion
other than his own personal recollection of that event. This means in
effect that, as Jesus was sent for trial, he certainly did not stand alone as
the accused. By his side was the eight-year-old Marcus Julius Agrippa –
probably one of the most embarrassing prisoners the Roman authorities could have held without express orders from Rome. I shall explain
as we proceed.

The idea that another associate had to have been present during the trial matches exactly what ancient Jewish sources tell us happened during trials of Christian sectarians. They typically interrogated one 'heretic' while another listened outside. The way the gospel is written supports this assumption. Various traditions identify a shadowy figure variously identified as 'the other disciple', 'the beloved disciple', or Mark, who was called John, as the only believing eyewitness to Jesus' whole ordeal.

In fact Mark being present at the Passion makes sense. How could anyone have believed his account of these details if he had not witnessed them first-hand? In the very same way the gospels tell us that, immediately after this trial in front the Jewish authorities, two prisoners were marched before Pontius Pilate – albeit none of them mentions explicitly that they were Jesus and Marcus Agrippa. Rather, the text presents the two miscreants as being Jesus and the aforementioned Barabbas. Our most reliable sources identify him only as 'a well-known prisoner'.[36] In some ancient traditions both men are called 'Jesus' – *our* Jesus and Jesus Barabbas. It was this cryptic Barabbas figure who was spared execution, while Jesus was condemned. The exact circumstances by which this happened are now obscured, almost to the point of being unrecognizable.[37]

In at least one of the surviving gospel narratives, it is claimed that there was an established Roman tradition of allowing one prisoner of the people's choice to go free at the time of the Passover. This claim has been almost universally rejected by scholars and seems to be a total invention on the part of the gospel writers.[38] So how can we account for the release of the second prisoner Barabbas in the gospel story? What could it have been that allowed a known criminal – someone already condemned to death – to be allowed to walk free and unpunished? The presence of the impending Samaritan Jubilee, with its tradition of allowing slaves and prisoners to be released, is the only suggestion that makes any sense, especially in light of the fact that at least some Christians understood that the arrest took place on Mount Gerizim, the Samaritan holy mountain.[39]

Reading between the lines of his own later testimony, it seems clear that Marcus Agrippa was originally an integral part of the Passion story, even if he is never referred to by name in the gospels. Here he is identified only as Barabbas. Why the secrecy and why Barabbas? The explanation for this will be revealed in Chapter 5.

Pilate addressed the assembled crowd on the night of Jesus' arrest, asking those assembled one very telling question that reinforces my belief that his actions were tied to the Jubilee and its traditions. Pilate said: 'Whom will ye that I release unto you? Barabbas, or Jesus which is called the Messiah, the King of the Jews?'[40] We have already noted that the 'followers of Mark' often read passages with a slightly different grammatical emphasis. It is noteworthy then that the same sentence here could just as easily be read as: 'Whom will ye that I release unto you? Barabbas or Jesus? *Which is called the Messiah, the King of the Jews?*'

In other words, the gospel might have put forward the question as if it were a referendum, in which the prisoner that the crowd chose to release was the person acknowledged as their Messiah. It is this understanding that stands at the heart of the old text of the Jewish historian Josephus, cited earlier.

The crowd had a choice between Jesus and another figure whose identity was deliberately shielded by the author of the gospel. The irony of Pilate's question, 'Which is called the Messiah, the king of the Jews?', is now lost on us. As we have already demonstrated, the ancient followers of Mark paid careful attention to the grammatical structure of each sentence in the text. Their version of the gospel had Jesus repeatedly deny that he was the awaited Messiah.

The original gospel set the stage for Jesus' trial by having the Jews initially make an entirely *false* charge that Jesus claimed to be their king, the Christ of the Jews. Even a superficial reading of the gospel demonstrates that Jesus never made a statement to this effect. If Jesus had done so, one would presume that the evangelist would have preserved it. The proper point then was that the real Messiah had been standing in front of the Jews throughout the ministry of Jesus – he was little Marcus Agrippa, also known as Barabbas. Their minds were blinded so as not to see the truth of the gospel.

The original statement of Pilate forced the Jews to release the one who *did not claim* to be the Messiah, the king of the Jews, thus liberating Barabbas. This is reflected in the old Latin Gospel of Nicomedus where Pilate asks:

> Which of the two, then, do you wish that I release to you? The people answered: release to us Barabbas. Pilate says: What then shall I do with Jesus? They say: Let him be crucified ... for he called himself the Son of God and a king. (The Gospel of Nicodemus, ch 9)

The point is that no one in their right mind could ever have claimed that the Jesus who died and went to heaven represented anything resembling the realized expectations of the Law and the prophets. This interpretation was forced onto Christians in a later period of their history through a systematic manipulation of the original gospel. The real story, as we have already emphasized, had the Messiah survive by the will of God, 'blinding' the Jews into getting the wrong man.

No one can claim to know exactly what happened next. One might suppose that both men suffered gravely as a result of the capture at the foot of the Samaritan mountain. It was now the morning of Friday March 23rd. Jesus was scourged and ridiculed before being nailed to a cross. By popular tradition he remained alive throughout the remainder of the day until the late afternoon, but it would not have been considered correct in the eyes of the law for crucified criminals to remain alive into the following day, the Sabbath, commencing at dusk.

Those supervising the execution would break prisoners' legs at such a time, so that their death would come more quickly. But according to tradition they found that Jesus was already dead. Again, according to the gospel accounts that remain today, Jesus' body was taken down and placed in a tomb nearby.

From dusk on March 23rd until the morning of March 25th we have no gospel account for what was taking place. As far as little Marcus, called Barabbas, was concerned, we can only work backwards from the central assumptions of the gospel. This concluding narrative is called 'the Passion' in English, which is typically traced back to the Greek word *pathe* in some form or another. Yet the ultimate source of the word is found in the Aramaic *yetzer*, which happens to have another meaning deliberately ignored in later Catholic interpretations. The same term can also be translated as the 'transformation of Christ' implying that someone else became Christ through Jesus 'emptying' on the Cross.

The idea is consistent with various statements found in the apostolic writings where Christ's death, burial and resurrection led to the transformation of the community as a whole. It was undoubtedly also for this reason that the Christians were frequently identified in the early Jewish writings as the *notzrim* or 'the transformed'. The one unmistakable point that emerges from the gospel is that 'Christ' only appears openly among the first Christians after Jesus was crucified.

It is not important to consider what the early Christians understood by 'the Resurrection'. For the moment it is necessary to see that, whoever this Christ was, he did not appear in the same physical shape or form as the living Jesus. The gospel tells us that Christ was only 'recognized' by the 'marks' on his body; a clear signal to Jesus' disciples that their master had come back from the dead in another body.

It is worth noting that the surviving Gospel of Mark ends abruptly before explaining any of these critical details. It's as if someone doesn't want us to know what happened after Mary discovered the miraculously opened and empty 'tomb'. Yet if we fast-forward to that post-Resurrection scene, the followers of Mark tell us that they happened to be in Mark's house while Mark's mother Mary was present too. They also tell us that, during the crucifixion, Mark and his mother were there when Jesus uttered his last words. So in many ways it doesn't take a genius to see what was taken out or obscured from the original gospel – all meaningful clues to allow us to piece together Mark's place beside Jesus.

As I see it there is a trail of evidence, beginning with the arrest narrative and ending with the events after the Resurrection, that demonstrate Mark's role as the real Messiah of Christianity. The pattern in the gospel finds its ultimate historical vindication in the parallel coincidence that one particular Mark, Marcus Agrippa, also claims in a separate tradition to have been released from imprisonment in Jerusalem on the morning of Sunday March 25th. It is an unmistakable confirmation of gospel miracle as historical fact.

We see the claim surface in a historical document associated with

Agrippa from the last years of the reign of his imperial benefactor Caligula (*c.*40). Marcus declares to his lord and master Caesar:

> You released me when I was bound in chains and iron ... you abated from me a fear of death continually suspended over my head; you received me when I was almost dead through fear; you resurrected me as if from the dead.[41]

The dating of Marcus Agrippa's release is absolutely certain – March 25th, 37 CE – as it was taken by Marcus Agrippa to be the first action of Caligula, as he was about to take the imperial throne.

So we can see that, though Jesus had died, Marcus had literally escaped death by the skin of his teeth. In the developing allegory that turned the whole event into a contemporary reworking of a vitally important story from the Old Testament, this fact would prove to be of crucial importance.

CHAPTER 4

AN ENTHRONEMENT

I t may seem to fly in the face of established convention to suggest that
the crucifixion of Jesus took place in March of 37 CE, or moreover
that Marcus Agrippa and his family were followers of Jesus. Yet what
are the reliable alternatives? (See Appendix A.) It is far more amazing
to realize that 'official Christianity' lacks any consensus as to when the
Passion actually occurred. Why is this the case? What was it about the
truth of Jesus' crucifixion that seems to have made ancient Church
leaders so vague and defensive?

I believe there was a secret so dangerous to the developing Catholic
Church that the exact circumstances of Jesus' crucifixion were ultimately
suppressed. However I remain convinced that with a little diligent
searching the true facts surrounding the Passion can be rediscovered. All
that is required is to assemble a mosaic of ancient testimonies, to help
restore what was originally present in the hearts and minds of believers
before the construction of Christianity as we see it today.

To this end it is important to recognize that the proof of any historical event or series of events cannot be ascertained by looking only at a
handful of facts. Rather, the final picture is somewhat like the poles of
a teepee, which individually could not support anything, but owe their
strength to the fact that there are many of them, all dependent on each
other. Just as the finished structure of a teepee becomes strong when all
poles are in place, so it is with historical clues relating to a specific event

or period in history. I hope that by the time all my 'poles' are in place, my readers will admit that the story I have to tell makes sense.

Little by little I hope to demonstrate that the number of strange associations and events linking the historically proven figure of Marcus Agrippa and the almost entirely fictitious St Mark are not coincidences at all. They occur because Marcus Agrippa and St Mark are one and the same person. I also want to show that it is entirely plausible that someone other than Jesus could have fulfilled the role of the Christ after the events of the Passion, and that the person who did so was Marcus Agrippa.

As a first step along this road we can look to see what St Mark's Throne has to tell us about events that took place in the months following the Passion, and how everything that took place was intimately related to Old Testament prophecies that the Jews and Samaritans simply could not ignore.

Marcus Agrippa claimed to have been 'resurrected' in Jerusalem in 37 CE, but contemporary historical texts tell us that, by the summer of the following year, he arrived in Alexandria for a visit that would shake the contemporary world. This, I am certain, is linked directly to the Throne of St Mark in Venice.

The existence of the throne poses a number of questions that the art experts who have previously looked at the artefact have never thought to ask. They have never questioned whether its existence relates to a specific event in history, though of course they are not in possession of the evidence provided by its various carvings.

We know the throne to be extremely old, and I will provide evidence to prove that it is even older than most experts have suggested. In Christian terms it is an anachronism, but if it was specifically made for Marcus Agrippa the dilemma it presents is resolved. I hope to prove beyond reasonable doubt that the Throne of St Mark was specifically manufactured for a ceremony that took place in Alexandria when Marcus Agrippa went there in 38 CE.

This visit, and in fact Marcus Agrippa's very rise to the rank of king, were only made possible because of the caprices of the new emperor of Rome, Caligula. But what was it about Caligula that made him *care* about this little prince from so far away? At this juncture it is worth pointing out that Caligula himself had the strangest upbringing imaginable. As a young and impressionable youth he spent a great deal of time with his uncle Tiberius on the island of Capri. There he was subjected to the many perversions and sexual distractions with which the aging emperor surrounded himself. Not least amongst these, and well documented by historians soon after his death, was his predilection for being surrounded by pretty little boys.

These unfortunate children were to be found all through Tiberius' palace on Capri. He called them his 'minnows'. They would swim naked around him in his swimming pool and nip his legs, and it is suggested that there was no perversion that was too great to feed Tiberius' appetite. This was no place to bring up an impressionable and highly-strung young man such as Caligula, and it is therefore probably no surprise when we look at Caligula's own life and reign as emperor that he showed himself to be eccentric to the point of madness. Undoubtedly his background and the influence of Tiberius played a part. Later events indicate that he had inherited his uncle's preference for sexual perversions.

By all accounts, Marcus Julius Agrippa was a positive charmer – a capricious child who could easily have endeared himself to Caligula. To be more charitable, we have to remember that, in addition to the peculiar circumstances into which Caligula had been immersed, his life was also surrounded by potential treachery, the caprices of an uncle who was all-powerful and, if his contemporaries are to be believed, barking mad, together with the possibility that he could fall from favour at any time and be executed at a moment's notice. Caligula may simply have been in need of friends who didn't want to kill him.

Though Marcus Agrippa was younger than Caligula he was astute and insightful. Both he and his mother, the calculating and intelligent Queen Salome, would have known Caligula very well while in Rome and would have backed their hunch that he would one day be emperor. Caligula was always susceptible to flattery. It can be seen from later correspondence that he received plenty of this from the young Agrippa. What other sort of relationship Caligula and Marcus Agrippa may have shared we will never know and, for the sake of modern sensibilities, it is probably better that we do not.

Some years after his deliverance, Marcus Agrippa would communicate his gratitude to Caligula and would place his good fortune and survival directly at the feet of the new emperor. Whether this was entirely true probably doesn't matter. Caligula responded positively and though as his reign went on he became far less predictable and even clinically mad, the young emperor never forgot his little friend nor failed to heap ever more honours upon him.

In fairness, historians have not always been entirely unbiased in their assessment of Caligula, especially at the start of his reign because when he came to power Caligula was popular. For some months he showed a genuine desire to improve the lot of the empire and to be worthy of the honour that had come to him. His preference for Marcus Agrippa may therefore have had a more practical aspect than simply the affection of a peculiar young man for his catamite. In any event, Marcus' elevation by Caligula did turn out to be fortuitous for both of them.

Tiberius died on March 26th, 37 CE. Two days later the imperial throne was handed to Caligula. The crucifixion of Jesus and the imprisonment of Marcus Agrippa had taken place three days earlier, on March 23rd. This means that the date of Christ's resurrection must have been on March 25th, just a day before Tiberius' death. On March 28th, Caligula was proclaimed emperor of Rome and almost immediately the fortunes of Marcus Agrippa changed dramatically.

If there is any conjecture about the place of Marcus in the story of Jesus' ministry or the Passion, there is absolutely none about his rise during and after 37 CE. All commentators from the period bear out that Marcus Agrippa's enemy, Herod Antipas, was stripped of his titles, and that the governor of Judea, Pontius Pilate, was removed from office and shamed.[42] According to Josephus this was on account of his poor handling of a Samaritan messianic gathering – which sounds suspiciously like the events surrounding Jesus' arrest, trial and crucifixion.[43]

The young Marcus Agrippa then received an honour from Caligula that had not been forthcoming since the days of Herod the Great. Marcus was given the province of Syria, together with lands formerly ruled by his uncle Philip. Even more importantly, he was allowed to hold the title of 'king'.[44] Although he owed a loyalty to Rome, at eight years of age this little boy became a reigning monarch, with all the rights and privileges implied.[45]

Yet something very odd occurred immediately after Marcus' elevation.

Instead of instantly setting sail to take possession of his kingdom, little Marcus prevaricated for over a year. The question that scholarship has been unable to answer is why he waited so long to claim his prize. Why, together with his family and advisers, did he not seek to take up the reins of power for such a long period? To make matters even more puzzling, even when Marcus and his entourage did set sail, they did not travel immediately to Marcus' new kingdom. Instead they travelled to Alexandria in Egypt. This visit to Alexandria seems to have been undertaken amidst considerable secrecy, but why should this have been the case?[46]

At first glance there is little assistance to be gained from the surviving historical record. What we do know is that, at the time Caligula came to power, the Roman prefect of Egypt was Aulus Avilius Flaccus. We know that Flaccus had been appointed by Tiberius and, according to the Jewish writer Philo, he had been for some years an exemplary governor. However, at about the same time as Caligula came to power a sudden change seems to have come over Flaccus. If the testimony of Philo's is to be believed, Flaccus appears to have transformed overnight into one of the great Jew-haters of all time.[47]

The whole scenario seems quite odd because there were many influential Jews in Alexandria, and Flaccus must have worked alongside them without trouble or incident. As we shall see, there may have been grievances between the Jews of Alexandria and its mainly Greek population, but the historical record does not indicate any major conflict until a period that coincides with the visit to Alexandria of Marcus Agrippa in 38 CE.[48]

Jews and Samaritans were an integral part of the fabric of Alexandrian culture. They had been present in the region ever since Alexander the Great had created the city that took his name. Alexander had intended that the city should become one of his chief ports and administrative centres, but that required a large and effective population. The new port drew individuals from across his huge domains, and that included Judea. So by the time Caligula became emperor, Jews were an essential part of a community that was crucial to Rome. In fact, Jews in Alexandria had been so successful that their community had become partly autonomous. They enjoyed their own districts, worshipped at their own synagogues and generally ran their own affairs – though at the same time they contributed to the running of Alexandria and formed an important part of its overall administration.

Alexandria was for the most part a very good place for Jews to live and work. That was, until Agrippa came to visit. The Jewish writer Philo, who himself lived in the city, denies the inference that the Jews were welcome and well treated in Alexandria. What is undeniable is that Marcus Agrippa's presence in the city suddenly threw the place into an uproar. It was at this time that the Roman governor Flaccus suddenly and inexplicably allowed an orgy of violence to take place against the Jewish citizens of Alexandria.

Any hope of trying to sort out the details of what actually took place from a superficial examination of the available evidence is necessarily doomed to failure. The only source we have to hand regarding the troubles comes from apologists for Marcus Agrippa – and in particular Philo of Alexandria.[49]

The fact that Flaccus was sacked from his position and called back to Rome, supposedly as a result of his 'mishandling of the situation', is hardly convincing proof that Agrippa should be totally exonerated of any provocation. In contrast to the love and affection Caligula clearly had for Agrippa, he had serious doubts about Flaccus, the prefect of Egypt, who had formerly been a staunch supporter of Tiberius. Flaccus had also previously been implicated in the plot that had been hatched against Caligula's outspoken mother Agrippina. This had ultimately led to her arrest and execution during the reign of Tiberius.

We might also suppose that Caligula had been receiving news about the way events were turning out in Alexandria and, though he may not have had any special concern for the safety of the one million Jews in Egypt, it was absolutely necessary that Alexandria continued to function effectively. The economic importance of Alexandria to the Roman Empire cannot be overstated.[50]

It is quite unfortunate that our sole surviving source on the subject of what happened in the city in 38 is Philo, a leader of the Jewish community in Alexandria. This is partly because Alexandrian tradition suggests that Philo was Marcus Agrippa's uncle.[51] So we find ourselves facing the daunting task of trusting the testimony of a family member when deciding whether the anti-Jewish riots in Alexandria in 38 were made worse or even inspired by Marcus' presence. Neither is Philo the easiest historian to read. His style is evasive and he is so verbose that it is easy to forget what his point in any particular section actually was. Of course this could be entirely deliberate. Philo makes the reader forget what the original question may have been by deviating into irrelevancies and abstractions. In other words he is the ancient equivalent of the modern politician.

Later in the book I will include a full chapter on Philo, whose presence and influence is pivotal to all that subsequently took place. But for the moment I will merely state that there is something about his description of events that took place in Alexandria in 38 that doesn't ring true. His account is filled with eloquent phrases and clever explanations but, in the end, it completely fails to offer any explanation as to *why* there was a persecution of the Jews in Alexandria at the same time as Marcus Agrippa's visit to the city.

Reading between the lines of what Philo has to say, it does seem that Flaccus might have suggested at the time that it was the visit of Marcus Agrippa that had caused all the trouble. Historians tell us that Flaccus was the first to give his explanation to the emperor concerning the riots and killings, but it is likely that little Marcus Agrippa was present in Rome when Flaccus gave his testimony.[52] Philo, Marcus' uncle, appeared in Rome much later, undoubtedly having been alerted to what his enemy Flaccus had reported and ready to counter his evidence.

Philo tells us that, after setting sail, Marcus Agrippa slipped his ship into the port of Alexandria, deliberately avoiding telling Flaccus that he had arrived.[53] From the Roman governor's point of view that was proof enough that Agrippa and his entourage were up to no good. According to Flaccus, Marcus Agrippa deliberately avoided signalling his arrival because he was secretly trying to stir up the Jewish population.[54] Philo vehemently denies these claims but, interestingly, he offers no coherent explanation as to why his relative needed to keep up a cloak of secrecy during his visit to the city.

When we carefully examine Philo's testimony, it is clear that he is merely counter-spinning Flaccus' original charges against the Jewish community, made during Flaccus' original audience with Caligula in the winter of 38 CE.[55] There are countless examples that prove this. Time and time again we see Philo has little choice but to acknowledge some of Flaccus' claims – yet he inevitably manages to turn Flaccus' arguments to his advantage.

As an example, when Flaccus claimed that the Jews were amassing armour and weapons in Alexandria, Philo acknowledged that this assertion was true, but only in part. Yes, stockpiles of arms were present in Jewish homes, but they were 'defensive weapons'. He similarly explained away Marcus Agrippa's failure to signal the appropriate authorities of his arrival by saying that his relative was 'so modest' that he didn't want the governor to make a big fuss over his arrival![56]

It is quite obvious that Philo avoided being truthful about events in Alexandria in 38 CE. With hindsight it is quite evident that he created a veritable smokescreen in order to obscure his and his family's involvement in the 'Jubilee plot'. This leaves us with the distinct possibility that Flaccus was telling the truth after all. Marcus Agrippa's visit to Alexandria was arguably the spark that set off the powder keg in the city.[57] Attacks immediately came against Jews and Samaritans that Flaccus allowed to take place, or else encouraged, in his role as governor.

So we are back to our original question: why did Agrippa come to Alexandria? The immediate answer could be that Agrippa was there to expand his influence, but almost certainly not only in his capacity as the king of a nearby state. We can imagine that his ever-ambitious mother Mary Salome was behind this effort. It has to be borne in mind that Agrippa had been 'miraculously' released from prison just a few months earlier. This was still the Samaritan 'year of favour', when messianic fervour was running high. Flaccus certainly seems to have made reference to this desire on the part of the Jews and Samaritans to accept Agrippa as their king when he made his now lost report to the emperor. Evidence for this occurs constantly in the writings of subsequent generations of Greek Alexandrians. It appears to be true that Marcus Agrippa, though more likely at this time his mother, was accused at the time of wanting to take over the world![58]

To get to the heart of the matter, we have to look at one particular piece of 'evidence' put forward by Philo. He says that Marcus Agrippa, the utterly modest young man he describes, was jeered in the streets by the Greeks of Alexandria, who were egged on by Flaccus. Philo suggests that shouts of '*Marin*' and '*Carabus*' rang out, both of which were words that are utterly meaningless in Greek but extremely significant in their Aramaic context.[59]

In Aramaic, a language not spoken by the Greeks of Alexandria, *Marin* means 'Lord', and many scholars have connected it to the cry of maran'atha – 'Our Lord has come!'.[60] Scholars also think that *Carabas* is an insult – a deliberately corrupted form of *Barabbas* – that is, the familiar messianic title from the Passion narrative that we examined in the last chapter. Philo's explanation of events also suggests that, having insulted Agrippa verbally, the Greeks then proceeded to abuse him in their actions too. Philo tells us that the Greeks caught hold of a poor, unfortunate fool from the streets of the city. He tells us:

> Setting him up there on high that he might be seen by everybody, [they] flattened out a leaf of papyrus and put it on his head instead of a *diadem*, and clothed the rest of his body with a common doormat instead of a cloak, and instead of a *sceptre* they put in his hand a small stick of the native papyrus which they found lying by the wayside and gave to him; and when, like actors in theatrical spectacles, *he had received all the insignia of royal authority, and had been dressed and adorned like a king*, the young men, bearing sticks on their shoulders, stood on each side of him instead of spear-bearers, in imitation of the bodyguards of the *king*, and then others came up, some as if to salute him, and others making as though they wished to plead their causes before him, and others pretending to wish to consult with him about the affairs of the state.[61]

I have deliberately emphasized words in the account indicating that what was being described here was a mock enthronement ceremony. Philo is as good as admitting here that there was indeed an enthronement in the city during Agrippa's visit, but in his version it didn't involve Agrippa – it was perpetrated by a mob of Greek hooligans who were trying to stir up trouble, eventually succeeding in their aims. Soon the poor Jews were being massacred and chased from their homes.

In all the commentaries I have ever read regarding this story, nobody seems to have noticed how utterly implausible Philo's argument is, when read in its totality. First, Philo says Marcus Agrippa was absolutely innocent, simply a victim of his own modesty. He then suggests in effect that it wasn't Agrippa's enthronement that caused the rioting and that the rioters themselves set up a parody enthronement that incited the anti-Jewish riots. These are both utterly ludicrous arguments that disguise the real truth originally reported by Flaccus. There was an enthronement in Alexandria, and it *was* a real one, designed for Marcus Agrippa. What else would have created such hatred from the Greeks of Alexandria?

As for the mock ceremony that took place in the streets, it is quite possible that Philo was reporting a real event here too. For example, when Triumphs were held in Rome to honour a victorious emperor or general, the vagrants, beggars and low-life of the city would invariably hold a parallel Triumph of their own, taking on a form very similar to the mock enthronement Philo describes. In other words it was a deliberately staged parody of something that had actually taken place.

The existence of the Throne of St Mark, which we know for certain was originally from Alexandria, lends weight to the belief that, in his estimation, Flaccus was quite justified in his accusations that the Jews were responsible for the disturbance. We should not forget that Marcus' arrival in Alexandria came only months after the events of March 25th in 37 CE. It was still the year of the Samaritan Jubilee and, what is more, Agrippa was on his way to receive the domain of his grandfather Herod the Great. If there was ever a time to celebrate Agrippa's rise to power, this was certainly the right occasion.

There can be little doubt that Marcus Agrippa was indeed crowned during his visit to Alexandria and – as I will demonstrate presently – it was the symbolism associated with this event that caused the Greeks to riot against his presence in their city.

Whatever the actual truth of the situation, it did Flaccus no good. Within a very short period of time Caligula had dispatched a squad of soldiers with a centurion at its head. In a totally clandestine operation they arrived in Alexandria at night and, in disguise, they made their way to Flaccus' palace. They found him at supper with friends and with a flair that would have done justice to any modern operation of its sort, they brought Flaccus out of the city under arrest before anyone really knew what was happening. The timing of the operation was significant and almost certainly no coincidence.

The Roman troops arrived at the festival of *Succot*, or Tabernacles.[62] It is at this time that Jews remember the period they spent living in the wilderness. In line with even modern traditions, Philo tells us that it was at this time of year that many Jews would normally have been living outside their houses in tents. Yet it is important to note what Philo *doesn't* say. The year 38 CE was considered by many to be the true year of the Samaritan Jubilee. The month of *Succot* represented the actual starting point of the celebration of the Sabbatical and Jubilee years.[63]

Did the Jewish and Samaritan citizens of Alexandria recognize little Marcus Agrippa, not only as the king of Syria, but also as something much more significant to their own lives and aspirations? The existence of the so-called Throne of St Mark, surviving to this day in Venice, most certainly seems to indicate that they did. There were strong reasons, explained in greater detail in the next chapter, why many Jews at this time might have looked towards Marcus Agrippa for their deliverance.

From the point of view of the Alexandrian Jews and Samaritans, what better time could there be for the Messiah himself to turn up and release them from the bonds of oppression and persecution? There is good circumstantial evidence to give cause to believe that it was in this year that Agrippa formally acknowledged himself as the awaited Christ of the Jews, and Philo's strange reference to the Hebrews of Alexandria deciding not to set up tents that year to celebrate the Feast of Tabernacles is also very suggestive.

Hebrews could not simply stop carrying out the Laws of Moses, even with persecutions going on around them. If this were true we would expect every generation of Jews throughout the ages to have abandoned various practices because it was too hard to continue following the customs of their ancestors.

There is another reason why the booths were not set up that year. It is well established that the setting up of tabernacles was connected to the expectation of the future appearance of the Messiah. Why would they need to set up the tabernacles if they considered that the Messiah had just arrived and made himself known – not merely in Judea but now also in Alexandria? In the mind of the inhabitants of Alexandria all of the old rituals and practices were now to be abandoned, because the year of the Messiah's arrival had come.

We can imagine the flurry of activity that took place in some local workshop at the news that Marcus Agrippa had arrived in the city. An order was placed for a throne suitable for the Messiah. Of course it could not be a full-sized throne because the Messiah in question was only nine or ten years old. But the finished product had to have all the symbolism, all the ornamentation and all the archaic mystery that was only right and proper for the once and future Messiah – the elected of God, who would rescue Jews and Samaritans and show them the way towards God's new world. As we shall come to see, the figurative carvings on the throne confirm absolutely that this was its original purpose. Together with the Hebrew and Samaritan inscriptions and another secret cipher of pictographic, numerical and alphabetical construction, they leave no doubt that, in the comprehension of the Alexandrians of the period, the Messiah was at hand.

If the *Succot* of 38 CE was good to Agrippa, it was disastrous for Flaccus. Caligula's revenge was sweet. He had no love for Flaccus in any case, but he obviously wanted to make it plain that he was not to be trifled with. Flaccus was tried for his crimes and sent into exile to a tiny island named Andros. Whilst he was there Caligula dreamed up various tortures to inflict on him, a man to whom this sort of isolation would have been a horror in itself. Eventually the emperor tired of his sport, giving orders for Flaccus to be executed.

Caligula had previously ordered that statues of himself should be set up in the synagogues of Alexandria. Marcus reported to the emperor how incensed the Jews of Alexandria were that pagan idols had been placed in their synagogues. Either as a mark of respect to his young friend, or because he wanted to placate his citizens, Caligula relented and allowed the idols to be removed. Peace was restored to Alexandria, together with its accustomed prosperity.

CHAPTER 5

THE MAKING OF A MESSIAH

It is not difficult to see how the arrival of this bright boy from Judea, who clearly had the ear of the emperor, could have seemed to the Jews of Alexandria like a manifestation of God's intervention. They were in fear of their very lives, and now, in the midst of their woes, a divine child, a king born of the ancient House of David, had been sent into their midst to scatter their enemies and to put right the wrongs of the previous dreadful months. Their reaction is not especially surprising. After all, the whole concept of a messianic deliverer went right back to the very start of Israel, countless centuries before Marcus Agrippa's time. It was written clear through the psyche of the entire nation.

According to tradition, and perhaps underpinned by at least some genuine events, the Hebrews, ancestors of the Jews and the Samaritans, had represented a series of client tribes, living and working amongst the Egyptians far from their point of origin. Over time the relationship of the Hebrews to their Egyptian employers had changed, until eventually they were recognized not as valuable foreign labourers but as slaves.

The Hebrews longed to be free. From within their midst arose a leader, a man chosen by God who would lead his people out of bondage and back to the lands that had been their point of origin, so many generations before. This man was called Moses and, after a period of discussion, argument and threats with the Pharaoh of Egypt, he eventually led the tribes out of Egypt and north towards Palestine. The

Children of Israel, as they are often known, wandered for decades. At the time they were probably quite unique amongst the peoples with whom they came into contact because of their insistence on worshipping a single, all-powerful deity.

According to tradition, close to the start of their journey north, in Sinai, Moses had climbed a mountain and at its summit he had been in the direct presence of God. God had spoken to Moses and passed to him a series of ten rules, by which the Children of Israel would be expected to live. The Ten Commandments were as follows:

1. I am the Lord thy God.

2. Thou shalt have no other God beside me. Thou shalt not make for thyself an idol.

3. Thou shalt not make wrongful use of the name of thy God.

4. Remember the Sabbath and keep it holy.

5. Honour thy father and thy mother.

6. Thou shalt not murder.

7. Thou shalt not commit adultery.

8. Thou shalt not steal.

9. Thou shalt not bear false witness against thy neighbour.

10. Thou shalt not covet thy neighbour's house nor thy neighbour's wife.

There are slight differences in the way that various sects within Judaism preserved the wording or divided up the text to derive ten specific *mitzvoth* or Commandments. Nevertheless, all Hebrew sects were united by these ten utterances that Moses received from heaven.

Of course, once the Children of Israel arrived at their destination in Palestine, beginning to carve out a homeland for themselves, the fairly basic and even primitive nature of the original Ten Commandments was hardly enough for good government or law. In any case, the Commandments could be interpreted in a number of ways. For example, what represents one's neighbour? Was it any other Hebrew, or anyone at all who might be living in close proximity?

Moses, the original deliverer of the Jews, had thought about this and, according to a well established Jewish tradition from deepest antiquity, independently of God or the original commandments, laid down a further series of 603 additional laws (Torah) that were much more complicated than the original ten.

As we shall see, not everyone in Jewish society accepted that all 613 Commandments of the Torah were equally binding, since the great majority had not been personally ordained by God. Arguments arose as to how the original Ten Commandments should be observed, let alone the laws laid down by Moses. Different groups developed, even within mainstream Judaism, and all of these had alternative ways of interpreting the Torah.

But Moses was not alone in being held up by the developing Jews as a divinely inspired messenger. There was also the first of the Jewish kings, David, a warrior. Through him the Children of Israel had been able to forge themselves a kingdom within the Promised Land. It is between these two quite different characters, Moses the law-giver and David the warrior-king, that the idea of the Messiah probably arose during the troubled centuries that followed.

While there is no explicit mention of a Messiah in the Torah (the original Law of Moses), his presence is manifest in countless cryptic references woven into the fabric of the text. These encoded proclamations were explained by means of oral traditions passed on through generations of believers among the Jews and Samaritans. Above all else, the Messiah would be 'like Moses'. Among the great things expected to coincide with his arrival was the revelation of a new Torah. The new messianic age would sweep away all that had been established before his advent and humanity would be finally reconciled with God through his more perfect Covenant.

Details regarding the Messiah are to be found scattered throughout the books of the Old Testament of the Bible. His character and actions took shape through the inspirations, visions and opinions of a series of prophets, all of whom contributed to the expectations of an entire nation. Through the long, tortured years of battle, slavery and servitude, the form of the Messiah stood high in the consciousness of the Jews.

From the Book of Isaiah we learn that the Messiah would be born of the ancient House of David and that he would be a warrior-king. This book also tells us that evil and tyranny would not be able to stand before his leadership. Isaiah also suggests that nations that have wronged Israel in the past will come to realize what they have done because the Messiah's message will be for all nations and peoples, not simply for the Jews. Other books indicate that barren land will become fertile and that cities once destroyed will be re-founded and rebuilt when the Messiah appears.

Meanwhile, the inspired prophets of old gave graphic accounts of the physical manifestations of the Messiah's appearance, as well as of the Throne of God, to which the Messiah is necessarily connected. When taken together it could be argued that the Messiah would appear in association with God's fiery throne, flanked by angels and seraphim. The descriptions are graphic and would have been well known by all those who studied the works of the prophets.

There is a great deal of difference between the Messiah as envisaged by the Jews and the Messiah of the European Christian tradition. Whilst the Christian Messiah, who is of course Jesus, goes to prepare a heavenly kingdom for his faithful, the Jewish Messiah is a much more tangible and worldly character. In antiquity at least, the Messiah was necessarily a monarch who successfully vanquished the enemies of Israel. In this regard, we inevitably come back to the same formula: the Messiah was necessarily like Moses. To borrow a formula from Philo, he would necessarily be king, high priest and prophet.

From the perspective of Jews living almost anywhere at the start of the modern era, it is easy to see how the more martial aspects of the promised Messiah would have been of the most significant interest. Lives were hard, taxes were high and the Roman war machine had enslaved their entire nation. What good would the Messiah be if he failed to address these issues?

If we now look again at the situation that prevailed in Alexandria at the time Marcus Agrippa arrived there and the almost immediate alteration in events as a result of his appearance, it is easy to see how the vast majority of Jews living in and around the city would have seen Marcus as being that very saviour they had been promised for so long. After all, had he not managed to get the statues of the emperor removed from their holiest places, their synagogues? Had he not been responsible for getting the hated Flaccus removed from power, banished and then executed?

Through a direct bloodline, Marcus Agrippa was related to the Hasmonean kings, who in turn could trace their lineage straight back to King David. Arriving in Alexandria, Marcus was undoubtedly credited with saving his people at a stroke. He seemed to be on especially good terms with the rulers in Rome – in fact from a local perspective it may have looked as though he had the new emperor in his pocket.

It is also abundantly clear that little Marcus or, more properly, those who were running his life at this time, did nothing to counter the suspicion that he was the Messiah. On the contrary, Marcus would go on to spend his whole life proving that this was exactly the position he held. To first achieve such an objective in Judea would have been difficult.

Alexandria represented a very different cultural climate to that of Judea. Here Jews and Samaritans, who had long embraced Hellenistic culture, were now actively reaching out to convert large numbers of native Egyptians and pagans. Marcus Agrippa might well have proved to be the exact sort of messianic symbol that would solidify these efforts in conversion.

Alexandria was unique in that it was essentially a Greek city even though it was situated on Egyptian soil. Native Egyptians living in the city did not have full citizenship status and even the rights of Jews were questioned. As the inherent inequality woven into the fabric of the city festered over time into open conflict, Jews and Egyptians were natural allies against what must have been seen as Greek oppression, especially when Roman rule became more established. In the eastern Roman Empire, Greeks, whom the Romans had overcome, nevertheless formed the cultural core and local power structure of the region. Later, on the decline of Rome in the fifth century, the eastern Greek sphere survived as Byzantium, while the western sphere centred in Rome fell.

Desperate people will clutch at any available straw, even if it comes along in the form of an eight- or nine-year-old boy. Is there any wonder that, when the assaults and killings ceased and people were allowed to return in peace to their property, they immediately assumed that the time of true deliverance was at hand? Was not King David only a small child when he killed the giant Goliath? Had not this divine child, Agrippa, stopped carnage and mayhem by simply being present?

It is my contention that the situation would only have been odd if Marcus Agrippa had not been earmarked as the long-awaited Messiah. Human nature and ego aside, Marcus Agrippa had good reason to believe that this was the case. His rise from the rank of a small renegade prince of a generally despised family of client rulers to that of the saviour of his people had been rapid – in fact, almost instantaneous. The circumstances surrounding his elevation appeared to parallel one of the most sacred parts of Jewish history and tradition.

At the very start of the Jewish story, long before the exile in Egypt and the struggles of the first kings, the Jews believed themselves to be descended from one man, the father of the entire nation, Abraham. The Jews believed that Abraham was born in Mesopotamia and that God had called on him to travel to the land of Canaan. Abraham fathered two children but, as far as the Jews were concerned, Isaac, born to Abraham and his wife Sarah, was his 'only' son.[64] Abraham's other son, Ishmael, born to his servant Hagar, was later cast out into the desert with his mother, to become the traditional father of the Arabs.

According to traditional Hebrew accounts, the circumstances of Isaac's birth were wholly miraculous. His mother was 90 and his father 100. The name *Isaac* was given by God to Sarah after He had visited her when she was still childless. He told the couple that she would give birth. Sarah was understandably dubious and she laughed. As a result the baby was called 'Isaac', which is a play on the Hebrew word for laughter. Isaac was henceforth always associated with miraculous deliverance and faith. He became the very symbol of the continued survival of Israel itself.

This was reinforced in what is surely the central story in the Torah itself. When Isaac was about nine years old, God told his father Abraham to take his beloved son and deliver him up for sacrifice. No doubt with a heavy heart, Abraham travelled with Isaac to Mount

Gerizim, which would eventually become the heartland of the Samaritans. There, Abraham prepared to kill his son as a necessary offering to God. At the last moment a ram was found with its horns entangled in the thick foliage of a bush, and God informed Abraham that the ram was to be sacrificed in place of Isaac. This duly took place and the event later became known as the *Akedah* or 'binding' of Isaac.

The story was used to emphasize the kind of faithfulness that the Hebrew religion demanded of its members. Abraham was hallowed as a great man because he was wholly devoted to his God, even to the extent of being willing to kill his own beloved son. Yet Isaac had an even more intimate place in the hearts and minds of Israelites in all periods of history. He was the one whose life had hung in the balance of this ancient drama. It was only thanks to the appearance of the ram that Isaac could live and go on to father the entire nation of Israel.

Henceforth, in almost every 'do or die' historical crisis that faced the Jewish people, the example of Isaac's binding is inevitably recalled. During the Holocaust of the 1940s, Jewish survivors in various parts of Europe outside of the reach of the Nazis routinely identified themselves as 'Isaacs'. Similar cultural remembrances are found in other periods of Jewish persecution throughout the ages.

As a result, it should hardly be surprising to consider that Marcus Agrippa would see in his miraculous 'resurrection' experience a connection with the Biblical narrative of Isaac. Indeed the very name 'Barabbas', that we have seen associated with him at the time of the Passion, brings home the idea clearly. Yes, Barabbas, like many original Aramaic words or phrases, can be understood in a variety of different ways. It could for instance be interpreted to mean 'son of the father'. The fifth-century Church Father Jerome takes the original Aramaic term to be *bar rabban* or 'son of the teacher'. Yet in my mind the most convincing explanation given the underlying context of the Passion narrative is to take the term to derive from *bar Abba* – son of Abraham.

Adela Yarbro Collins, in her various works on the subject of the original gospel writer Mark, notes that the name Barabbas undoubtedly means 'the son of Abba', where Abba is a diminutive form of Abraham.[65] Citing other scholarly arguments that support her thesis, she goes on to say that the Abraham hypothesis is bolstered by other New Testament passages that '... refer to Abraham as "father" or imply such an appellation; Matt 3:9; Luke 16:24, 27, 30; Gal 3:7, 16, 29.'[66] Indeed Jews and Samaritans to this day identify Abraham as the father of their community.

Our idea of a messianic 'son of Abraham' being bound and ultimately freed during the Passover confirms what many scholars have already noted about the gospel. The original evangelist clearly took a historical event and made it conform to the well-known story of the binding of Isaac. Not only does Jesus' and Marcus' arrest at Mount Gerizim play into this assumption, but also the artificiality of having one sacrificed in the place of the other does too.

All of this inevitably leads us back to the Throne of St Mark. The plate section contains a close-up of the panel on the throne that is immediately above the seat. The carving shows a large ram standing in front of a bush or tree. This was clearly meant to represent the ram that appeared in the story of Abraham and Isaac. The real question, however, for any Jew who would look at the depiction is, *where is Isaac? Why doesn't the real subject of the whole narrative appear in the depiction on the throne?* There are countless representations of this Biblical scene that have come down to us from various ancient sources. None ever depict only the ram. The very idea would seem quite absurd.

The solution is immediately obvious when the inscription on the front of the throne's seat is translated. 'Isaac' is clearly understood to be the one enthroned in 38 CE. That is why the crowds were shouting 'Barabbas' in the first place – a year earlier at the time of the Passion. In other words, little Marcus, the nine-year-old boy, was seated in the foreground, and Jesus the ram caught in the foliage of the bush is placed in the background. This act of sacrifice by Jesus at the time of the Passion stands behind Marcus Agrippa's eventual triumph, and the little boy never forgot it. He eventually went on to develop the first gospel narrative into a sort of modern day *Akedah*.[67]

Marcus Agrippa and his family must have claimed to have been followers of the prophet Jesus. As I will go on to show, Jesus was quite emphatic that, in his presence and ministry, he was a herald to the arrival of the Messiah whom, he implied, was already in the midst of his followers. There is plenty of evidence to link Marcus to Jesus. We also have the knowledge that Marcus was imprisoned at the time of Jesus' capture and ultimate execution. In the allegory that took place at the time of the crucifixion, Jesus was offered up as the sacrifice so that Marcus could go free and show himself to be the Messiah.

So let us return to our earlier discussion of the place of 'bar Abbas' in the gospel. He is released while Jesus is sacrificed in his place. It is Jesus' experience that becomes the basic ground of Christianity. Jesus' sacrifice becomes the central act that sets in motion the 'transformation of the Messiah'. The gospel narrative goes out of its way to demonstrate that, throughout his ministry, Jesus regularly acknowledged that he knew what his end would be. The earliest interpretations of St Mark's gospel understand that Jesus' death cleared the way for the manifestation of Christ – he himself was not the Messiah of the Jews. Of course, if this is true, it also necessarily leads us to the following question: *if Jesus wasn't the Christ, who was he?* The answer was well known to ancient observers. It even adorns the entranceway to our oldest surviving church.

Jesus was the *Chrestos*, a Greek word that roughly corresponds to 'the Good' or better yet 'the Right One'. The title was widespread in the early Church, even if it was shunned by the authorities in Rome. It had and still has a central place in the Markan tradition. It is the most common title in the traditions of Coptic Christianity. To check this, open virtually any Alexandrian psalm book and see the number of times Jesus is called *pi-khrestos*. The regular use of this title is quite staggering.

When we take into account that no early gospel ever explicitly attaches the name *Christos* or Christ to Jesus' name, we have the beginnings of a great mystery. Jesus' messianic status wasn't an open-and-shut case, even within the orthodox branches of Christianity, let alone the so-called heretical traditions. There were many who held that he was simply the one chosen to be sacrificed on behalf of someone else.

It is easy to see that the story of the *Akedah* was understood to be playing out once again in the events of the Passion. As in the case of Isaac, it looked at first as if young Marcus would meet his fate as a sacrifice, but instead Jesus the teacher willingly accepted this role.

This may well be the original reason why Jesus became known as 'the Lamb of God'.

In just one case out of many in which the so-called Throne of St Mark proves its real origins and purpose, the figure of the ram caught in the bush carved into the backrest of the throne shows definitively that those who ordered its creation knew full well what had happened in Judea the previous year, and they understood its symbolism only too well. Jesus, the sacrifice, had died so that Marcus, the Messiah, could survive and fulfill his mission.

In the comprehension of the Jews and Samaritans of Alexandria in 38 CE, there was no doubt about who Marcus Julius Agrippa actually was, and what he represented. Every facet and nuance of the Messiah is to be found somewhere on the alabaster throne. The inclusion of the ram caught in the bush is merely the first way in which this remarkable surviving artefact tells us about a pivotal event that in so many other ways has been eclipsed by later events and more or less forgotten. The Throne of St Mark is actually the throne of Marcus Agrippa, a man once considered not only to be a genuine Jewish King, but also the very redeemer of his people.

CHAPTER 6

ALLIED TO MONSTERS

Eventually Marcus Agrippa and his family left behind the adulation they had received in Alexandria and sailed on to make another impression in Marcus' new lands. With him went the empire's gratitude that the little boy had managed, against all the odds, to defuse a situation that may have led to massive starvation in Rome itself, since Alexandria was one of the chief ports for the shipment of grain from the Nile delta in northern Egypt. We can also be sure that the new emperor gained in popularity as a result of his own efforts to alleviate a potentially troublesome problem for the empire, and particularly for Rome itself.

As it turned out, Marcus Agrippa stayed high in Caligula's favours even long after most of the emperor's former friends and allies were quaking in their sandals. But with the passing of time, as far as the empire was concerned, things went from hopeful to bad and from bad to worse. Caligula's famous excesses drained the exchequer to such an extent that he soon ran out of money. Only a couple of years into his reign he began to invent ever more ingenious ways of extorting money from the richest and most influential citizens in Rome and beyond the city.

This had started earlier, as a reflection of Caligula's perverse and frightening sense of humour. Soon after his accession the young emperor was taken desperately ill. Sycophantic senators and others swore oaths that they would gladly give up their own lives if the emperor's life could be saved. Upon recovering, and by now proclaiming himself to be a god, Caligula took them at their word and insisted that they should commit suicide, making him their chief beneficiary. This plan worked so well Caligula thought up a variant of it once the money began to run out. He announced that it would henceforth be mandatory for everyone to mention the emperor in their wills. Once they had done so, he put pressure on the richest of them to commit suicide. Then he picked up the loot.

Caligula's determination to achieve the status of a god was a cause of singular horror and utter hatred from many directions. True, Augustus had been deified after his death, but he had worked long and hard to support Rome and, in any case, he had never made any suggestion during his lifetime that he might aspire to becoming 'as one with the gods'. Augustus shied away from such proposed honours. If being a god during his own lifetime wasn't enough, Caligula raised his favourite horse to the rank of senator. This insulted all the great Roman families whose members held this hallowed office. He even caused a severe famine by commandeering all the grain ships to create a pontoon bridge across the harbour at Ostia.

Things eventually came to such a pass that nobody's life was safe any more. Had Caligula only realized, he was providing the best possible reason for his own assassination. The conspirators had little to lose. Their lives would most likely be worth nothing in any case, whereas if they disposed of a man whom everyone now hated, they might become heroes. The assassins were led by disaffected members of the Praetorian Guard – some of the highest-ranking guards had a particular hatred of Caligula because he constantly embarrassed them with menial duties and ridiculous passwords. So it was planned that Caligula should be assassinated and that the Roman republic should be reinstated after three generations of dictators.

Caligula was ambushed outside the circus in Rome on January 24th and hacked to death. And so, at the age of 28, ended the reign of a deranged psychopath. It might also have spelled the end of young Marcus Agrippa. He was still only 14 years of age and his power and prestige lay firmly in the hands of whoever happened to be ruling the empire at the time. Fortunately for Marcus, who always seemed to live a charmed life, the next emperor appears to have been just as fond of him as Caligula had been, though probably for quite different reasons.

The Praetorian Guard might have connived at Caligula's death, but many of the soldiers in Rome were against a restoration of the republic. The emperor's bodyguard did very well out of their duties in Rome, so the moment Caligula was dead they cast around for another representative of the royal family. Unfortunately Tiberius and Caligula had disposed of most of the possible candidates. The only person with sufficient credentials left was Caligula's middle-aged uncle, Claudius. As Caligula lay bleeding from his mortal wounds, Claudius was found hiding in a wardrobe, expecting to be murdered at any moment. Instead the soldiers declared him to be the new emperor.

The Senate was already in full session, praising the murder of the tyrant and planning the restoration of the republic, when news came to them that Claudius had been pronounced emperor. With discretion being the better part of valour, talk of a republic was soon forgotten and everyone agreed what a fine emperor Tiberius Claudius Drusus Nero Germanicus would make.

In truth they couldn't have picked a less likely emperor. Claudius was already 51 and lame. He had a pronounced stutter, had never been a soldier, and slobbered like a child. He was considered by everyone who was anyone to be a virtual idiot. But the reality was rather different. It was true that Claudius had been damaged at birth and that he had physical difficulties, but he had a good mind; he was an expert in Greek and Roman literature, and he spoke and read a number of languages – some of which were extinct. Either Claudius' family had overlooked his good points in view of his infirmities, or nobody had ever taken the trouble to find out exactly how bright he was. For most of his life he had been left alone to get on with his studies in private. Since it was generally accepted that he was an imbecile, nobody had bothered to murder him.

So what could young Marcus Agrippa expect from the middle-aged emperor? As things turned out he could have expected a great deal. Much has been written about Claudius. Writers from nearer to his own time were dismissive both of his character and his influence. More modern experts have treated Claudius in a fairer way. If he had come to the throne at a younger age and without some of the health problems that dogged his reign, we might even remember him as one of the greatest emperors Rome had. His administration was capable and Rome flourished under his rule. It might be suggested that although it was clearly the deranged Caligula who had been responsible for Marcus Agrippa's rise, it was to Claudius that Marcus owed the consolidation of his assets and sufficient time to cement his plans for the future.

Above all, Claudius was a scholar. Though he was kept busy as emperor, he never forgot about the libraries where he had whiled away so much of his life before his unexpected rise to power. We know from later accounts of Marcus Agrippa that he too was very committed to books and learning. Despite Marcus being only around 14 when Claudius came to the imperial throne, the two would have had much in common. Both were especially interested in history and languages. A very important factor in their relationship was that Claudius was quite definitely not anti-Semitic. On the contrary, he was more than fair in his dealings with Jews, both in Alexandria and wherever they lived in the Roman Empire and he did his very best to right the wrongs that had taken place in Alexandria. He showed in his dealings with all groups and races that he was even-handed and fair.

Early in Claudius' reign, disturbances once again broke out in Alexandria. The Jews there, fearful of what had happened previously, sent not one but two delegations to the emperor. He listened very carefully to what they had to say and eventually composed a 'letter to the Alexandrians'. The letter was not wholly created to benefit the Jews. For example he made it plain that they must not move new families into the city en masse. This was to prevent Jews from eventually outnumbering gentiles, but Claudius did grant them far more rights as citizens than they had enjoyed before. He made it absolutely plain that harassment of Jews would not be tolerated. According to Josephus, Claudius then went on to restructure and make official the rights of Jews across his empire.

Can we see Marcus Agrippa in these actions? It seems likely. Marcus spent a good deal of time in Rome and would probably have consulted with Claudius on a regular basis. We can also infer from Marcus' relationship with Claudius, as with every other stage and facet of his life, that the old emperor was as vulnerable to Marcus' intelligence and charm as everyone else seems to have been throughout Marcus' reign.

Though there is little in the way of hard evidence on a balance of probabilities, it is more than likely that Marcus Agrippa already knew Claudius quite well. With his winning ways, Marcus would have appealed to the emperor's good nature. Claudius would have been only too aware of the singular service Marcus and his family had afforded the empire by their handling of the situation in Alexandria, and it is clear from the evidence we have that the new emperor was at pains to make his gratitude known.

Marcus Agrippa's uncle, Philip, had died before his own rise to power. He had been the king of Gaulanitis, Batanaea, Trachonitis and Auranitis, to the north of Galilee and in Syria. In 54 CE Claudius granted to Marcus all those parts of Philip's kingdom that were not already in his hands. It is also more or less certain that Marcus had control over the Temple in Jerusalem, because he appears to have held the right to appoint the high priest there.

With careful rule by Marcus, and thanks to Claudius' steady hand on the tiller of the empire, things remained generally quiet in Palestine for the next few years. Claudius expanded the empire in many directions, not least including Britain, which his armies invaded in 43 CE.

It has been suggested, more or less ever since his own lifetime, that Claudius was far too trusting of a series of Greek freedmen, who he engaged to run much of his regime on his behalf. But it must be remembered that Claudius was not a young man when he came to power and that he did have significant physical difficulties, probably caused by cerebral palsy. All things considered, he stabilized the position of emperor for at least a few years. Unfortunately, despite his success as emperor, his private life was a disaster and, after several unfortunate marriages, Claudius was eventually poisoned by his final wife, Agrippina. He died on October 13th, 54 CE. Once again Marcus Agrippa, now grown to full manhood, would have had reason to wonder who Claudius' successor would be.

The man who took the throne after Claudius was his great nephew and adopted son. Nero by name, he would go down in history as one of the most peculiar and ultimately unsuccessful of all Roman emperors. Like his relative Caligula, he was also deranged. Poor Nero was not temperamentally fitted for the role he was expected to undertake. His chief interest in life was a study of the arts. Nero was a great builder of theatres and circuses, choosing to live a life of total opulence.

From a personal point of view Nero could be charming, courteous and affectionate, but like all the Claudian emperors he had a fierce temper and was extremely dangerous when crossed. He had his own mother murdered, not to mention his former wife, and those surrounding his court perpetually had to watch their backs – as had been the case during the reign of Caligula, though probably less so under Claudius.

As far as can be ascertained, Nero and Marcus Agrippa got on very well. The new emperor was younger than Marcus and it seems that Nero turned to him for advice on Eastern matters. The two also shared a love of the arts, so they had much in common. We know that Marcus Agrippa was not only a scholar but also that he revelled in the same creative instincts that motivated Nero. During Nero's reign Marcus received new territories, in particular the city of Tiberius and parts of Peræa, east of the Jordan River.

It is with Nero's reign that we come to the incident that more than any other sets the seal on the life and influence of Marcus Julius Agrippa. By the year 66 CE Marcus was 39 years of age. After an unlikely start to his reign, he had consolidated his early acquisitions, managing to steer a careful course through what must have been difficult times. At all stages, his ability to change with the times and cultivate successive emperors had kept him not only alive, but at the very centre of Roman politics in Palestine and beyond.

What happened in 66 CE was probably inevitable. The first of the major uprisings in Judea seems to have been partly spurred by the fact that Marcus was not in Palestine when it began. As was often the case, Marcus was in Alexandria, so he was not able to use his charm and influence to calm matters at their outset.

What the final spark was, we will never know. Certainly there was great disaffection on account of the extraordinarily high taxes placed on ordinary people in Jerusalem and across Judea. There was also a food shortage at the time. What made matters worse was that the Temple in Jerusalem, which had been in the process of being rebuilt since the time of Herod the Great, was now completed. Many hundreds of workers employed on the site for generations were thrown out of work. It is also possible that the Temple's presence at the heart of the city acted as a stimulus to nationalistic fervour.

Probably the most likely reason for the revolt was that many of Agrippa's Jewish subjects decided to use his own tactics against him. Just as mother and son had been involved in plots in Galilee and Alexandria to overthrow the rulers of territories they coveted, the rebel leader Josephus and his kinsmen might well have plotted much the same thing, but now in reverse. Whatever Marcus might have been to his beloved Alexandrians and to a great percentage of his own subjects, he was still of the Herodian dynasty, which was especially hated by the revolutionaries and some of the fanatically religious sects of Judea. Now it was Agrippa who had everything to lose: his Jewish enemies did their best to prove that he could not effectively control his subjects. It is not only in our own period of history that fanatics and fundamentalists use every means possible to destabilize regimes of which they do not approve.

What began as a series of small incidents went from bad to worse when some citizens of Jerusalem were killed in a tax riot. In a bid to restore authority the Roman governor, Gessius Florus, foolishly had a number of bystanders crucified. Marcus' wife, Berenice, was present when the trouble began, but it was quite beyond her ability to prevent the subsequent escalation. Marcus returned as soon as he received news of events, making an impassioned appeal for calm, but to no avail.

The result was an armed insurrection which eventually turned into a full-scale war. Whether or not Marcus Agrippa was genuinely surprised by this turn of events cannot be known for certain. It is clear from the uprising itself that Marcus was nowhere near as popular throughout parts of Judea as he was in Egypt. Whether or not the turn of events in 66 CE surprised him, there is no doubt what he thought about the situation henceforth.

There were groups within Judean society, such as the Zealots, that were looking for any excuse to take up arms against the Romans, and without doubt against their Herodian rulers if they had a chance. But in reality it was the power and influence of a few specific families that allowed the uprising to take place. Doubtless, as with all civil wars, the vast majority of the population simply wished for a peaceful life, but once the swords and shields were removed from their hiding places and the call to arms went up, almost everyone was affected in one way or another.

Marcus fled with his family to Paneas, now Banyas city, near the northern perimeter of Galilee. There he consulted with the Roman authorities. As it turned out, the war was long and bloody and the rebels against Rome at first gave good account of themselves. Meanwhile Marcus judged his actions extremely well. Now was the chance to prove even to the rebellious Judeans that he really was the promised Messiah of his people.

CHAPTER 7

THE MESSIAH'S WAR

With its newly quarried stone shining brightly in the heat of the Palestinian sun and its vast bulk sitting squarely and massively on its hilltop mound, no building could have polarized opinion more in 66 CE than the Temple of Jerusalem. For countless centuries the Temple had remained the focus of Jewish life for the whole region. It contained the Holy of Holies, the set-apart, venerated place where God's communion with man was made manifest. It was here that the legendary Ark of the Covenant had originally been placed, though it is probable that the Ark had been lost or hidden before the destruction of the first Temple.

According to tradition, inside the Ark had been stored the broken remnants of the stone tablets created by God, together with replicas of the replacements made by Moses. The Ark had held God's most important instructions to his people. Whether or not they were still to be found anywhere in the Temple, the laws remained binding. They were the rules by which the people of the Lord were expected to live their lives.

Despite the reverence for the Holy of Holies, the Temple complex was a hive of activity. Priests came and went; businesspeople sold souvenirs and the necessary sacrificial victims for the use of devotees. Much like St Mark's Square in Venice or Westminster Abbey in London, the Temple in Jerusalem attracted thousands of visitors each year – the more so now that people could come and see its vast Herodian architecture and the amazing craftsmanship that had gone into its construction. People made wonderful things in those far-off days, but the very best of what they could create was always reserved for the gods – or, in this case, the One God.

To orthodox Jews, especially those whose families had always dedicated themselves to this place, the Temple was unique, inviolate and perpetual. The very prospect of Judaism surviving without it would have been unthinkable. Had it not stood here, on this site, since the days of King Solomon? Was it not an inimitable part of both tradition and that special relationship with God that none but the Jews enjoyed?

But of course there were other opinions regarding the Temple. Those who believed that Jesus had been sent by God as the last and greatest of His envoys knew that the survival of a Temple constructed of stones and mortar was now little more than an abstraction. Jesus' very words had been 'I will destroy this Temple and establish another'. The radicalized Galileans who had supported Jesus, listening to his words, must have developed into natural allies of the Samaritans, who had always viewed the Jewish temple with contempt. Two hundred years earlier a Jewish king had dared to desecrate the Samaritan holy place, and much of the northern kingdom longed for the opportunity to return the favour.

Between these competing factions stood Marcus Agrippa and the Galilean principality, part of his domains. In terms of population Galilee was more or less evenly split between Jews and non-Jews. Agrippa almost certainly began his rule trying to be the king of all of the people but, as divisions worsened within his domain, he was ultimately forced to take sides. Unlike the Jews and Samaritans of Alexandria, who would have followed him to hell if necessary, the vast majority of the Jews in his holdings further north simply refused to recognize his authority. But why might Agrippa have been unpopular? Part of the reason was that much of the Jewish population was scandalized by the growth of the Jesus faith throughout his domain. The capital city, Tiberias, was almost wholly devoted to a semi-pagan cult that was flourishing there.

At the same time, rabbinic reports also confess that their efforts to convert non-Jewish Galileans to the Jerusalem-based Judaism were proving fruitless. Galilee was increasingly becoming divided along ethnic lines and Agrippa aligned himself *against* the most powerful

Jewish faction – the Pharisees. The Pharisees are mentioned repeatedly in the New Testament, and Jesus regularly crossed swords with them. They were an old sect that had originally been responsible for the Temple. Their version of Jewish Law was strict and conservative, leaving no room for modernization or compromise.

Marcus Agrippa had powerful enemies amongst the Pharisees. There was one priestly family in particular that stood out as being powerful enough to challenge his authority. This was the Goria clan. It had a patriarch named Nicodemus at its head, claiming Josephus (later the historian of the Jews) as a member. Many scholars in the recent past have approached the Jewish War as if it were entirely based on lofty principles like 'freedom from imperialism'. But these weren't the only goals of the aristocratic families that ran Jerusalem. They had too much to lose if everything fell apart.

These men were not fools. They must have realized that a band of poorly trained peasants could never hope to defeat the Roman army. What is more, wealthier Jewish families had vested interests in Palestine and would have lost everything if the situation spiralled out of control. It is therefore hard to believe that Nicodemus, as the head of one of the richest and most elevated Jewish clans, was willing to throw all caution to the wind simply for the sake of liberty. There must have been an underlying financial vested interest that motivated wealthy Jewish families to organize and take part in a rebellion.

It cannot be coincidental that Galilee happened to be the epicentre of most of the action in the Jewish War. Galilee was the source of most of Marcus Agrippa's income. It was the breadbasket of the region, filled with farms, fisheries and other natural resources. It seems certain that Galilee was the prize on offer and that these powerful Pharisaic families were using religion to manipulate willing foot soldiers for their own specific ends.

Josephus himself was the leader of the Jewish insurgents in Galilee. We can see from his later writing that he employed persuasive rhetoric to conceal what must have been his family's motivation for stirring up the uprising. To portray the rival Herodian faction as 'enemies of the people', Josephus emphasized that Jews had a duty to rebel against Marcus Agrippa to save their religious institutions. Josephus speaks of the Herodian rulers as '… departing from the traditional customs and gradually corrupting the ancient way of life … and neglecting those things which had formerly induced piety in the masses'.[68] This is especially rich, coming from a man who, quite early in the war, changed sides and became a Roman citizen.

Nevertheless, words like this must certainly have resonated with the average Jew on the street. In the end, it was probably what encouraged them to go to war against Marcus Agrippa and his Roman allies. Throughout Josephus' writings (and especially in *Vita*, his apologetic work) we find frequent references against Herod Agrippa for establishing synagogues and buildings with images of living creatures, appointing uncircumcised high officials and having an underlying tendency to introduce innovations within religious life. But despite his own private agenda Josephus was probably speaking the truth. As we shall see, being a Messiah meant rebuilding Judaism and making it fit for a world of uncircumcised gentiles. All the same, the words of Josephus motivated the religious-minded, who might have been sitting on the fence prior to the uprising.

Marcus Agrippa's connection with 'foreign ideals' certainly did act as a great stimulus to his enemies. Yet they were not in themselves the cause of the revolt. As Richard Horsley notes in his *Galilee: History, Politics, People, Josephus* '… has much to explain about his own and other aristocrats' role in the great revolt'.[69] Josephus' surviving account attempts to portray the ensuing violence as a series of random outbursts of social dysfunction, but this is far from being the case.

The protagonists certainly knew how to take advantage of the existing imperial system. They could justifiably point to the fact that even a simple complaint about Roman taxes in any public forum could lead to random crucifixion. In quiet corners and in the shade of houses, whisperings arose. The whispers turned to shouts and then some hotheaded youth threw a stone at a Roman soldier. In an instant, Palestine was at war.

Despite his best efforts to turn the tide of disaffection, Marcus Agrippa was powerless to prevent his people from exploding with a white-hot anger. He could do nothing to quell the cries of 'liberty' that sounded all across the land. He could not root out the stores of carefully made and preserved armaments that had been waiting in dusty corners for decades. He could not dissuade even the most humble woodcutter or street sweeper from picking up their axe or broom and making of it a weapon of war. On the contrary, there were sections of the populace that saw Marcus Agrippa as a 'bad Jew', an interloper, a puppet of the Romans and everything the Messiah should not be. Disaffection was everywhere and it spoke in numerous tongues.

In all probability it was no more than Marcus had expected for years. Together with his allies the Romans, he doubtless took stock of the worsening situation. They watched and cooperated, to determine the best strategy for dealing with the unrest. Marcus Agrippa had a keen intellect and the Roman authorities already knew he was someone who could be trusted. When it was suggested that this was the right time to seize the initiative and attempt to solve 'the Jewish problem' once and for all, Agrippa's opinions must have received serious consideration.

It is said that the revolt started in Caesarea, and that it had been provoked by Greeks. Apparently they had been sacrificing birds to their pagan deities directly outside a local synagogue, which incensed the locals. What followed demonstrates that preparations for an uprising had been in hand for a very long time, though there is no doubt that the Romans were initially surprised by the organization and fighting prowess of the locals.

The son of the high priest, Eliezer ben Hannania, led a vicious attack on the Roman garrison based at Jerusalem. Marcus Agrippa and his wife Berenice were resident in the city at the time and had to flee for their lives to the safer area of Galilee. Alarmed at what was taking place, Cestius Gallus, the Roman governor of Syria, marched his troops into Judea and clashed with the rebels at the battle of Beth Horon. The battle was fought between two towns on the road from Jerusalem to Lod (now Lydda, the location of Tel Aviv airport). The site was significant because it had witnessed a much earlier battle in which Judas Maccabaeus had been triumphant against the Seleucid Empire around 166 BCE.

Gallus has been criticized for his handling of this battle, which took place between November 4th and November 8th, 66 CE. He was essentially a civil servant, not a seasoned army commander. As a result he made a few tactical errors resulting in the loss of a nearly an entire

Roman legion. The Jewish forces are said to have been outnumbered almost 5:1, and lightly armed in comparison with the Romans. However, they had tactical advantages in that they knew the terrain, and they were assisted by Gallus' ineptitude. Gallus failed to seize the high ground and hilltops with disastrous results, as the rebels poured down burning arrows and every kind of missile on the legionaries below. Romans excelled in hand-to-hand pitched battles but, using guerrilla tactics, the Jewish rebels never gave the Roman soldiers the sort of battle they preferred. The result was a rout, a severe embarrassment to Gallus and of course to Nero. Most tragic of all for Rome's pride was the tenth legion's loss of its *aquila*, or standard, whilst retreating. This was an insult that would have to be avenged, even if it meant sending every legion of the Roman army to Palestine.

Utterly panicked by the loss of so many soldiers, the emperor Nero now turned to one of his most able generals. This was Titus Flavius Vespasianus, better know these days as Vespasian. Vespasian came from a family of mule breeders from the Sabine country of Italy. He had worked his way through the ranks of the Roman army, fighting with distinction in Britain and on other frontiers. By 66 CE he was a hard-bitten, rough-speaking warhorse of 51.

Vespasian brought with him two full legions, eight cavalry squadrons and ten cohorts of auxiliaries. He made his base at Caesarea Maritima – a city originally built by Herod the Great, lying about halfway between modern Tel Aviv and Haifa, on the Mediterranean coast. He then began systematically to clear the coast and the north of the region of rebels. Like all Roman commanders Vespasian relied heavily on terror. Thousands of men, women and children were either slaughtered or taken as captives and sold into slavery. Nevertheless it took until 68 CE before the north was brought to full submission.

While Josephus was ultimately captured in the field and changed sides, his brother Simon bar Giora escaped to Jerusalem. A bitter civil war broke out in and around the city. Anyone who advocated capitulation was summarily executed by the Sicarii and the Zealots, the most fanatical of the rebels. Owing to fierce in-fighting, all the leaders of the revolt in the south of the region had been killed by other Jews before the Romans had a chance to face them in battle.

The position of Jerusalem was hopeless, but its inhabitants simply would not give in. The factions within Jerusalem that had been fighting amongst themselves now came together to defend the city, but it was too late. Although Jerusalem was well defended, the Romans had been practising siege warfare for centuries. They camped around Jerusalem and built their own wall around the entire city. Anyone who managed to escape from Jerusalem was caught between its own walls and that of the Romans. There, facing back towards the Holy City, they would be crucified so that they could be seen by those atop the ramparts.

While the siege was taking place, the emperor Nero committed suicide on June 9th 68 CE in Rome after a military coup and Vespasian was called back to Rome. After a brief but bloody struggle a permanent successor appeared to lead the Roman world. In the meantime, command of the Jerusalem siege fell to Vespasian's son, Titus Flavius Vespasianus, known to history as Titus.

Fighting in Judea died down somewhat while Vespasian was away and it wasn't until the middle of May in the year 70 that Titus was ready to storm the huge walls of Jerusalem. By this time his father was the emperor, and he was in a position to offer any support necessary. For months Titus' sappers had been building siege engines and his troops had been constantly training, readying themselves for what everyone knew would be the final battle for the city.

The forces of Titus eventually broke through the third wall of Jerusalem and captured the fortress of Antonia, on high ground near to the Temple Mount. Josephus, by now fully integrated into Roman ways and an officer in its army, did his best to negotiate a surrender, but to no avail. It is almost certain that, by this time, Titus and Marcus Agrippa had already decided to destroy the Temple as part of their common plan to sort out Judaism once and for all.

When attacks were made from the high ground of the fortress of Antonia, the walls of the Temple began to burn and, by the end of August, it was razed to the ground and lay in ashes. Some of the defenders escaped through underground tunnels but most fought to the bitter end in a series of protracted house-to-house skirmishes that made the Romans pay dearly for their prize.

According to Josephus the Roman soldiers were furious that they found so few citizens to kill, once they finally held the whole of Jerusalem. Probably as a means of keeping them occupied, Titus ordered that the city and the Temple should be systematically torn down. He made an exception of a few towers and walls that he ordered to be spared, so that people in future could see how great Jerusalem had once been and how mighty had been the Roman war machine to destroy it so thoroughly.

Some Zealots remained and spasmodic fighting went on for a while. But finally it came to an end after the siege and destruction of the mountaintop fortress of Masada in April of the year 73 CE.

Throughout the war Marcus Agrippa survived the uprising as a staunch ally of Rome. It would be too easy to accuse him of capitulating or watching as his countrymen fought and died in a futile attempt to free their land from the oppressors. To Marcus the drama that was playing out before his eyes was entirely in accord with scriptural prophecy, directly associated with his own rank and station as the much-heralded Messiah.

One eventuality came about as a result of the Roman intervention in the region that, paradoxically, would assure Marcus of continued Roman support and offered him many relatively untroubled years to pursue his religious intentions for the Jews of Judea, Alexandria and anywhere else they might be living. Titus, Vespasian's son, would, like his father, one day be the emperor of Rome, but during those long, hard, dusty years when he commanded his father's troops in Jerusalem, he must have been in Marcus Agrippa's company a great deal. Yet it wasn't Titus' relationship with Marcus Agrippa that is remembered by history, rather, it was his growing fascination for Marcus' wife Berenice. This would become such a passion that it would go down in history as one of the great love stories of all time.

The love affair between Titus and Berenice would do much more than cause a potential scandal within Rome and threaten Titus' eventual power base. It would contribute to the creation of a religion that would become more powerful and influential than any before or since.

CHAPTER 8

LIFTING THE VEIL OF
VERONICA

Berenice represents one of the most intriguing and yet little under-stood women in Jewish history. She is remembered as a woman of great beauty, but in Rome she was considered to be a scheming and shrewd Eastern queen. At the time she appeared, Roman society already had preconceptions about what such exotic sirens could do to them and their society.

Decades before, Rome had been torn apart and very nearly destroyed because of another Eastern queen, better remembered today than Berenice. This was Queen Cleopatra, the ruler of Egypt, who had first seduced Julius Caesar and then Mark Anthony. According to tradition her feminine wiles had caused disaffection and civil war throughout the empire and, although there is only a grain of truth to this assertion, Cleopatra is still remembered as a scheming political animal, a temp-tress and a 'femme fatale'.

If her reputation is such today, we can imagine what was said of her in Rome only just beyond living memory of the damage that was done to the empire. Mighty armies clashed in horrendous and destructive civil war for the sake of Cleopatra and her oriental throne. As a result, the slightest suggestion that the whole tragedy might be repeated again, with another emperor falling for such a woman, must have caused near-panic at the heart of the empire. There is no doubt that Berenice, no matter what her many virtues might have been, was judged by Romans as being another Cleopatra.

Because of this, her ultimate story is one of tragedy, loss and eventual obscurity – ideal material for the playwright and novelist. Quite a few versions of the story of Titus and Berenice have been produced over the years and, although most of these are now out of date, if William Shakespeare had ever chosen to turn his pen in that direction Berenice would now doubtless be as famous as Cleopatra.

Readers may be surprised to learn that Berenice was not only the wife of Marcus Agrippa, she was also his sister. It might seem odd for a man who claimed Jewish descent to marry his own sister, but there are reasons why the move was expeditious and also why it did not even contradict Jewish law. We are told that Berenice had already been married and widowed before she became her brother's wife and Jewish law stated that a man had a responsibility to maintain and cherish his sister if she became a widow. Further to this, the only relevant Jewish law forbidding an association between a man and his sister stated that 'he must not make use of his sister's nakedness', which need not necessarily be interpreted as an instruction that he could not marry her,[70] so one could certainly develop a legal justification for Agrippa's 'incestuous' marriage.

As things turned out, whether or not the marriage contract between Marcus and Berenice was odd, it was certainly a good move. The fortunes of Marcus Agrippa in later life would rest fairly and squarely on the fact that he was married to Berenice, as well as upon her famed beauty and her naturally amorous nature.

Berenice was almost certainly a couple of years older than her brother Marcus, though she had been widowed at a very tender age – probably long before her marriage was ever anything more than an understanding and a contract for the future. We know this because we are also aware that her marriage to her brother Marcus took place while he was still relatively young.

We will presently be taking a close look at the Christian gospels, to see how well documented Marcus Agrippa actually is in the very earliest written reports of Christianity. There we will find not only numerous mentions and inferences of Marcus' presence, but also that of his mother Mary Salome and of his sister Berenice. There is an early and very powerful tradition among even the earliest Catholic sources that Jesus' mother did not appear anywhere in the narrative describing his ministry. This Mary was Mary Salome, the mother of Mark.

Even though Marcus' mother has kept her name through the misinterpretations and the deliberate falsifications of the Church Fathers, Berenice has taken on another name in Christianity – though it is one that is directly connected to the name by which she was known at the time. Generations of devout Christians have prayed to this Eastern temptress, without being remotely aware of the fact. She became one of the most famous icons of the Catholic Church, and all because of a small piece of cloth!

Berenice is a Macedonian Greek name (originally Bernike or Berenike) changed to its Latin form, which is Veronica (by way of Veronike). She is still called Bernike in Greek to this day – the difference being only a matter of language. Veronica is a much-loved saint of the Church and, although she is not mentioned by name in the present canonical gospels of the New Testament, she does feature heavily in Catholic worship. She is mentioned in the 'Stations of the Cross', a sort of journey undertaken by certain Christians during their worship. The Stations of the Cross represent specific stages in the trial, crucifixion and burial of Jesus. Veronica appears at station number six, the title of which is 'Veronica wipes Jesus' face with her veil'.

Perhaps in a rather unlikely attempt to give some actual substance to the character of Veronica, who appears to come from nowhere and to return to nowhere, the Church eventually associated St Veronica with a woman who touched the hem of Jesus' garment and was healed.[71] There are also other legends about St Veronica, one of which associates her directly with a Roman emperor, though the emperor mentioned is Tiberius, not Titus.

What is in no doubt is that St Veronica eventually achieved cult status within the Church, all because of the veil she is supposed to have used to wipe Christ's face. The reason this incident was remembered is because, in popular tradition, an imprint of Christ's face was left on the veil, which henceforth became a treasured religious relic.

This tradition of the wiping of Christ's face by Veronica – who locally must have been called Berenice – may well support an underlying truth. As we shall see, there would be very good reasons why those who eventually perverted the original gospels would have been happy to lose this little story. However, popular tradition does not always rely on written evidence and, if the story was already circulating widely before the gospels we know today became 'law' to the Church, it would doubtless have survived, even without verification from any of the gospel writers.

We know that Marcus had already been taken off to prison by the time Jesus was crucified, but his mother and sister could well have been present at the crucifixion. Indeed there is every reason to believe they were. The gospels clearly tell us that, present with Jesus' mother Mary at the time of Jesus' execution, was another Mary – Mary Salome. If Marcus' mother was present, then it is highly likely that her daughter Berenice would also have been there. Nor is it unlikely that, as a follower of Jesus the teacher and prophet, Berenice might have wiped Jesus' face when his suffering was at its worst. Not only is this the action of a devotee, it is also entirely in keeping with what is known of Berenice's nature. Despite the reputation she gained in Rome, all those describing her declare that she was not only very beautiful but also brave, with a kind and attractive nature.

What actual relationship Marcus Agrippa had with his sister-wife Berenice is not known. We can infer that there was a great fondness between them because Berenice spent so much of her life with Marcus, but whether the marriage ever had any physical dimension we can never know. We might perhaps infer from Berenice's ultimate and long-lasting love affair with Titus that this had not been the case, but here we are in the realms of speculation. However it is also entirely likely that Marcus, clearly a driven individual, was so committed to his crown and his cause as the Messiah that he forsook normal romantic relationships. Certainly there were no children mentioned in association with Marcus, either with Berenice or any other woman. As far as we are aware he died childless.

If Marcus Agrippa was not only associated with the origins of Christianity but in large part responsible for them, it perhaps isn't too surprising to find that his sister Berenice has also found a cherished place in early Christian stories.

Locally, her name St Berenice remains as one of a precious few saints whose cultic centres are native to Palestine. Her shrine in Caesarea Philippi (Paneas, now Banyas or Banias) was once famous throughout the Western world. The list of early and important Church Fathers who made pilgrimages there is astounding. Amongst them are Euschius, Sozomen and Philostorgius, to name but a few.

Eusebius, the bishop of Caesarea (*c.*263–339) wrote that her place of residence '… is shown in the city', and '… that remarkable memorials of the kindness of the Saviour to her remain there'.

In a church in Caesarea Philippi is to be found an important statue that is claimed to have been in existence from the time of the Apostles. Eusebius described it in the following terms:

> There stands upon an elevated stone, by the gates of her house, a brazen image of a woman kneeling, with her hands stretched out, as if she were praying. Opposite this is another upright image of a man, made of the same material, clothed decently in a double cloak, and extending his hand toward the woman. At his feet, beside the statue itself is a certain strange plant which climbs up to the hem of the brazen cloak, and is a remedy for all kinds of diseases. They say that this statue is an image of Jesus. It has remained to our day, so that we ourselves also saw it when we were staying in the city. (Eusebius, *Church History*, Book 7, Ch 18)

It is quite noteworthy that Eusebius had some hesitation and was clearly not certain that the man depicted in the statue indeed was Jesus. His exact words are, 'They say that this statue is Jesus', but he seems somehow unwilling to acknowledge this claim himself.

In what immediately follows, Eusebius seems to recognize that there is something about this statue of Berenice that contradicts his basic assumptions regarding the earliest period of Christianity. How did a religion that supposedly developed from a group of impoverished workers and fishermen manage to produce such an impressive artistic representation? If the surviving gospels are correct in their descriptions of Jesus and his followers, none of them could possibly have afforded the kind of grand palace associated with Berenice, or indeed even the statue in question. Yet Eusebius concedes that the statue is contemporary with the very beginnings of the Christian story. Whatever artist was commissioned for this work was a person of great talent and an individual who presumably would have been accustomed to receiving significant payment for his skills.

John Malalas, a prominent sixth-century Byzantine scholar, seems to know something of a connection between this Christian saint and Marcus' sister when he speaks of:

> Berenice, the sick woman of yore, set up in the midst of her own city of Paenada (Paneas) a monument in bronze adorned with gold and silver. It is still standing in the city of Paenada. Not long ago it was taken from the place where it stood in the middle of the city and placed in a house of prayer. One Batho, a converted Jew, found it *mentioned in a book which contained an account of all those who reigned over Judea* (author's emphasis).[72]

We get a little more information from *Macarius Magnes: The Apocritus*, a fourth-century work that defends Christianity against the objections of pagans. In Book 1, chapter 6, the anonymous author tells us:

> Concerning Berenice, or the woman with the issue of blood … Berenice, who once was mistress of a famous place … was made whole by a touch of the saving hem of His garment. For the woman, having had the record of the deed itself nobly represented in bronze, gave it to her son, as something done recently, not long before …

A 'queen of a certain place'. This is a very telling phrase and adds to my assertion that Berenice Agrippa was one and the same as St Veronica or St Berenice.

John Francis Wilson, the former head of New Testament studies at Pepperdine University in Malibu, California, suggests caution. He argues that *Macarius* must have been mistaken and suggests that the writer '… conflates [fuses] the story of a haemorrhaging woman with that of Berenice, the sister of Herod Agrippa'. Wilson's example is particularly interesting because he led an excavation in the city, discovering both the palace of the Herodian Berenice and the shrine of the Christian saint of the same name.

Is 'the House of Berenice' the fortress she is known to have shared with her brother and the site of many of her encounters with her lover Titus? We get the sense that it is most likely the place where the organization of the campaign for the reconquest of Palestine took place. This is made manifest in Josephus' description of Vespasian coming to the fortress in Paneas in Caesar Philippi:

> ... in order to see the kingdom of Agrippa, while the king [Agrippa] persuaded himself so to do (partly in order to treat the general and his army in the best and most splendid manner his private affairs would enable him to do, and partly that he might, by their means, correct such things as were amiss in his government). (*Jewish Wars*, Book 3, Ch 9)

Josephus goes on to say that:

> There [Vespasian] refreshed his army for twenty days, and was himself feasted by King Agrippa, where he also returned public thanks to God for the good success he had had in his undertakings. (*Jewish Wars*, Book 4, Ch 2)

Vespasian's time in Caesarea Philippi was limited because:

> ... as soon as [Vespasian] was informed that Tiberias was fond of innovations, and that [Magdala] had revolted, both of which cities were parts of the kingdom of Agrippa, and was satisfied within himself that the Jews were everywhere perverted, he thought it seasonable to make an expedition against these cities, and that for the sake of Agrippa, and in order to bring his cities to reason. (*Jewish Wars*, Book 9, Ch 3)

The rest of the history of the Jewish Wars has various members of this quartet, Vespasian, Titus, Marcus Agrippa and Berenice, passing in and out of the fortress – a building that, during the period immediately after the war, seemed to have passed exclusively into the hands of Berenice. Fortunately the fortress still stands to this day. It demonstrates the highest degree of skill and workmanship and is unequalled in size in this part of the world, though only the bottom half of the structure remains today. Most of the stones from the top half were later re-used by Byzantines, Arabs and Crusaders.

Nevertheless, what remains is impressive. The entire palace complex is over 130 m (400 ft) long. The exact width of the building has not yet been determined, but it is likely that it is nearly as wide as it is long. It had five levels and ten arched passageways, some of which have been excavated and a proportion of which lie under existing roads. Those parts excavated so far include a huge bathhouse with a caldarium (a steam room), a Roman-style basilica, a military tower, a *cardo maximus* (a paved street lined by colonnades), a fountain with a pool, a courtyard, vaulted rooms and a fortified gate. The scattered remains of mosaic floors have also been discovered.

Most walls in the palace were originally decorated with thin sheets of marble attached by iron nails to 1 m (3 ft) thick, solid limestone walls. Parts of the palace still have marble and other imported stones decorating its walls. Most of the decorative stone was imported by sea from Greece and Italy through the Phoenician port city of Tyre. The vast expenditure certainly points to the incredible wealth of Marcus Agrippa and his sister-wife.

Wilson writes of the palace saying that, 'The building was not only an engineering marvel, it was also an example of the finest and most expensive interior design available in the early days of the Roman Empire.'

The quality of work on this palace is so exceptional that Wilson suggests the stonemasons who built the palace may have been loaned to Agrippa by a Roman emperor, possibly Titus. On the east side of the building are the remains of an elegant basilica, with marble floors and walls. In the apse, the walls were covered with mosaics. It was the first time that such fine mosaics from such an early period had been found in the region and it is believed that the basilica was Agrippa's throne room.

The palace in Banias was certainly not simply the administrative centre during the war; it was undoubtedly the place where Berenice and Titus began their long-lasting but ill-fated love affair. Some have argued that the magnificence of the palace architecture demonstrates the guilt and sorrow Titus felt for eventually breaking off his marriage proposal. It is possible that the sumptuous nature of the palace is merely another reflection of his affection for Berenice. Josephus speaks of Titus,

... [solemnizing] the birthday of his brother Domitian [thereby having] inflicted a great deal of the punishment intended for the Jews in honour of him for the number of those that were now slain in fighting with the beasts, and were burnt, and fought with one another, exceeded 2,500. Yet did all this seem to the Romans, when they were thus destroyed ten thousand several ways, to be a punishment beneath their deserts. (*Jewish Wars*, Book 7, Ch 3)

So, having identified the sprawling palace of Berenice in modern Banyas (Banias), what about the cult of St Berenice that so many of the Church Fathers mentioned? Wilson notes that the description of the wonderful statue provided to us by Eusebius doesn't quite match the story that comes down to us of Jesus healing the sick woman. The woman in the gospel narrative is depicted as touching Jesus from behind. This statue meanwhile had the woman supplicating before the man, and each had outstretched arms. Because of this Wilson concludes that the statue does not represent the story in the gospel text and therefore cannot be a Christian depiction. Wilson does however offer some ideas about which group of people the statue might have represented:

> The statue was most likely of great antiquity, nevertheless several possibilities have been suggested. The group described by Eusebius could plausibly have been a contemporary depiction of, say, Titus and Herod Agrippa II's half-sister Berenice, who were Roman lovers prior to Titus' ascension to the imperial throne. This might explain the appearance of the name Berenice as that of the woman healed of the haemorrhage in certain Byzantine church histories. (John F Wilson, *Banias*, p 91)

Other accounts of the same excavation undertaken by Wilson tell us:

> Excavations at Banias have revealed a large basilica that is almost certainly a very early Christian church. The building was constructed directly over structures dating to the Herodian and Roman periods (first century ce) and numerous architectural elements of these buildings have been incorporated into it. The fine grey granite columns which are widely scattered all over the site today probably were incorporated into the church from an earlier Roman building, as were the well-made

column bases found near the wall of the church. Particularly striking is the reuse of finely carved white limestone fragments in the walls and even in the foundation trenches. The building was very large but was itself destroyed and its stones reused to build towers and walls of the medieval fortress … The basilica was located directly in the centre of the city, its atrium opening directly onto the Cardo Maximus. This important location suggests that it was the seat of the bishops of Banias … it was likely also the repository of the 'statue of Christ' as well. (Ibid, p 96)

Wilson seems to leave out some critical details about the exact location of this basilica that make the central characters in the statue all the more obvious.

The basilica is actually on the east side of the original palace of Berenice. Indeed, when I asked Prof Wilson how wide a distance separated the two buildings, he told me 'twenty yards at the most'. Another study has determined that 'the basilica was Agrippa's throne room'. As such, and assuming that the image of Christ went back to the Herodian period, Marcus Agrippa would have of necessity been looking at the statue of himself and his wife Berenice on a very regular basis.

When the Jewish War ended, Titus went back to Rome to be with his father and Berenice went with him. It was said she lived alongside him in the palace, where he treated her as if she were his wife. And well she might one day have been, were it not for the fact that the old warhorse Vespasian, who had been robust all his life, suddenly became ill in June of 79 CE. As he lay dying, he joked with his aides at the expense of his Claudian predecessors. Virtually his last words were reported as being 'Dammit, it looks as though I'm becoming a god'. He died on June 23rd, to be replaced on the imperial throne by his eldest son Titus. This situation left Titus in something of a cleft stick with regard to Berenice. Despite her best efforts she was unpopular in Rome and, while living with Titus as his effective concubine was one thing in the eyes of the Roman populace, having her as the emperor's wife was something entirely different.

Through thick and thin across the previous few years, Titus had been absolutely loyal to Berenice, despite the fact that she was a good ten years older than he. But once he took the imperial throne there was nothing else for it: she had to go.

Very reluctantly he sent her back to her own country, where she disappeared into obscurity. It is said that Titus may well have intended to bring her back to Rome once things calmed down and his power base was secure, but that was not to be. His reign lasted only two years until 81 CE, when he died on an expedition to the Sabine country, reportedly in the same farmhouse where his father had died.

The story of Berenice and Titus is the stuff of genuine tragedy. It is interesting to speculate what would have happened to the Roman Empire had Titus lived longer and had he been able to have Berenice by his side. Even more interesting is the thought of what might have taken place if they had borne a son together, for in such a case the blood of the House of David might well have flowed in the veins of the dynastic rulers of the Roman Empire.

CHAPTER 9

INSIDE A MESSIAH

Marcus Agrippa's commitment to his Roman allies cannot be doubted for a moment. From the second he was released from prison by Caligula, Marcus continued to show loyalty to his overlords for the remainder of his life. It was a long life, because Marcus Agrippa retained control of his kingdom until around 100 CE. We know he lived this long because an inscribed lead weight was found in Tiberias that mentioned his 43rd regnal year, which must have occurred around 98 CE.

By this time the emperor of Rome was Trajan, which means Marcus Agrippa held his territories and ruled over his kingdom under no less than *ten* different emperors. At a time when to be in a position of authority and even to outlive one emperor was something of a feat, Marcus' life was truly remarkable.

It has been suggested by some historians that there wasn't really much left for Marcus Agrippa to rule after the first Jewish War. Thousands of his subjects had died and still more had been sold into slavery, and almost all of these were Jewish. But clearly the territories were not empty after the war because at least half of Marcus' subjects were not Jews and probably remained generally unaffected by the war and its aftermath. In my estimation, once all the evidence has been amassed, the war and what followed constitute proof that Marcus Agrippa did indeed believe himself to be the promised Messiah of his people and that he continued to view himself as such right up until his death. Let me explain.

There will be those who quite understandably suggest that a Messiah of the Jews who supervises what amounts to a holocaust upon his own people is something of a departure from what orthodoxy would suggest for a redeemer and a heaven-sent servant of the one true God. But such a response clearly fails to address what Jews expected from their Messiah or what Marcus Agrippa himself took this position to mean.

It is worth looking again at what some of the expectations of the Messiah were, as spelled out in different parts of the Old Testament. Thus we will be able to see how successful Marcus Agrippa was – in his own terms, if not through the eyes of history.

One of the primary expectations of the Messiah was that he would bring about a situation under which all nations and people would worship the God of Israel.[73] The Book of Zechariah tells us that, after the Messiah appears, all the world will turn to the Jews for spiritual guidance. Zechariah 8:23 says:

> In those days ten men from every language of the nations shall grasp the sleeve of a Jewish man saying, 'Let us go with you, for we have heard that God is with you'.

It was also prophesied that the Messiah would bring peace to the world, though there is nothing to suggest that this state of affairs would be achieved without bloodshed and misery on the way. It is made very clear time and again that those who fail to recognize the Messiah, or who fail to follow his lead and instructions, can expect nothing good from God. In Deuteronomy, from 18:15 onwards, we find Moses talking to his people. He says:

> The LORD your God will raise up for you a prophet like me from among your own brothers. You must listen to him ... I will raise up for them a prophet like you from among their brothers; I will put my words in his mouth ... If anyone does not listen to my words that the prophet speaks in my name, I myself will call him to account.

Of course it was only human nature for Jews of the first century to take extra note of extracts from their holiest and most ancient books that served nationalistic goals. People still do that today. Quite naturally there were many Jews living in Palestine in the days of Marcus Agrippa who expected that the Messiah would direct his warlike intentions against the Romans – that he would cause the nation to rise up and throw out the invaders once and for all. Nevertheless it is important to note that this wasn't the only messianic school of thought in Jewish antiquity. The earliest text of the rabbinic tradition – the *Mishnah* – has a story of how the ancient sages actually acknowledged Marcus Agrippa as this awaited figure.

All of this gets swept under the carpet nowadays because of today's resurgence of Israeli nationalism. Marcus Agrippa isn't the sort of figure that modern Zionists would wish to see as the eternal flame of their tradition. Nevertheless a careful examination of this story and subsequent rabbinical commentary makes clear that it was well known to Jews of all times. Indeed, Christian commentators throughout the Medieval and Reformation periods attacked Jews for their continued belief in 'the Messiah Agrippa'.

The whole subject of the Jewish remembrance of Marcus Agrippa as the Messiah is best left as the subject of a separate work, although I have outlined a brief sampling of the material in Appendix C. However, it is appropriate to mention the earliest reference in the *Mishnah*, in which we are told that, on a particular sabbatical year or Jubilee (the text is not specific in that regard), Agrippa was acknowledged by the greater body of sages to have been the awaited Messiah.

Agrippa is portrayed as doing what Jewish kings had always done during this festival – he read from the scroll of Deuteronomy. The purpose of this exercise was to remind the Jewish people of what their ancestors had endured in the past. Yet it is equally clear that Agrippa's actions on that day were filled with symbolism. Jewish custom prescribed that a king should sit while carrying out the reading. This was intended to show deference to the high priest who retained the singular position at such times.

The story tells us that Agrippa boldly stood as he read each line from his scroll. The symbolism was obvious to everyone who had gathered there. It was intended as a fulfilment of the line from Deuteronomy we cited earlier, where God says to Moses:

> I will stand a prophet from among your own brothers, and I will put My words in his mouth, and he shall speak to them all that I command him.

Clearly Marcus Agrippa standing to undertake the reading was a break from tradition, intended to make a statement. Marcus Agrippa was announcing that he was the promised Messiah and that he would eventually create a new and perfect Law.

The text tells us that he stumbled a little in his reading when he came upon a prohibition set by Moses on Jews placing a foreigner as their ruler. We have to remember that his Herodian ancestry made many people think he was more Arab than Jew. Nevertheless the reassuring words of the consensus of Jewish leaders made clear that they accepted him as fully Jewish, showing that they felt he was enough 'like Moses' to be the Messiah. 'Do not fear Agrippa,' they declared, 'you are our brother, you are our brother.' Thus they confirmed him as a king and a prophet from 'among their brothers'.

Marcus Agrippa was a Jew, but he understood the Romans all too well. After all he had spent much of his time in Rome and had been carefully schooled in Roman ways. He knew what 'being Roman' could offer anyone who embraced citizenship, but he was astute and clever, so he must have also understood the many shortcomings of life under the empire. What he was clearly seeking for 'all' his people was a new way forward. We know from historical sources that he was a great scholar. Indeed the rabbinical theological tradition associated with him made him a perfect candidate to have been the founder of Christianity.[74]

According to the Jews, the Messiah was one who would bring a 'more perfect' revelation to Israel, thus rendering the old commandments and ordinances utterly useless. In short, the task of the Messiah was to start again from scratch. Old laws would no longer be valid and a new Covenant with God would be established. Catholic Christianity later shunned such radicalism from its seminaries, nevertheless it was clearly present in the earliest days of the faith and was intimately associated with a strict authoritarian figure named 'little Marcus'.[75]

In his time, Marcus Agrippa was a modern man with a good understanding of the realities surrounding him. This has to be the case because, unless he was a very shrewd and intelligent individual, he could not possibly have held on to his lands and titles through such difficult times. His recognition of what the Messiah should be was radically different to that of the Jewish nationalists, who in reality simply wanted to maintain the status quo in terms of their own power base. Marcus saw the potential for a new way forward, but he possibly suspected from the start that his dreams might never become reality without a significant amount of bloodshed and misery on the way.

We can see a situation in which the peculiar coincidences surrounding his early years led not only Marcus Agrippa, but also his immediate family, to reach the conclusion that this little prince genuinely was the Promised Messiah. This, under the circumstances, would have seemed quite rational and wasn't simply a matter of his mother, sister or other relatives trying to manoeuvre events to suit their own ends. As we shall presently see, for at least a year prior to the crucifixion, the prophet and herald Jesus had made it abundantly clear that little Marcus indeed was the Messiah. To him would fall the task of rescuing not only the Jews, but the whole of humanity.

In the cynical age that we inhabit today, we can perhaps be forgiven for believing that everyone has 'an agenda' and that if Marcus did put forward the suggestion that he was the Promised Messiah, he probably did so only to suit his own purposes. But it is equally likely that Marcus believed that he had been sent by God to do great things – almost everything we know about him tends to suggest that this was the case. If he had entertained any doubt at all about his true status, the tumultuous reception he received in Alexandria, not simply as a child but throughout his life, must have confirmed that he was a special person engaged in a very specific task. If all the Jews he encountered throughout Palestine had been as receptive and willing to make necessary changes as the Jews and Samaritans of Alexandria, the whole history of the Near East may have turned out to be quite different. Unfortunately for Marcus Agrippa and for Judea, this was not the case. In particular Marcus had to deal with sects such as the Pharisees.

The Pharisees are a difficult group to describe or to fully understand. The word 'Pharisee' comes from the Hebrew פרושים or *perushim*, from פרוש or *parush*, which means 'apart' or 'separated'. Pharisees sprang from an earlier group known as the *Hasidim*, a sect of especially pious individuals who had shown a great hatred for and opposition to the Greek influence that had crept into Judaism from the time of Alexander the Great onwards.

Most inhabitants of the region, though Jews, were non-sectarian, so they could not be classified as Pharisees, but the Pharisees were respected and enjoyed a high degree of power. Way back in time, Herod the Great's reign had been beset with difficulties created by the Pharisees and other devout Jewish sects; they never accepted him as a rightful Jewish king. In the intervening period the Pharisees had not changed: they were as opposed to Marcus Agrippa as they had been to Herod the Great. In fact, to them, there was no difference. Both men were not quite Jewish and, in their cooperation with the pagan Romans, they were in fact regarded as traitors to Judaism.

If the Pharisees were not bad enough, Marcus also had other groups to deal with. Amongst these were the Zealots, a sect that found popularity amongst the poor because of their radical nationalistic agenda. War leaders such as Josephus before his 'romanization' could be classified as both Pharisee and Zealot, a combination that bred men who were totally alien to cooperation of any sort with the Romans. Unless Marcus had been willing to raise an army and attack the Roman forces head on, he could never have found favour with the Zealots or their followers.

Marcus held his titles for 28 years before armed rebellion broke out and the first Jewish War commenced. During this time we can be certain that he did everything possible to bring peace to his troubled lands. True, some of his actions may have seemed provocative to more militant and conservative Jews. For example, he was accused of raising idols in certain synagogues and was already putting into place some of the changes that his status as the Messiah demanded, but he was a man who believed himself to be on a divine mission – one he was determined to carry through, no matter what the consequences.

It is clear from the historical evidence that the Romans, and probably Marcus too, were somewhat taken by surprise by the suddenness and ferocity of the armed uprising that took place in 66 CE. Since Marcus was in Jerusalem at the time the garrison there was attacked, it is possible that he was one of the primary targets of the rebels. But together with his wife Berenice he escaped to Galilee. From there he cooperated fully with Rome in order to sort matters out once and for all. The Jewish homelands had been a thorn in the side of the Roman authorities for many decades and now, with many of their legionaries dead and one of their famous 'eagles' (*aquilae*) captured, the Romans were not about to pull their punches for anyone. If Marcus Agrippa had refused to cooperate with Rome's response he would have been removed from power and most probably executed.

He must have used all his skills as a negotiator and scholar to maintain his position, because client kings who failed to control their own territories were almost never left in positions of authority. What usually happened under such circumstances was that the monarch was removed and the lands in question were taken under the direct control of Rome. In the mind of Marcus Agrippa the factions that simply failed to see sense and come to terms with the realities of the world had signed their own death warrants. Just like the Romans, Marcus Agrippa wanted to sort things out in Judea – even if that meant a protracted and bloody war.

There can be no doubt that many innocent people were caught up in the fighting, though this state of affairs was clearly brought about as much by the rebels as by the Roman army – in the siege of Jerusalem, inhabitants of the city who genuinely wanted to surrender were mercilessly butchered by their fellow Jews.

It seems quite evident that, after nearly three decades of patient rule and countless frustrations at the hands of the conservative elite, Marcus Agrippa finally asserted his authority as the Messiah he believed himself to be. But those historians who suggest that all he was left with at the end of the war were empty lands are far from accurate.

Marcus' new way survived. The Temple and all it had stood for was deliberately and totally destroyed, doubtless with Marcus present to see it happen. The inhabitants that remained would not be bothered by the Pharisees or the Zealots again – at least not for a long time. Marcus had bought himself some breathing space, during which he could put his new policies into action without the interference of nationalists. Whether deliberately or simply as a result of the serendipity that seemed to follow him throughout much of his life, Marcus not only retained his titles and lands, but his sister became the chosen one of a man who would undoubtedly one day be emperor of Rome.

What was infinitely more important was that Marcus Agrippa's 'new covenant', a philosophy meant for *all* people, not simply for Jews, may well have found its way directly to the top. When we read about the nature of Titus, a man who revelled in war and martial pursuits as a young man, we find a dramatic change came over him later in his life. This became singularly evident when he took up the reins of power as emperor. Titus had conducted the war in Judea with great ferocity, even by the standards of Rome, and when he returned home he showed again just how ruthless he could be. He became the commander of the Praetorian Guard, the emperor's personal bodyguard. From this position of power he quickly eradicated anyone suspected of disloyalty to the emperor, sometimes having them executed on the spot.

Because of these actions many Romans feared that when Titus became emperor he would become another Tiberius or Caligula, but they must have been astounded by what actually took place. As one of his first actions as emperor, Titus called a stop to trials based on treason charges. Treason had come to mean not only actions but words, so that anyone slandering the emperor or his family was liable to execution. But Titus said this: 'It is impossible for me to be insulted or abused in any way. For I do naught that deserves censure, and I care not for what is reported falsely.'[76]

Previous informants, of which there had been many, were now banished from Rome. It was even reported by Suetonius that if Titus ever realized that he had done nobody any particular good throughout his working day he would say: 'Friends, I have lost a day.' Although his reign was short, Titus was remembered with great affection and respect for decades after, and is set apart as one of the potentially great emperors who lacked only sufficient time to put his plans into action.

None of this is to infer that Titus became a plaster saint. He was the leader of the greatest empire in the world at the time and acted as such. But he developed a kindness and an understanding that not only belied his earlier brutish nature but which truly puzzled those around him. How much of this came from his association with Marcus Agrippa and, even more importantly, Berenice is impossible to say, but that Titus became more 'Christian' in the terms the word is often used, there is little doubt.

CHAPTER 10

THE GOSPEL TRUTH

If Marcus Agrippa, the last king of the Jews, was truly the unquestioned Messiah for tens of thousands of people during his lifetime, why is he almost totally forgotten today? Surely, if Christianity began as Marcus' own self-created mystery religion – a deliberately created offshoot of Judaism – we should still be aware of this. How is it that Jesus, a self-confessed warm-up to the main act, now has star billing in a show dedicated to his memory?

The story of the ultimate failure of Marcus Agrippa's new covenant is a complex one. It has much to do with the way people have always been able to manipulate facts, figures and especially past history to suit their own ends. This process still goes on today. Consider for example the immediate legacy of President John F Kennedy. At the time of his tragic death his stature was so high in America and throughout the world that he was genuinely spoken of as some latter-day King Arthur. His period in office was, quite surprisingly now, referred to as 'the Camelot years'.

With the passing of time the world came to learn that this elevated statesman, like all human beings, had feet of clay. His methods have been questioned and some of the people with whom he did business have been discredited. President Kennedy's personal life has come under close scrutiny and been found wanting. Even some of the honours paid to him after his death, such as the change in the name of Cape Canaveral to Cape Kennedy, have been reversed.

Now, something of a backlash is taking place and President Kennedy is once again being talked about with greater affection than for the last couple of decades. Was he a genuine superhero of the 1960s or an all-too-willing tool of an oppressive, unjust and incredibly corrupt capitalist system? It all depends on whose book you read and the context of the time in which you read it.

The case of J F Kennedy only goes to prove how quickly the perceived character and integrity of a leading statesman can take a nosedive, even in a society where media coverage is all around us. How much easier therefore would it have been to whitewash an equally famous person out of existence 2,000 years ago? Few could read and, even if they could, there were no newspapers, magazines or television screens to offer opinion and comment. History was, in those far off days, whatever those that had power and authority wanted it to be.

But we should not allow this state of affairs to discourage us from making the best attempt we can at unravelling the secrets of the past. In the case of Marcus Agrippa there are sizeable clues, such as a boy-sized throne with a massive story of its own to tell. There is also a written legacy, if only we recognize it for what it truly is – or rather what it once *was*. Marcus Agrippa left us a unique insight into what he believed and how he thought that, as God's chosen Messiah, he could achieve his world-changing objectives. Strangely enough this written testimony is known to anyone who has had anything to do with Christianity. It ranks as one of the most holy of all Christian documents and yet virtually nobody knows who wrote it, when it was penned or what it is actually trying to tell us. It even carries Marcus Agrippa's name to this very day, because we know it as St Mark's Gospel.

Wait a minute though. Isn't St Mark's Gospel exclusively the story of the ministry of Jesus? Moreover, this gospel doesn't stand alone; it is only one of four such books in the New Testament, so what makes it any different from the others, and how could it possibly be about anything other than what we have been brought up to believe? To answer these questions we need to know a little more about all of the gospels of Christianity.

Any outsider, having learned the basic facts, might be led to believe that the central concepts in Christianity are quite straightforward. The faith relates to a man named Jesus who gathered a group of disciples together in order to preach the gospel. His message was a doctrine of peace. It so enraged the Jewish authorities that they arrested, tried and quickly crucified him. After his followers buried his body in a tomb just outside Jerusalem, he rose from the dead, thus fulfilling a promise he had made to them while alive.

Word spread of the amazing miracles of this man. In due course God sent his Holy Spirit into chosen evangelists to establish a written testimony about his ministry in four books or gospels. Other books followed later but it was the gospels that were the cornerstones of the faith. Out of these four pillars the Christian Church was established. According to its adherents, the eventual triumph of this simple faith from its humble origins in Galilee to a worldwide religion proves that Jesus indeed was the Christ of the Jews.

Most people from a Christian background are brought up to believe that the four gospels of the New Testament, when taken together, represent a truthful account of the life and ministry of Jesus. This isn't a surprising attitude because the gospels have been around a long time. But while most of us have lost touch with our ancient past it is important to remind the reader how completely removed, even in remote times, the average Christian believer was from the events being described, or indeed from seeing the holy texts upon which the tradition was originally based. When the gospels did eventually arrive the vast majority of believers were barred from reading them due to illiteracy. Even to those who could read, faith in Jesus came first and then, in due course – when and if the adherent was sufficiently trained in official Church dogma – the fourfold nature of the gospel was finally revealed to him.

The important point to keep in mind is that few people openly questioned the 'great mystery' of the New Testament – that it was God's will that there should be four different accounts of Jesus' life instead of one. It was only after a thousand years of Catholic dominance in Europe that a few daring scholars during the last century openly proclaimed that these official claims were completely unscientific. In their opinion there had to be a better way to explain how the fourfold New Testament canon got its start than simply by relying on what the first Church Fathers considered an act of faith.

Beginning around the time of the Reformation, it became unfashionable to limit oneself to a supernatural explanation for the presence of four separate gospels. For one thing it seemed obvious that there were undeniable literary traits in each of the texts that proved that they belonged to separate human authors. What is more, at least three of the gospels, those of Matthew, Mark and Luke, parallel each other and, in some specific instances, even seem to be identical. Clearly this is not likely to be the case if the four gospels were genuine, first-hand accounts of a series of historical facts that had been written independently. One has only to look at witness reports from a modern crime in order to see how diverse accounts of the same events tend to be when viewed through different eyes.

The problem of the three gospels of Matthew, Mark and Luke has been worried over for so long that the situation has become like a huge ball of string that has been kicking about in a drawer for generations. It has now become so tangled that any hope of finding a place at which to begin sorting it out seems hopeless. Nevertheless it is in the nature of human beings to try to bring order to chaos, so scholars across the ages, especially since the 19th century, have attempted to work out once and for all who wrote what when, who copied from whom and why such a complicated situation came about in the first place.

For a long time it was thought that the Gospel of Matthew had come first. After all, it appears first in the canon. What is more, early Church writers and scholars *believed* that Matthew's was the first gospel and later generations were not inclined to argue with those individuals who were, by this time, revered and considered holy. It's as if we should imagine that, because these people were chronologically nearer to the events that are being discussed, they must necessarily have been in a better position to understand what happened and when. To modern sensibilities this is a very strange and distorted point of view. One might as well suggest that just because the emperor Caligula believed himself to be a god – and was believed to be so by those people whose lives were contemporary with his – we still have to accept his divinity today. There are times when distance from an event or a series of events can and should bring greater clarity and a dispassionate approach.

The situation is compounded by the fact that Christians, like so many other religiously inclined people, are conditioned to *believe* rather than to prove their case. The Church Fathers would not be seen as reliable witnesses in any court of law today. Not only were they influenced by their own time and the circumstances in which they lived, but also their very notion of truth was inexorably different to ours.

There are still many devout believers, but generally speaking we live in an age of science, when something is taken to be true only if it can be proven. Unfortunately, when it comes to the gospels, who wrote them, when they were written and who influenced whom for what reason, many of the components necessary to build a working and replicable experiment are missing.

That hasn't prevented thousands of people from trying to get at the truth, though even here it has to be remembered that many of those who have undertaken the exercise were, themselves, ardent and sincere Christians. Though laudable in one sense, this probably makes their efforts somewhat tarnished before they began.

The Gospels of Matthew, Mark and Luke, set apart as they seem to be from the Gospel of John, are together known as the Synoptic Gospels. The word *synoptic* comes from two Greek words that mean 'together' and 'seeing'. The term was coined as early as the 16th century, possibly by Georg Siegel, but it was in the 18th century that people really began to look at Matthew, Mark and Luke in an objective manner.

Throughout the years different experts looked intently at the gospels and it seemed as though each had his own idea about which of them had been written first, and when. As better forensic techniques developed it seemed that there might actually be a gospel missing. It was suggested that there were elements common to some of the existing gospels that most probably came from an entirely different source. This supposedly lost gospel became known as *Quelle*, German for 'source', usually referred to as 'Q'.

The Q theory reigned for quite a while until some scholars worked even harder at the problem and came to the conclusion that the mysterious Q might not exist at all. It was quite possible, they asserted, that

Mark alone was the definitive voice and that what we see in Matthew and Luke is simply a series of later embellishments. It now seems to be generally accepted that, of the three surviving synoptic gospels, Mark was the first to be written. There are dissenters to this point of view, but they are fewer in number these days than they have ever been.

A fairly recent proposal that becomes possible only because we now have biblical scholars who are not necessarily Christian, or who retain a genuine impartiality, is that none of the gospels can be taken at face value and that they were all substantially altered in the second century. One of the greatest exponents of this theory is David Trobisch, Throckmorton-Hayes Professor of New Testament language and literature at Bangor Theological Seminary in USA.

Trobisch has literally taken the gospels apart and has concentrated on all sorts of nuances that would not even have occurred to experts in the past. In particular he looked at forms of language, abbreviations and sacred name contractions in order to judge the genuine originality of each gospel. The result of his efforts was a developing conviction, ably proven by evidence, that all of the gospels were responsive to the same sort of editorial processes at the same time. He looks towards a single publisher of the gospels in the second century CE only, after which the books were reproduced elsewhere.

The implication is clear: if the gospels all respond to the same publishing procedure and so share so much in common, they cannot be viewed as being reliable source documents about specific and actual events. There is strong evidence that the four canonical gospels as we see them today were all contrived from a single earlier source document which has itself been lost or deliberately abandoned.

Perhaps one day some fortunate archaeologist will bring to light, in some hidden cache of documents like those found in Qumran or in Nag Hammadi, Egypt, a version of the gospels so contemporary with the events it reports that its authenticity cannot be doubted. But for now we can only rely on the documents we have. The early Church Fathers were in the business of creating a religion and there were many factors that contributed to their behaviour and attitudes. They had to deal with the political realities of the world in which they were living. Compromises had to be made and, as the Church hierarchy began to develop, documents already in its possession were scrutinized carefully and alterations made to eradicate potential problems – either religious or political.

We have good evidence in the level of composition that the four accepted gospels appeared in the same place and at the same time. David Trobisch points out that this is evident in the level of conformity in language. In all the gospels, words such as *Theos* (God), *Kyrios* (Lord), *Iêsous* (Jesus) and *Hierousalêm* (Jerusalem) are written in an abbreviated form with a horizontal line on top. He took this one stage further, pointing out that these are not old shorthand symbols because they take just as long to write as the full form of the words. These special words, or *nomina sacra*, appear for the first time with the gospels. They constitute a publisher's informing of the reader that what he is reading could only be part of the fourfold gospel.

It is obvious therefore to Trobisch and others that the fourfold gospels were produced at the same time and in the same place. They appeared in Rome in about 172 CE and went on to become the accepted gospels of the developing Roman Catholic faith. This may not of itself stand as irrefutable proof that the accepted gospels are actually much altered and fractured versions of one single, original gospel, but the possibility seems more than likely.

In the knowledge that so much has been done to alter a story that is understood very little, a fundamental question has to be asked. That is, did Jesus build the Church or – just as likely and in some ways more so – did the Church build Jesus? While such a process would be virtually impossible to achieve in the high-tech, information-laden society of today, it wasn't half as difficult at a time when few could read and when communications across national and geographical boundaries were strictly limited.

One might ask the very reasonable question, why are there four gospels in the first place? This has not universally been the case. We have to take account of those early Christians who used a version of the gospels known as the *diatessaron*. The diatessaron, which means 'out of four', is generally taken to be a harmonization of the Gospels of Matthew, Mark, Luke and John. Most of the material from all four is used, and all tell a common story.

Supposedly the most famous diatessaron was written in about 175 CE by an Assyrian named Tatian. It got rid of the ambiguity that came from four separate works and made of Jesus' life and ministry a narrative story that was about 75 per cent the size of the four gospels combined. Tatian's was far from being the only diatessaron, versions of which were at one time used in church services across a wide geographical area.

I mention the diatessaron not as a further confusion, but simply to point out that not all early Church traditions relied on the four canonical gospels. Rather they used a synthesis of them, as in the case of Tatian's diatessaron. There is sufficient evidence to suggest that many early versions of Christianity relied on a single version of the gospels – though it almost certainly was not a compilation as in Tatian's case.

I hope to prove in due course that all the various versions of the gospels, and the diatessarons that appeared, were ultimately responsive to one original gospel. We could call this the Gospel of St Mark, which would accord with most expert opinions today, but even then we would be only half way to the truth because the Gospel of St Mark as we see it today is no longer in its original form. In a sense it is just as divorced from the truth as are the Gospels of Mark, Luke and John.

Information on authorship of the gospels relies entirely on Church tradition and is particularly responsive to a corpus of work known as the *Works of the Ante-Nicene Fathers*. This is a collection of short passages, essays and commentaries written by Christian scholars, generally dated to the period before a great Church council, the Council of Nicaea, held by the Emperor Constantine in 325 in Anatolia (now Turkey). In this case and in the collections of post-Nicene Christian documents, we find a series of traditions that have become so enmeshed into Christianity that they are treated as 'gospel', which in many cases they most definitely are not.

Unfortunately there is no historical reference to St Mark the Evangelist outside the gospels themselves. 'He may be this, he could be that ...' are the responses of Christian scholars when dealing with St Mark, and indeed most of the saints from this early period. This state of affairs is not their fault and it isn't down to sloppy research; it's simply that there isn't a single word about St Mark the Evangelist from any contemporary historical source, and hearsay – no matter how spiritually imbued – is not the same as independent testimony.

It's as if an inquest is being held into the death of a specific individual who is known by name, whom everyone claims once existed but nobody met. Some witnesses have sent letters to the court in which they claim to have known the deceased, but the writers of the letters can't be traced either, let alone turn up and give evidence. The coroner may reluctantly draw the conclusion that the proceedings are rather pointless since there is no body, no reliable witnesses and absolutely no tangible proof that the deceased ever existed.

As with so many other characters in the gospels, each commentator has taken the story of St Mark as he or she learned it and, maybe without any real intention, has elaborated upon it just a little. As a result the spectre begins to gain some sort of human shape but in all honesty, the finished form still lacks substance. It is not enough to say that, because the Gospel of St Mark exists, there must have been an evangelist by the name of Mark who wrote it.

The descriptions we have of St Mark are presented by the Church, not as a biography, but rather as a 'hagiography', the dictionary definition of which is 'a worshipful or idealized biography'. We are told that he was sometimes called John Mark and that he was the son of Mary, a woman living in Jerusalem who is also mentioned in the gospels. St Mark is supposed to have associated with St Peter and St Paul and it is suggested that he eventually travelled to Rome. Tradition also suggests that he founded the Church in Alexandria.

His authorship of the Gospel of St Mark is said to have dated from around 60 CE. It was written in Greek, for the sake of gentile converts to Christianity. St Mark's evidence for the life of Jesus is said by some to have been derived from the testimony of St Peter, who was one of Jesus' disciples.

Where St Mark was born or where he died are matters of conjecture, about which even the Church admits it has no evidence. Like so many characters associated with the very foundation of Christianity as we know it, St Mark comes from nowhere, goes to nowhere and in the middle writes something upon which an entire faith is founded. But even if St Mark actually did exist we know that his gospel, along with those of Matthew, Luke and John, was at least re-written in about 172 CE, and there is a nagging doubt as to whether there were originally four gospels at all. On the available evidence it seems much more likely that the four gospels as we know them today were gleaned from an original single work. On the way they were altered and annotated in order to suit the needs of a growing Christian Church that had begun to gain ground and that was hardly likely to allow the truth to get in the way of a good story.

It is my contention that there was indeed only one original gospel and that it was, as experts agree, written by a man called Mark. Now using evidence, rather than hearsay and conjecture, I want to prove to the coroner that there is indeed a body and that there are plenty of witnesses to attest to the fact.

CHAPTER 11

THE SUPER GOSPEL

By now the reader has become familiar with the standard scholarly model that explains the origins of the canonical gospels. These days most truth-seeking academics suggest that the oldest gospel was written by an otherwise unknown historical figure named Marcus who lived some time in the late first century. Who this Mark actually was seems to remain a total mystery according to most experts. All that can be ascertained for certain is that his gospel is the oldest of the four canonical texts.

The most likely explanation for the situation is that, before the arrival in 172 of the gospels we know today, there existed in antiquity one original gospel – one *full* text in which all the narratives about Jesus and the disciples were held under one roof. Such examples, later to be known as *diatessarons*, are usually thought of as being 'gospel harmonies' of the established Church. But we would do well to remember that this is a name afforded by people who would come to reject them in favour of the four separate gospels.

I prefer to call this text a 'super gospel' owing to the fact that it represents something fuller or more complete than the shorter texts with which we are more familiar. Nevertheless most scholars identify them by the derisive term employed by their Greek-speaking detractors – diatessaron, or 'synthesis of (the) four'. But what is difficult to know is which came first, the chicken or the egg. It remains a distinct possibility that the diatessaron form, as it turns out to be incorrectly named, was both known and used in certain Christian circles long before 172.

Why does all of this matter for our theory of the origins of the gospels? Well, for one thing, the earliest Church Fathers do not speak of 'gospels', the plural but rather 'gospel' in the singular. When they cite long sections of text, rather than just a sentence or two, it is inevitably a citation from a super gospel rather than being from one of the familiar canonical texts. As the eminent New Testament scholar David Trobisch notes, the whole idea of a fourfold gospel appears only in the mouth of one particular Church Father living 150 years after Jesus was crucified, and even then his argument is barely convincing.

The man in question is Irenaeus, whose date of birth is not known, though he almost certainly died at the end of the second century. Irenaeus was the bishop of Lugdunum in Gaul (now Lyons in France) but he spent much of his time in Rome.

If we read the writings of Irenaeus carefully we notice right away that he doesn't say what theologians would like him to say – that the fourfold set of gospels had always existed from the beginning of Christianity. Instead he emphasizes that they 'ought' always to have existed. In other words, he can't identify one single person before him who ever used the four gospels. Irenaeus claims that he inherited the fourfold gospels from his own teacher, Polycarp, but a little determined research shows conclusively that Polycarp never used anything other than a single document – he was familiar only with a super gospel.

As a result of arguments like this, Trobisch and others have suggested that Irenaeus invented our four canonical New Testament texts himself. Many people familiar with the supposed diatessaron texts that have survived down to modern times notice that they look uncannily like a fuller Gospel of Mark. This suggestion stems from the fact that the first words of the diatessaron parallel those of the modern and accepted Gospel of St Mark.

In one of the super gospels, known as the Borgian Diatessaron, we see the survival of a tradition connecting the material to an author named Mark. The opening words acknowledge an acrostic behind the names of the four familiar evangelists. An acrostic is a poem or series of lines in a document in which certain letters are intended to spell out a quite separate but significant word. This is a form of code, implying that a man with the name of Mark was ultimately responsible for all the texts. We read in various forms the declaration:

> Matthew the elect, whose symbol is M, Mark the chosen, whose symbol is R, Luke the approved, whose symbol is Q, and John the beloved, whose symbol is H. (Borgian MS 1)

In the parallel Latin text the letters derived from each name are M, R, K and A. It isn't too hard to piece together what the original editor is really saying: the diatessaron, or super gospel, was written by *Marqeh* (Mark), and this is the specifically *Samaritan* Aramaic rendering of the Roman name of Marcus. The implication has somehow been missed by various generations of scholars who have studied it. The editor is clearly pointing to an ancient tradition that Mark didn't just write the material that made its way into the gospel carrying his name in the West. *Mark was the author of all the material that eventually and falsely appeared under the name of four other supposed gospel writers.*

None of this should come as a surprise to anyone who has ever studied the Coptic Christian faith of Alexandria. An oral tradition that has passed from generation to generation, despite all sorts of hostile foreign pressure, says much the same thing, albeit in a slightly different way. The Alexandrians tell us that Mark was more than just another evangelist; he was a kind of eyewitness reporter who had a first hand experience of all the words and deeds of Jesus and put them down on paper.

The Alexandrians emphasize that any reader can quite literally 'see' Mark standing there beside Jesus, witnessing his ministry in the text of the gospel itself. Their tradition lists a number of scenes in the narrative in which Mark is clearly recognizable as being present. What reinforces this impression is that Mark is very often self-evidently present in versions of the gospels other than that attributed to St Mark himself. In other words we find his shadow being cast over the supposed work of Matthew, Luke and John.

Let me try to spell this out more clearly. As an example, Alexandrian tradition says that Mark was present at and wrote down a description of the marriage at Cana. This was the well-known story in which Jesus turned water into wine. However the Marriage at Cana narrative is not found in the Gospel of Mark. Rather we find it in the modern Gospel According to John. But the Alexandrians are insistent that Mark was present. They also assert that Mark penned the story of how, after the crucifixion, Christ appeared before the disciples in a house, the doors of which were shut. Yet this story no longer appears in a gospel ascribed to Mark but rather that according to Luke.

It may come as a surprise to some readers to learn that there is still a sizeable Christian community in Egypt, despite the centuries-long influence of Islam in the region. This Christian presence owes nothing to much later Western European influence in Egypt – it is home-grown, dating a long way back. By far the majority of Christians in Egypt belong to the Coptic Church. According to tradition the Coptic Church was founded directly by St Mark in the middle of the first century CE, and Copts are adamant that the founding of their Church took place in year 42 CE. As a result it might be expected that the Christians of Egypt, and of course one of its major cities, Alexandria, would hold a special regard for St Mark. But in reality the situation is far more complex than simple adulation for the founder of Egyptian Christianity.

The title with which St Mark is most commonly identified by the Copts is that of the 'Beholder of God'. This title appears and reappears countless times in the Coptic liturgy. The use of this title is necessarily rooted in the idea that the apostle Mark (who rather confusingly was also called John), alone of all the disciples beheld Jesus (that is, God), who was crucified at the Passion. However in the canonical Gospel of Mark used in the orthodox Christian tradition and shared by all peoples of the former Roman Empire, no mention at all is made of Mark's unique status.

All of this begs the question: where could the Alexandrians have got the idea that Mark had a unique status and that he had beheld and written down countless scenes that are no longer attributed to his authorship? The only possible answer that makes any sense at all is that the original historical literary composition written by the real apostle Mark was a super gospel – what traditional scholars would call a diatessaron. It is worth repeating that the very name diatessaron is therefore entirely misleading. This super gospel didn't represent an attempt at harmonizing four supposedly original texts: rather, the situation was the other way around. There was one original Gospel of Mark that was in turn deliberately and quite consciously divided into four shorter compositions. This was clearly done in order to eradicate some unwanted text in the original composition.

It is impossible at this distance in time, and without the necessary evidence, to know exactly why Irenaeus took upon himself the job of creating four disparate gospels out of one original. Interestingly, buried in Irenaeus' own apologetic work *Against the Heresies* is an acknowledgement that a group of 'heretics' devoted to Mark made the suggestion that Irenaeus was 'in the pocket' of the wicked Emperor Commodius. If we put all the pieces together we end up with the very real possibility that the fourfold canon was developed at the behest of the Roman emperor of the period.

All of this begins to make sense, even to those who have never heard of Marcus Agrippa or the suggestion that he, rather than Jesus, may have been the promised Messiah. Ancient sources are insistent upon the point, and it wasn't simply Jews who believed this. The earliest Christians in Alexandria were not only devoted to an apostle or 'spokesman of God' named Mark but also, from the first century on, the earliest Christian voices from Alexandria share the Jewish understanding that Marcus Agrippa rather than Jesus was the Messiah prophesied by Daniel.

The first Christians of Alexandria most certainly had unique beliefs regarding their beloved St Mark. It is also clear these same people held as sacred the fact that Mark wrote the original super gospel, from which all our canonical texts were later derived.

It cannot be disputed that the oldest Catholic Church Fathers from Alexandria were all connected to this rival super gospel written by Mark. Clement of Alexandria, a Christian apologist, missionary and theologian (150–c.216) referred to it by the title either of the secret Gospel of Mark or indeed as the Gospel of the Egyptians. Under its latter name, the Gospel of the Egyptians is mentioned in accounts from antiquity as being genuine and well-known. In the last century a letter was discovered that had been sent by Clement to a certain believer named Theodore. In this letter Clement states explicitly that there were two gospels written by Mark – a short one which made it into the New Testament (our canonical Gospel of Mark) and a fuller secret text that the Alexandrians kept hidden from everyone else. This document and what it suggests about St Mark's super gospel has certainly unsettled many scholars.[77]

Even Irenaeus, who seems to have created the four gospels we know today, and probably did so as a result of an imperial command, made mention of St Mark's super gospel. He attacked members of Clement's own 'secret' tradition, identifying them as possessing a fuller Gospel of Mark that added many new and unfamiliar stories about Jesus. Both in his letter to Theodore and in his other writings, Clement makes it clear that members of his tradition had to hide or even deny their faith in this 'other' Gospel of Mark for fear of the authorities at Rome.

So strong was the Egyptian faith in St Mark's original gospel that there were relentless persecutions in Alexandria. Clement eventually had to flee the city to avoid death. Most scholars characterize these persecutions as being perpetrated against all Christians. But if this were true, one would expect that the first people to be arrested would have been the bishops and dignitaries in the Church appointed from Rome. It is therefore very strange that Clement – who speaks in whispers about a secret Gospel of Mark – was run out of town, but that the official overseer of the Roman Church in Alexandria, a man identified as Demetrius, remained there, totally untouched by the attacks, for almost 50 years!

Maybe this isn't as surprising as it seems. Demetrius could not have been a native Alexandrian. The various legends related to him in Coptic literature always stress his foreignness. The underlying suggestion is that people such as Clement had much to fear when Demetrius came to town. His overt mission was to keep an eye on the locals and make sure that they were enforcing the official orthodoxy of the Commodian period, which was of course rooted in the claims regarding the 'heaven-sent' fourfold gospel. In other words the developing Christian Church in Rome was already beginning to champion its own doctrines over those of any other form of Christianity.

The same pattern can be seen playing out over the course of the life of Clement's successor in the Catechetical school (more about this in chapter 15), a man by the name of Origen. It is true that in his writings Origen never once mentioned the existence of a secret Gospel of Mark, but this is almost certainly because Origen, knowing what had happened to Clement, went to far greater lengths to hide his 'heresy'. Whereas Clement openly identified himself as a Gnostic, the charges against Origen were much slower to take hold, simply because he was more careful about publishing his true beliefs.

In almost every page of Origen's works we hear him toe the party line regarding the fourfold gospel. He even wrote countless commentaries on each of the texts. His commentary on Matthew survives only in an incomplete form. Nevertheless enough of the material has come down to us that we can uncover something rather odd about his methodology. Despite the fact that he openly claimed to be writing a commentary on one particular gospel text, that of Matthew, Origen's exposition consistently follows the diatessaron at every turn. It is so uncanny that at times one can't help but feel that he and his followers were secretly communicating with one another between the lines.

It was probably inevitable that the Church in Rome would smell a rat. Origen was eventually discovered to have deviated from 'true orthodoxy'. He was tortured and eventually made his way to Palestine. What is not at all surprising is that it was Demetrius, the hatchet man from Rome, who was ultimately responsible for his expulsion. After arriving in Caesarea, Origen remained very influential despite the charges of heresy levelled against him, and many stories developed about his true beliefs.

In a letter to Theodore Clement had explicitly stated that:

Mark came over to Alexandria, bringing his own notes ... [where] he composed a more spiritual gospel for the use of those who were being perfected. Nevertheless, he yet did not divulge the things not to be uttered, nor did he write down the hierophantic teaching of the Lord, but to the stories already written [in the canonical text] he added yet others and, moreover, brought in certain sayings of which he knew the interpretation would, as a mystagogue, lead the hearers into the innermost sanctuary of that truth hidden by seven veils. Thus, in sum, he prepared matters, neither grudgingly nor incautiously, in my opinion, and, dying, he left his composition to the Church in Alexandria, where it even yet is most carefully guarded, being read only to those who are being initiated into the great mysteries.

Clement goes on to curse a group of philosophically inclined Christian heretics for taking this text and spreading it around the world. Against them he says the true believers in Mark '... must never give way; nor, when they put forward their falsifications, should one concede that the secret gospel is by Mark, but should even deny it on oath. For, "not all true things are to be said to all men".'

When we add up all the facts that are available there seems to be general agreement that the original gospel text emerged from Alexandria, a city that, in a Christian sense, is still devoted to Mark to this day. We are left with the impression that there simply must have been a genuine faith associated with the original gospel that was also suppressed. This inevitably leads us back to Marcus Agrippa.

I have already demonstrated the sort of impression Marcus Agrippa made on the population of Alexandria when he arrived there as a boy, sent at the request of Caligula to spy on the Roman governor and to help stop the pogrom that was taking place throughout the city. Now the strands are beginning to pull together. It is not simply a coincidence that the names Marcus and Mark are so very similar. Neither is it in the least surprising that the little alabaster throne currently to be seen in Venice is known as the Throne of St Mark. It becomes more and more evident that Marcus Agrippa and the gospel writer and apostle St Mark were one and the same person.

CHAPTER 12

THE HEBREW MESSIAH

The gospels of the New Testament, as they stand today, or even the diatessarons that still exist, can only take us so far in our search for the original Gospel of St Mark. This is, for the moment, lost to us. It isn't out of the question that copies of it lie sleeping in some forgotten vault, like the scrolls of Qumran or the Gnostic Gospels of Nag Hammadi, both caches of documents that have come to light in recent times. Neither is it totally unlikely that, at the back of some forgotten shelf in a dark and dusty old Coptic Church somewhere in Egypt, a copy of this lost work still survives.

In the meantime all we have are snatches of St Mark's original composition. In a way it is remarkable that, after so many years of editing, annotation and deliberate falsifications, we can still see Marcus at all through the ensuing gloom. But see him we can, because he was there when events were unfolding and his presence remains. Mark was the boy who was surprised in the night alongside Jesus and his disciples. It was late and the eight-year-old had doubtless been asleep. The gospels tell us that he was covered only by a towel and that when he was apprehended he slipped out of his modest covering and ran away naked. Though, as we have seen, he didn't get very far.

Mark was at the Marriage of Cana and doubtless witnessed the Sermon on the Mount. He was with Jesus at the end of his life and was the Barabbas that the crowd bayed to save; and later he represented the 'risen Christ', when the disciples were gathered together after the crucifixion.

But of the true nature of Mark, alias Marcus Agrippa, as he originally appeared in the gospel of his own construction, we have nothing. This is hardly surprising since those who chose to alter the very mystery religion that Marcus Agrippa had created cannot be expected to have left us glowing accounts of his presence alongside Jesus.

Nevertheless, slowly but surely we are adding the poles to the teepee, on our way toward proving the central claim of this book – that Marcus Agrippa believed himself to be the Messiah of Jewish tradition and that he was the writer of St Mark's original gospel. In order to offer more evidence we can look again at what we know regarding the writer of St Mark's Gospel. Scholars have ascertained with some degree of certainty that St Mark was a Jew, though one who nevertheless sought to make his work accessible to Gentile readers.

Whoever scholars over the years thought the gospel writer Mark was, an overwhelming body of scholarship has already been brought to bear on determining *when* he wrote his original gospel. The vast majority of academics date his authorship to the period of the Jewish War. Some say it was before, others during, and a few maintain that it was shortly thereafter. But it is uncanny how uniform the opinion is that the gospel was composed 'around 70 CE' and of course by a man named Mark.

Why is everybody so convinced of this? There are two reasons. The first is that the earliest Church Fathers all connected Mark's composition to the death of St Peter, who was supposedly another important disciple of Jesus. The second reason is that the words of St Mark make it appear that Jesus prophesied the imminent destruction of Jerusalem and its Temple. In other words, Jesus is understood to have said 'The destruction will be in 70 CE'.

In his gospel, Mark uses the same passages from the Book of Daniel that were also used by Jews and the first Christians to argue that Agrippa was Christ. This is what Daniel said:

The Messiah shall be cut off and will disappear, and the people of the prince that will come will destroy the city and the sanctuary ... [H]e shall make a firm covenant ... and cause the sacrifice and the offering to cease, because of the abomination of desolations, until the decreed extermination will pour down upon them. (Daniel 9:26–7)

Also the surviving gospel tradition most closely associated with the historical Mark says:

And when ye see the unclean sign of desolation, spoken of in Daniel the Prophet, standing in the holy place, he that readeth shall understand. (Diatessaron 42:4)

Mark further emphasizes that Jesus or 'God' came down to earth to confirm the sanctity of the original prediction from Daniel. Later in the story of the developing Church someone felt compelled to alter Mark's original words, leaving us a 'yes' to the 'abomination of desolations' in 70 CE but a 'no' to the coming of the Messiah in the same year.

What exactly is the 'abomination of desolations'? Experts have argued over this strange phrase for centuries. The prophet Daniel makes it clear that it is something associated with the Temple – perhaps a pagan idol or a totally inappropriate act or a sacrifice on the holy ground. Some commentators suggest that this phrase relates to an event that happened in 167 BCE, when the Greek ruler Antiochus set up an altar to Zeus in the Temple at Jerusalem, but this can hardly be what Daniel was talking about, or indeed Mark. There was no Messiah around in 167 BCE. The 'abomination of desolations' that appears in both Daniel and Mark is more likely to be related to 70 CE, when messianic fervour was at its height. Indeed this interpretation of Daniel is shared *both* by official Judaism and Christianity.

The earliest texts of the Jewish historian Josephus attempt to clarify what Daniel meant when he uttered his prophecy about the last days of the Temple. The reconquest of Jerusalem by Agrippa's imperial backers represented nothing short of a 'victory of the Cross' over the forces of Judaism. In other words, Daniel foretold the coming of Christianity and more importantly that its Messiah would appear only at the time of the destruction.

Here we find yet another ancient witness for the understanding that Jesus wasn't the Christ but the Messiah's messenger. His words and deeds proved that someone else would appear in another time and place just as Daniel had predicted. Who was Daniel's Messiah? The one startling truth that emerges from an examination of all ancient Christian witnesses is that Jesus wasn't the Messiah predicted by *this* prophet. He lived too early to figure directly into the history of the destruction of the Temple. Indeed the earliest witnesses of the tradition confirm Marcus Agrippa as this figure. Only in later times was the understanding systematically silenced.

So how could the developing Christianity confirm the 'abomination of desolations' as being associated with the period immediately before the destruction of the Temple, and yet at the same time deny the presence of the Messiah? The passage in Daniel is quite clear: first the Messiah appears, he is 'cut off' (he is attacked or at best ignored), and then Jerusalem and the Temple are destroyed. There is no ambiguity at all. What is more, not just the Jews but almost all the earliest Church Fathers, especially in Alexandria, adhere to the same formula, in spite of the later 'correction' to the text. It has to be this way because Marcus Agrippa was quite deliberately recreating the prophecies of Daniel in those days immediately before and during the destruction of the Jerusalem and the Temple.

There is little doubt why someone made this alteration. It was all part of the ongoing war against the secret meaning recognized by various Gnostics to have been implanted into the text by the original author. The changes made to the gospel in order to have the Messiah appear in some vague 'future period' not only openly contradict what Daniel wrote in this passage, but also fly in the face of almost all the other 'Son of Man' references put by the author of Mark into the mouth of Jesus.

As countless experts have noted, Mark makes Jesus inevitably speak in the third person about this 'Son of Man'. Jesus never said 'I am the Son of Man', nor 'I will come back as me', but rather he suggests that the Son of Man is some other person who is to fulfil all the messianic prophecies of Jewish scriptures.

By this logic, is it safe to assume that Mark, who wrote the gospel, was considered by many to be the Messiah? Given that there are almost no other notable Jews named Marcus anywhere in the surviving Palestinian documents of the period, Marcus Agrippa is certain to be a 'person of interest' or even a 'suspect' in the 2,000-year-old unsolved mystery of the identity of the original author of the gospel. Yet we can take this even one step further.

Origen of Alexandria, a man who was active in the third century, cites 'Jewish historical texts' – undoubtedly Josephus himself – as recognizing Agrippa as the Messiah of Daniel 9:26. Our oldest accepted manuscripts of Josephus by contrast come from the twelfth or thirteenth centuries. By this time all reference to Agrippa the Jewish Messiah had been systematically removed from the text. Origen himself accepts this scriptural interpretation, making it highly probable that at least some, if not all, of the members of his ancient Alexandrian Christian community made the connection between Marcus Agrippa, the Messiah, and St Mark the evangelist.

It is not so hard to see how this understanding would have developed. Anyone who has ever read Mark's gospel from beginning to end sees Mark has written the text in order to use Jesus as a confirmation of a particular application of Daniel's prophecy concerning the events of 70 CE. If the historical conquest of the Temple represented the 'abomination of desolations' (Dan 9:27), the Jewish people's historical rejection of Marcus Agrippa necessarily represented the fulfilment of the line preceding – that is, 'The Messiah will be cut off and will disappear' (Dan 9:26). Indeed it is absolutely amazing to see that, when we read the earliest histories of Josephus, this is exactly what happens to Agrippa – he is 'cut off' and then suddenly vanishes into thin air.

If we look a little closer at these earliest texts of Josephus we see Marcus Agrippa consciously moulded into an exact replica of the Messiah figure of Daniel. The author claims that, just before the start of the war, he went before the rebellious Jews at the start of the revolt, pleading with them to turn back from their wicked designs. In Hebrew copies of Josephus the identification of Agrippa with the office of the Messiah is explicit. In the remaining early traditions we see Marcus specifically reference the very prediction from Daniel 9:24–7 in the exact same way that his historical counterpart 'St Mark' did when writing the gospel.

Marcus Agrippa's desperate appeal to his Jewish contemporaries includes a warning to his listeners that their actions will lead to the results foretold by Daniel:

Did not scripture say these things would happen? Was it not written that all the sacraments of the temple would be profaned? Those things already too frequently profaned are displaying their strength and all the influence of their mysteries. The temple has been contaminated with human blood, the couches have been filled with bodies, the altars covered with gore. Battles have been fought on the Sabbath, transgression has occurred while the temple is defended not by its usage and the solemnity of its festivals but by bloody battle … *you will be the originators of the greatest loss*, since the inconsolable development of all these evils will be ascribed to our blame which we are supporting … May love of your country move you. If consideration of your hostages, of your wives does not call you back, let contemplation of the most sacred temple recall you, spare at least our religion, spare the consecrated priests, whom the Romans will not spare, nor the Temple itself … I have omitted nothing, I have warned of everything which pertains to our safety. I recommend to you what I choose for myself, you consider closely what is advantageous for yourselves. I wish for there to be peace with the Romans for you and me. If you reject it, you yourselves take away my association. *Either there will be common good fortune, or peril without me.* [Author's emphases.] (Latin copy of *Jewish Wars*, Book 2, Ch 9)

This is surely the smoking gun for which we have been looking. It is the critical missing link that connects St Mark, the original historical author of the gospel, and Marcus Agrippa the Messiah predicted by Daniel. For the time Agrippa is recorded as having made these statements, is almost the same day, month and year as most authorities say his counterpart St Mark framed the original gospel around this same prophetic text.

Is this mere coincidence? Could there have been two Marks living in the same place and at the same time, using the same words from Daniel to predict the destruction of Jerusalem and its Temple? I hardly think so. We also have to consider the almost universal chorus of early Christians and Jews who use this same scripture to prove Marcus Agrippa as the Messiah. The gospel suddenly seems to have Agrippa's fingerprints all over it. When we add to the mix the fact that the Church Fathers repeatedly report that the followers of Mark believed that the original evangelist wrote the gospel to prove his own advent, the idea seems confirmed. As one ancient Catholic witness notes, 'the party of Mark' understood that '… Christ wrote the gospel. [But this is absurd]. The gospel writer did not refer to himself; he refers to him who he is proclaiming – Jesus Christ'.[78]

The idea that Marcus Agrippa wrote the gospel is hardly a pie-in-the-sky argument. Ancient texts witness the fact that many in antiquity interpreted the gospel very differently to today. There are very good reasons for connecting St Mark with Agrippa.

We can see from his text that the apostle Mark was quite fascinated by the Herods. He went to great, even inexplicable, lengths to claim that members of Herod's house were followers of Jesus right from the beginning of his ministry. It is also noteworthy that Salome, the real name of Agrippa's mother, appears only in Mark's gospel. Marcus Agrippa himself appears as 'John', the beloved disciple (a name still ascribed to him as his Jewish name by the Coptic Church). As Derrida, the contemporary French philosopher notes, Marcus' sister and wife Berenice (Veronica) has been all but removed from the surviving texts. However, as we have seen, she does survive in the Passion of the Christ and in various ancient Church documents, legends and other early references to the gospel.

With all this evidence, it is hard to deny that Marcus Agrippa was indeed the original author of St Mark's Gospel, yet we can do better still. If we go beyond the reconstruction of the lost original text we can also see Marcus Agrippa's influence on the gospel by reminding ourselves of his well-documented attitude toward the concept of 'heavenly Torah'.

Marcus Agrippa is repeatedly identified in rabbinic texts as firmly holding the opinion that only the Ten Commandments came from heaven. The rest of the Torah was written on the authority of Moses. There can be no doubt that whoever the original author of St Mark's Gospel was, he shared Marcus Agrippa's attitude toward what is often called 'the minimalist position' regarding the Torah.

The great Jewish scholar Abraham Heschel points to the story that appears in all of the Synoptic Gospels, in which Jesus is made to outline the differences between the Christian and Jewish position on divorce (Matt 19:4, Mark 10:1–12). The Pharisees argue that the Torah allows for the dissolution of marriage based on what is plainly spelled out in

Deuteronomy, that is, 'When a man hath taken a wife and hath lived with her, and it come to pass that she find no favour in his eyes ... then let him write her a bill of divorcement and give it in her hand, and send her away out of his house.'

This argument, as Heschel notes, necessarily assumes that all 613 Commandments of the Torah came from heaven. Meanwhile, Jesus' counter-argument proves that the original writer of the gospel did not subscribe to this point of view. St Mark makes Jesus a mouthpiece for his understanding that commandments such as the one on divorce did not come from God but instead were established only on the authority of Moses. This is why Jesus responds to the arguments of the Pharisees by declaring that it was only Moses who '... gave you leave to divorce your wives' and that 'from the beginning it was not so'.

Heschel's arguments point directly to the underlying similarity between St Mark and Agrippa. Indeed, if St Mark were not Agrippa, we would have to accept that he was another Jew by the name of Mark, contemporary with Marcus Agrippa. He would be highly literate, with full knowledge of the events surrounding Jesus' ministry, and a man who also happened to hold many of the same beliefs as we know to have been held by Marcus Agrippa.

We can also look to Clement of Alexandria for notification of Mark the gospel writer's attitude to the timing of the Messiah's arrival. In his Alexandrian Gospel, Clement points to an important textual variant. In his fuller text the words '... after the resurrection they will neither marry nor be given in marriage' are tacked on at the end of Jesus' rebuttal of the Pharisees. This emphasizes something that is never properly spelled out in traditional approaches to the New Testament. It is quite clear that for Mark the gospel writer *the messianic age did not begin with Jesus' ministry.* Throughout the entire period of his ministry, right until his crucifixion, the old Law (for Agrippa this meant the Ten Commandments) was still in force. However, as observed through Clement's voice, with the appearance of the Messiah a new Law would be established which would render the old Commandments null and void.

It is also interesting to note that most people misinterpret the word 'gospel' to mean something like 'the teachings of Jesus'. Nevertheless an examination of the Palestinian cultural environment from which the gospel grew counters this point of view.[79] It has escaped the notice of most scholars that the Qumran texts actually identify the Torah as the 'glad tidings' or 'gospel of Moses'. In other words, the gospel dispensed to the Apostle Mark, by revelation, was taken to be nothing short of the new and indeed completely divine Torah from heaven. Of necessity it therefore superseded anything that had gone before.

It is also worthwhile looking at the specific title held by St Mark in his association with the gospel. He, like the other gospel writers and eventually the disciples as a whole, is referred to as an 'apostle'. The title 'the Apostle' is especially interesting owing to the fact that it is a formal title of Moses in Jewish and Samaritan literature. Moses is consistently identified as the one 'sent by God' to establish the Torah, in the same way the Copts still see Mark as the one disciple uniquely chosen to 'behold God' and to write down the gospel, the new Law of Christ.[80]

In Near Eastern literature the world 'apostle' meant 'divine spokesman'. The Catholic development of twelve apostles, or indeed the very concept of an apostle as one of many ambassadors of a certain religious view, dilutes the original point. The one called 'apostle' in such a cultural setting is necessarily the Messiah – like Moses. There can be only one apostle in the messianic age owing to the fact that God decreed that only one apostle – Moses – had the authority to speak for Him. In short, it may be possible in early Jewish linguistic terms to have a 'multitude of angels' but not a 'multitude of apostles'.

Neither should we overlook the fact that the *Mishnah* does indeed make an apparent reference to Agrippa with this very title – *apostolos* – in its account of the destruction of the Jewish temple.

All of this leads us to our most persuasive proof yet that Agrippa didn't simply *write* the Gospel of Mark. He established it as a kind of new messianic Law for Israel. An ignored folio of the *Shabbath Tractate* from the Babylonian Talmud demonstrates in very explicit terms that the gospel *had become the law of the land in Agrippa's kingdom in the period immediately after the destruction of the Jewish Temple*. How could any of what is being described here be true unless Agrippa was the Mark who wrote the original gospel?

What is clearly needed is a total re-evaluation of traditional values. The Talmud identifies the Jews as being governed by the gospel in the period immediately following the destruction of the Jewish Temple. This is almost never mentioned in any modern study of the period. From the same period we also see repeated mention of Jews assembling in clandestine gatherings. In order to ensure that everyone present was against the ruling authority, all present had to pronounce a curse against Christians which went as follows:

> And for the apostates let there be no hope, and may the insolent kingdom be quickly uprooted in our days. And may the Christians and their sectarians perish quickly. And may they be erased from the Book of Life and may they not be inscribed with the righteous. Blessed art thou, Lord, who humblest the insolent.

This is the so-called *Birchat ha-Minim*, the Blessing of the (Christian) Sectarians. It is definitely from the late first century. Traditional scholarly models have never known what to do with it. When all the evidence is taken on board it becomes obvious that the word 'Christianity' in this context means something markedly different from the Christianity we know today. Marcus Agrippa believed *he* was the Christ (the Messiah) and he ruled accordingly.

There are always two sides to every story. The fact that many Jews of his own period hated Marcus Agrippa doesn't mean that everyone was against him. On the contrary, if we go outside the borders of Judea, we encounter a very different perspective on Marcus Agrippa. The Church Father Justin tells us that by the second century everyone in Justin's native land of Samaria had gone over to a form of Christianity that would now be called deeply heretical.

Is it possible to demonstrate that contemporary Samaria venerated Marcus Agrippa as the Messiah? We already know that, whoever St Mark was, he believed that only the Ten Commandments came from heaven, because when Moses instigated the other laws he did so on his own authority. If we could find an important teacher or leader named Mark who had such beliefs and existed at the heart of Samaritanism during the same period, there would be no further ambiguity.

In fact there is such a teacher, and he is known to the Samaritans as 'Marqe, son of Titus'. I first came across him during my research into the existence of a super gospel, where I repeatedly found his name mentioned. Marqe is the specifically Samaritan Aramaic rendering of the Latin name Marcus.

The character known as Marqe is extremely important to early Samaritan theology yet, as a person, apart from his hymns, poems and his theological Magnum Opus we know very little about him. There are innumerable reasons for identifying the collection of Marqe's hymns and writings as being second-century creations at the very latest. In particular the works of Marqe make it plain that, during his time, Samaritans were actively engaged in converting others to Samaritanism. However, this practice was officially forbidden by the Roman Emperor Constantine at the beginning of the fourth century. The Church Father Origen makes it clear that Samaritans were also banned from carrying out these practices in the third century. These are indications of an early authorship on the part of Marqe. In addition, an early rabbinic tradition identifies the period leading up to and including Hadrian's rule as the latest possible date for Marqe's composition. Hadrian was emperor between 117 and 138.

For all sorts of reasons we can assume that the Samaritan people stayed loyal to Agrippa and the cause of Rome through to the end of the second century. As James Montgomery, author of *The Samaritans: the Earliest Jewish Sect* notes, on page 87:

[The hundred years] ... between the beginning of Herod's grace to the land of Samaria down to the fall of the Judean state was the happiest age, we may assume, that the Samaritan sect has experienced in its long history. The land enjoyed the favour first of Herod and then in general all his official successors; its value was recognized, from the days of Herod to those of Vespasian, as affording a sure foothold against the tumultuous Jews.

I would further suggest that a messianic candidate seen as meting out the appropriate vengeance against the Jews for desecrating the Samaritan altar almost 200 years earlier certainly would have been accepted as genuine. The destruction of the Temple in Jerusalem could have looked like a deliberate and necessary retribution when viewed from a Samaritan perspective. The only question now is whether the

Jewish acceptance of Marcus Agrippa as the Messiah necessarily carried over to their Samaritan cousins.

A careful examination of the texts and hymns attributed to Marqe should leave no doubt in the minds of anyone that Marqe was at one time identified as the Messiah of this culture – or, if one prefers the language peculiar to the Samaritans, he was a prophet like Moses. To this day the surviving orthodoxy continues to preserve his memory as someone of very special significance.

The literature associated with Marqe forms the core of contemporary Samaritan theology. His writings represent the proper interpretation of Moses' Torah, which is the beating heart of the Samaritan religion. Outside of his written words, we know only a handful of facts about him. Yet at the same time his influence is so great that we literally have no idea what Samaritan religion looked like before his coming. In this respect alone he is properly identified as something approaching a Messiah, albeit one who has become subordinated to the original authority of Moses.

The text called *The Teachings of Marqe* offers a perfect example of the paradox that Marqe represents in the Samaritan tradition. The author instructs his readers how they are to read and interpret various sections of Genesis, Exodus, Numbers, Leviticus and Deuteronomy, using mystical forms of allegory that sometimes defy explanation. There is clearly a truth lurking beneath all these cryptic allusions and ciphers, and it is very much Mark's truth. The author feels no need to explain where he received his knowledge. He doesn't refer to any contrasting views or alternative readings. His authority is unquestioned and his opinions are the very definition of orthodoxy in the community. Yet the Samaritans make it explicit that he was never a high priest.

This doesn't make sense except under very specific circumstances. Marqe was the only figure in the Samaritan constitution that could have trumped the authority of the existing high priest – which surely means he must have been the Samaritan community's awaited Messiah.

So what are the arguments in favour of Marqe being the 'second Moses' of the Samaritan community? The first is tied to that famed Jewish fascination for numbers related to religious passages. The

Samaritans note that the name Marqe is a numerological equivalent for Moshe (Moses) – the letters in each case add up to 345. In other words, just as Moses himself can speak of the coming of 'one like him' in terms of the name Shilo (whose letters also add up to 345) the name Marqe would undoubtedly have been interpreted in its day as having messianic significance.[81]

A copy manuscript of *The Teachings of Marqe* from the St Petersburg Museum makes the situation even more explicit. It identifies Moses as the 'prophet of the favourable period' and Marqe as the 'prophet of the period of turning away'.

Finally, there is the statement of the Samaritan document called *Tulida*, which lists the chronology of high priests in the community. It says that Marqe '… was the originator of the wisdom'.[82] To say that Marqe 'originated the wisdom' is another way of saying that he wrote out the new Law. Marqe was a prophet like Moses who came and revealed a more perfect Law, just as the original lawgiver had himself predicted would happen in some future period.

So, we have a man whose name is Marqe (Mark, Marcus) living contemporaneously with the period in question. He was a lawgiver to the Samaritans and a man who had the power to overturn the Law of Moses. He wasn't a priest but yet he is venerated to this day as being one of the founders of modern Samaritanism. What is more, he has gone down in history as being 'Marqe, son of Titus'. True, Marcus Agrippa was not related to Titus, soon to be the Emperor Titus, but he did become one of his staunchest supporters. All Roman emperors were 'fathers of the empire', which is what this epithet undoubtedly means.

We know for certain that the Samaritans achieved something of a golden age whilst Marcus Agrippa was king, and it looks very much as if they adopted him as their own special Messiah. If this is not the case, and if Marcus Agrippa, St Mark and Marqe of the Samaritans are not one and the same person, the level of coincidence attending these matters arguably goes beyond anything credible or even imaginable.[83]

CHAPTER 13

THE SEEDS OF GNOSIS

As the secrets of Marcus Agrippa's throne gradually become known, it will be seen that the foundations of the beliefs of this remarkable man were already laid before he was even born. We now know that his crowning as the Messiah of his people took place when he was only nine years old. No matter how precocious a child might be, he is hardly likely to have thought about life and his beliefs to any great extent at such a tender age. To this end, in order to appreciate all that followed in his later life, we need to look closely at the child in his times, and at the very important family connections and cultural circumstances he enjoyed.

We know very little about the personal background of Salome, Marcus' mother. This is especially unfortunate because there is no doubt that this rather mysterious woman played an important part in the earliest years of the last Jewish king. But we do have a good understanding of what was happening at the time, and of the strange cultural suffusion that was present in both Judea and Alexandria at the beginning of the first millennium.

Is it possible that Salome was from Alexandria? The likelihood cannot be ruled out. We know that Marcus was related to the philosopher, politician and writer Philo of Alexandria, referred to as being his uncle or cousin, though in historical terms 'cousin' is a cure-all for almost any sort of close relationship. Marcus' father was of the Herodian dynasty with the blood of the old Hasmonean kings of Israel flowing in his veins. There isn't any indication of Alexandrian relations on this side of the family, and so it stands to reason that Philo might have been related to Salome.

Bearing in mind all that happened, this makes sense. We might even suppose that Salome was brought up in Alexandria before eventually travelling to Judea in order to marry Marcus' father, Aristobulus. It was from his father that Marcus derived his Hasmonean blood that, by default, meant he was 'of the House of David'. We also know that Marcus' father died when the boy was still very young and it is therefore inevitable that Marcus fell under the guidance and support of his mother in the years leading up to his acceptance as the promised Messiah in Alexandria.

The city of Alexandria was a home to many Jews, of which Salome may have been one, but it was also one of the most important cultural, philosophical and religious melting pots to be found anywhere in the empire. It was even more cosmopolitan and free-thinking than Rome itself. For this the city could thank its founder, Alexander the Great, because at its inception Alexander had brought together people from across the whole of his own vast empire so that the place might flourish and grow more readily.

A sizeable proportion of the citizens of Alexandria at Marcus' time were Greeks, but most were Greeks who had lived in the place for many generations. They had become a very special species of Egyptian Greeks, to whom the world owes so much in terms of the birth of reason and ultimately science. Few people realize that the most famous queen of Egypt, Cleopatra, was not of Egyptian stock. She was a direct descendent of Ptolemy, one of Alexander the Great's most trusted generals. She was therefore ultimately Greek. Yet in the conception of most people she represents the absolute epitome of Egypt, with its strange customs and age-old religious practices. Cleopatra proves just how Egyptian the Greeks of Alexandria eventually became. At the same time it has to be recognized that it would have been utterly impossible for the Jews of Alexandria, no matter how much they tried to preserve their own traditions, to be unaffected by their cultural surroundings.

We can surmise that Marcus' mother, Salome, was brought up in these surroundings and, even if this was not the case, she clearly had

Alexandrian blood and thus was still susceptible to its rich suffusion of culture and religion. It also has to be recognized that Galilee plays a pivotal part in our story. This region had a population that was almost as cosmopolitan as that of Alexandria. Only half of Marcus' eventual subjects were Jewish and that means many other religious imperatives were being played out across the region. The Jews of Galilee would have been quite familiar with temples to Diana, Aphrodite, Zeus-Jupiter, Apollo and innumerable other deities of ultimately Greek and Roman origin. But aside from their own religion, the Jews of Galilee, like those of Alexandria, would have been most familiar with Egyptian deities, of which Osiris and Isis were by far the most important.

Osiris was the Egyptian god of life, death and fertility. Aside from Amun (with whom he was in any case associated) he was the most revered and certainly the most loved god in the huge Egyptian pantheon. The story of Osiris is one of majesty, treachery, death and ultimate salvation. Ancient stories said that Osiris had been the most popular of the gods but that the affection the other gods had for him also made him the target of jealousy. In particular, Osiris was hated by the god Set. Set eventually tried to kill Osiris by locking him into a sarcophagus and casting it adrift on the River Nile. Fortunately for Osiris he had a faithful wife and sister, Isis, who eventually found the coffin and was able to free her beloved husband. Still not content, Set chopped the body of Osiris into pieces and distributed them throughout the world. Isis searched the world for the fragments and reassembled them. One of the legends suggests that she then inseminated herself with Osiris' detached phallus and bore a son named Horus.

We can immediately see how such a story would have resonance for Salome. According to our reinterpretation of Josephus, Salome's husband Aristobulus was killed by Herod Antipas, which would certainly not be surprising when we consider the feuds that pervaded this most dysfunctional of families. For all we know, Aristobulus was murdered whilst Salome was carrying Marcus in her womb. The clever, calculating and extremely astute Salome would have leapt upon these circumstances in a moment, seeing the clear parallel between her own situation and that of Isis. This meant that her son, once he was born, would be synonymous with Horus, the son of Isis and Osiris. What makes this scenario even more likely is the great reverence with which Horus was held in Alexandria. To the Greeks there he took on a very slightly different persona. They called him Harpocrates and he was the embodiment of the sun rising each day at dawn.

Harpocrates was, for centuries, depicted as a naked boy with one finger of his right hand up against his mouth. Probably for this reason he became known as the god of secrecy, though it is just as likely that this gesture responds to the fact that he was already known for his divine secrets. This ensured that he became the centre of one of the most important mystery religions that ever appeared in Alexandria and beyond.

What exactly is a mystery religion? The term 'mystery' in this context is derived from the Latin word *mysterium*, which relates directly to secret rites and practices that lay at the heart of many religions flourishing in the time of Marcus Agrippa. In many of the mystery cults there were 'degrees' or stages of initiation. In other words a willing aspirant would first of all know very little about the deepest truths of the cult to which he had come. Only with the passing of time and after sufficient indoctrination and lessons would the willing supplicant gradually be introduced to the deepest mysteries that lay at the heart of any particular cult. Once in possession of them, it was suggested, he would at last understand and be as one with the Godhead.

There is little doubt that many of the mystery cults to be found throughout Western Europe and into the Near and Middle East during this period were closely related to one another. Many of them are now known as Osiris-Dionysus cults because at their heart there lay more or less the same dying and rising gods or demigods. These had many names in different locations, Attis, Adonis, Dionysus, Osiris and others, but the main themes remained essentially alike. A favourite mystery cult in Alexandria was that related to Serapis, a Greek/Egyptian counterpart of Osiris. As in many such examples, Serapis (Osiris) was so closely related to his son Harpocrates (Horus) that the two were virtually synonymous. This might be better understood in the realization that Horus was not simply the 'son' of Osiris, he was actually a *reincarnation* of Osiris.

What makes the cult of Serapis all the more interesting is the fact that it was once closely associated with Christianity. Just a few short years after the eventual death of Marcus Agrippa, a man by the name of Hadrian became emperor of Rome. In a work known as the *Augustan History*, a late Roman collection of biographies, we find a letter from Hadrian to a friend, in which he talks about religion in Egypt during his own time. We can take it that this letter was written sometime around the year 100 CE. This is part of what Hadrian had to say:

> The land of Egypt, the praises of which you have been recounting to me, my dear Servianus, I have found to be wholly light-minded, unstable and blown about by every breath of rumour. There, those who worship Serapis are, in fact, Christians, and those who call themselves bishops of Christ are, in fact, devotees of Serapis.[84]

This little passage is very telling, because it not only infers that there was deep religious confusion in Egypt at the time but also it directly associates the two religions of Serapis and Christianity, almost supposing them to be interchangeable.[85]

This immediately locks us back into Salome and her almost certain reverence for the story of Isis and Harpocrates. In her own mind Salome doubtless 'was' Isis and she would use every breath in her body to demonstrate that her fatherless son was nothing more or less than a direct personification of Horus-Harpocrates.[86] Harpocrates, as the Alexandrians saw him, reeked of mystery rites. As indicated, statues always show him with his finger against his lips, signalling silence, yes, but also giving a strict instruction to his devotees that the more they learned about him and his rites, the less they should say to non-adherents of the faith.

The fact that Marcus eventually married his own sister Berenice may not seem to be a very Jewish thing to do, but it is certainly extremely Egyptian. The gods and goddesses of the Egyptian pantheon frequently married their brothers or sisters, as indeed did the pharaohs for countless generations. Isis was not only the wife of Osiris, she was also his sister, and the fact that Salome must have allowed or even suggested the union of Marcus and Berenice displays her Egyptian religious leanings all too clearly.

If the conjoining of siblings seems odd, the contemplation of a marriage between the pagan practices of Egypt and the strict monotheistic beliefs of Judaism is even stranger. But it seems that this is a big part of what took place when Marcus Agrippa took on the mantle of the Messiah. It clearly could not have been his personal suffusion; it simply had to have been thought up by his mother Salome.

How could this possibly have come about? Of course we don't have sufficient evidence to say for sure, but what seems extremely likely is that Salome found herself to be a widow with many enemies, her husband murdered as a result of the fanatical feuding of his own family. Doubtless Salome fled to Rome, if she was not already there, and with her she took at least one daughter and a son, soon to be born. She most likely felt safe in Rome, until rumours regarding plots against the aged tyrant Tiberius in Capri came to her ears. Whether or not she took part in such plots cannot be known. But she certainly built bridges with Caligula, and encouraged her son Marcus to keep company with this strange young man who would soon be emperor.

When Tiberius rallied and learned about the plots in Rome, Salome fled with her children back to Galilee. There she fell under the spell of a charismatic preacher and prophet. She and her small family became his disciples. Salome might have hit relatively hard times but she was nevertheless a royal princess. Jesus earmarked her little son Mark as his successor and, if we are to believe what Marcus later wrote, recognized him as being the future Messiah.

Salome may not have actually hatched her plans for Marcus until those fateful few days when everything seemed to happen at once. Jesus was crucified, Marcus was arrested and then released, Tiberius died and Caligula came to power. Thanks to Marcus' strange but fortuitous relationship with Caligula he was raised immediately to the rank of king, whilst his wicked uncle Herod Antipas was deposed and murdered. In the mind of Salome it must all have been so obvious. Through his association with Caligula, Marcus, as Harpocrates-Horus, had avenged his father's death and now rose to become the saviour of the world.

It worked as well in Jewish terms as it did in an Egyptian sense. Even the sky had foretold of Marcus' eventual greatness. He had been raised or, more properly, 'resurrected' with the rising sun on the day of the spring equinox. Clearly then, Marcus was earmarked by God not only

Full view of the Throne of St Mark.

Dorigo (1989) is the most recent scholar to acknowledge that what now appears as the top piece or crest of the throne was added much later. The throne itself was cut from one piece of alabaster. The 'crown' or corona is either a distinctly separate piece of alabaster or else an original that was cut off and re-sculpted at a later date.

Samaritan inscription – The four characters on the left-most portion of the inscription represent the three Samaritan letters *alef shin lamed* with the last two letters separated by a character called a geresh (a device used in Hebrew to show that a word is special). The letters spell out *eshel* or 'the tamarisk'. This is undoubtedly the earliest part of the inscription. The letters appear in 'reverse order' (it would be natural to read Hebrew right to left and not left to right as here). The letters direct the attention of the initiated viewer to the image of the tree on the backrest.

The square Hebrew 'mirror writing' inscription which reads – 'the sitting of Mark Evangelist of Alexandria'. These 'mirror letters' are inferior in quality when compared with the three Samaritan letters. They represent a later addition reminding Alexandrians of the individual who originally sat on this throne and when he occupied it.

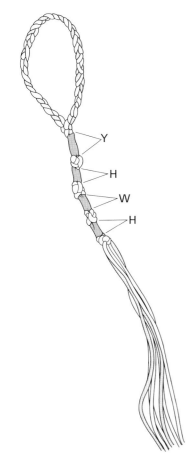

A *tzitzit*, or fringe (left) – Sephardic Jews have long employed 'numbered things' to represent letters of their alphabet. The fringes on the corners of the prayer shawl, or *tallit*, form deliberate patterns which spell out the name of God – they begin with ten loops, followed by two knots; then five loops followed by two knots; then six loops followed by two knots; and finally five loops followed by two knots, thus spelling out the name. In some traditions the loops of the fringes are made to spell out 'God is one'.

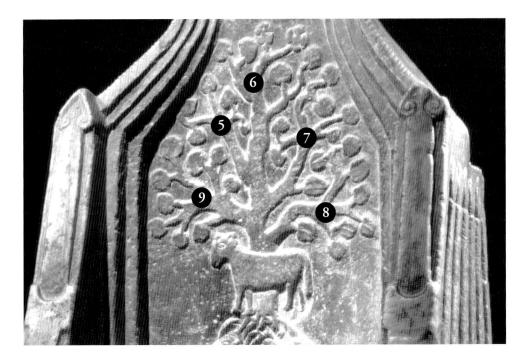

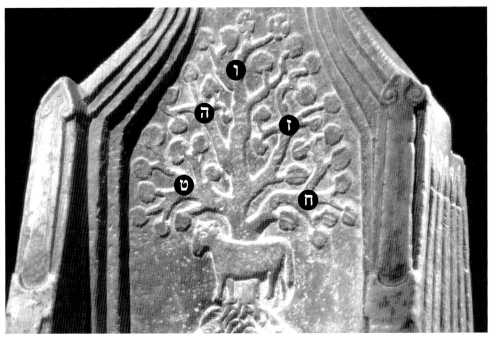

UPPER IMAGE The Jewish tradition of using 'numbered things' to secretly spell out hidden messages explains why the image of the tamarisk on the backrest appears asymmetrical. Each branch has a specific number of fruit to represent a particular letter of the Hebrew alphabet.

LOWER IMAGE When the numbers of fruit are converted to Hebrew letters a secret phrase emerges in Aramaic – 'the ninth vision'. There can be only one reference in mind here. Zechariah is a book containing nine visions – these were all vouchsafed in one night, and are of a symbolical character. Zechariah also happens to be the ninth prophet in the canon of Old Testament writings.

Left side (with bull) – The bull represents the underworld. Notice that no palm tree is represented here since at this stage the 'sprout' is symbolically 'buried', waiting to be 'reborn'.

Right side (with man) – The man represents the emergence of Mark the 'sprout'. Notice that the man is dressed as an evangelist but is not bearded, which would be a typical sign of manhood.

Back of throne (eagle and lion) – The lion prefigures Mark's eventual attainment of a Jewish kingdom. He is standing above the tamarisk tree that prophesied the crowned messiah. The eagle is rising above the world, carrying the gospel in its beak. This represents Mark ultimately manifesting himself as the historical messiah of Israel, revealing the new Torah.

The emergence of the palm tree into a rising sun. The Hebrew word *tamar* (palm tree) has the same numerological value as the word for sun (*shemesh*). Notice that the final image in the series is the eagle raising the sun. Van Luhuizen-Mulder (1988) notes that the representation of this eagle 'looks very much like that of the Tutankhamun falcon', which was a solar image.

to represent his own people but, as had been suggested for the Messiah since Old Testament times, the whole of humanity. He proved the fact by calming a dreadful revolt in Alexandria and doubtless saving the lives of thousands whilst he was still only nine years old. His simple presence had been enough to work this miracle, together with the magical hold he seemed to have over the Emperor Caligula.

Even at the time of Marcus' death, many decades after these first incredible events, people were having difficulty disentangling Christianity (Marcus' new religion) and the worship of Serapis. This is proof positive that Judaism had 'gone Greek' under the guidance and planning of Marcus Agrippa. Not only is Agrippa ranked by Jews throughout the ages as 'One of our own men who understood the Greek philosophy', but his secretary Justus was one of the leading men of his age to interpret Jewish scripture through neo-Platonic exegesis.

We don't know how long Salome lived but there is little doubt that it was long enough for her to realize that the faith she had shown in the cult of Isis and Osiris had brought tremendous rewards. She would undoubtedly have sung the praises of this Egyptian pair to Marcus all the time he was growing up and while he was at his most susceptible. In his short life prior to being declared both king and Messiah he had lived in a variety of places, under a host of different cultural practices amidst a cacophony of different religious beliefs.

It would have been absolutely impossible for Marcus Agrippa to have been left untouched by the events of his sudden rise or the inevitable conclusion that, all things taken into account, there was a pronounced element of divinity involved. He would have been educated not only in Judaism but would also have come to understand the sort of Greek philosophy that was so important to his relative Philo in Alexandria.

The Platonists were saying that all gods were one god. Their religious counterparts, those who would eventually become known as Gnostics, were professing that this divinity, though known by many names, could be directly approached by anyone. Marcus Agrippa considered himself to be its chosen spokesperson and would make the fact known – no matter what the sacrifice might be.

CHAPTER 14

THE ALEXANDRIAN
CONNECTION

There is a persistent suspicion raised among contemporary scholars that when Marcus and his party had arrived in Alexandria in 38 CE, together with his bodyguards, he had gone straight from the harbour to the house of his relative Philo. This is not at all unlikely. The city was in a state of ferment and Jews were in danger everywhere. Under normal circumstances a dignitary such as little Marcus would have been welcomed to the city by the Roman governor. Yet Agrippa did not alert the governor of his presence. Instead he arrived quietly at Alexandria and may even have left so quickly afterwards that Flaccus could not question his motives for being there.

The question of what Philo, little Marcus and his entourage were doing during this mysterious visit has puzzled scholars. We can say with certainty that if anyone could offer the new boy king the protection he needed it was Philo, who was not only extremely rich but was also one of the leading citizens of Alexandria. He had travelled to Rome regularly as an emissary for his people and on behalf of the Egyptian capital. Even as the renegade he had become, Flaccus would hardly have allowed any harm to come to Philo.

Philo of Alexandria is one of the most interesting men of his period. Although we don't know exactly when he was born or when he died, we do have a great deal of information concerning his ideas and it is possible to show how they were a direct product of the heady atmosphere into which he was presumably born and in which his attitudes developed.

Part of Philo's heritage came about as a result of events that had taken place centuries before he was born. Ptolemy, Alexander the Great's general, who had became the ruler of Egypt, had ordered that the Torah of the Jews should be translated into Greek, so that he and his fellow Greeks could better understand the motivations and beliefs of the Jewish faith. A better understanding of Judaism would assist in the efficient governance of Alexandria, but the flow of information would be far from one-way. It didn't matter how traditional and how zealous the Jews of Alexandria may have been in their devotion to their ancient Hebrew God, they were surrounded on all sides by people of other beliefs and, in particular, by the powerful forces of Greek philosophy. This would have had a profound bearing on their thinking, and especially so in the case of Philo.

Philo was a direct product of this heady mixture of influences. He may have been a man of business but we know that much of his adult life was spent in research and writing, which is one of the ways we know he was wealthy. But other information tells us of his standing, both financial and in a civil sense. Philo's brother, a man named Alexander, was called 'the Albarch', which almost certainly means that he had a very high standing amongst the Jews of Alexandria and probably had an important administrative function relating to Rome. This Alexander had been a great friend of Claudius long before he took the imperial throne. He was so rich that it is suggested that even Jewish kings borrowed money from him.

Alexander's son, Tiberius, would grow to be a great ally of Rome and eventually became Roman Procurator in Judea – at the time of the Jewish uprising! The office of procurator was extremely important. The dictionary definition is, 'an officer of the Roman empire entrusted with management of the financial affairs of a province and often having administrative powers as an agent of the emperor'. Tiberius, who must also have been a relative of Marcus Agrippa, must therefore have been cooperating heavily with Marcus, Vespasian and Titus during the conflict in Judea. One could hardly envisage a more influential family than that from which Philo sprang!

In Philo we are left with a portrait of an individual who managed to be 'all things to all men'. There is virtually nothing written about him that is not complimentary. He wasn't afraid to directly confront Emperor Caligula, the most mercurial of individuals, and he was recognized as being a good and devout Jew. Yet at the same time Philo's praises are sung by advocates of Greek philosophy. He was also earmarked by the early Christians as an advocate of their faith.

Fortunately for us, much of what Philo wrote in an apparently long lifetime still exists, and we have a very good picture of an individual who did all he could to reconcile Judaism with modern ideas of the time – as befitted the needs of the Jewish population of Alexandria. Philo was a great advocate of Plato, also incorporating the ideas of Aristotle into his own reasoning. He believed in the one, all-powerful God of Judaism, though with caveats, but he approached the divinity through *Logos*. To the Greek philosophers, Logos was the governing principle or reason, in distinction to superstition or simple acceptance. It is the cornerstone of science and, without it the modern world could not exist. But to Philo, Logos was more than a Greek explanation for sound, clear, thinking – it epitomized the very words of God as they appeared in scripture and law.[87]

Yet this explanation reveals only one part of Philo's belief system. For him, the Logos was nothing short of a divine hypostasis – a second god – that belonged in the religion established by Moses for the people of Israel.[88] It cannot be coincidental that the elusive St Mark appropriated it and made it the centre point of his gospel. Today Jesus is explicitly identified as the Logos, and the term would most likely have annoyed Jews in Palestine.[89]

Philo was close to obsessive about the written words of Judaism, but this does not mean he took everything he read in a totally literal sense. After all, there were passages that contradicted each other, and not everything the student of ancient Hebrew texts could read made any particular sense. Philo believed that it wasn't just what was apparent in the words that mattered, but also the codes or ciphers that underpinned the words. For this reason it was absolutely crucial to look at an entire text, even giving great weight to punctuation and sentence structure.

When all of his writings are taken together, it is clear that he conceived 'the Logos' as 'the wise architect' that established the hidden meaning of various passages. If one was initiated into His mysteries it was possible to distinguish when a particular passage had a specific hidden meaning that did not come across at first reading. Such passages could be recognized in a number of different ways. For example, one might find a repeated doubling of words in the text or the presence of superfluous words that appeared to have no real part to play in a specific phrase or sentence. Attention could also be drawn by a constant repeating of a phrase or sentiment, and once such a special passage had been recognized, there were ways in which to deal with it. A different meaning for a passage may emerge if the punctuation was ignored or rearranged, or if specific phrases were looked at in a different way or swapped around.

Philo believed that there were also specific words that had a deeper, hidden meaning. A good example of this was Philo's repeated insistence that almost every one of the patriarch's wives described in the Torah was really a representation of the female divine hypostasis or 'Wisdom'. Philo's system of logic was fiercely complicated by present standards and must have led to countless hours of interpretation, organization and juxtaposition before the final truth of a passage could be ascertained. But though extraordinary in many ways, Philo was only following the dictates of Jewish mystics right back to the dawn of time.[90]

The obvious parallels between Philo's mysticism and the opening words of the gospel are extremely striking; its declaration that 'the Logos was with God' from before the beginning of Creation is entirely Philonic. In other words, because the words or ideas that made up the written text 'came' from God, they were clearly 'of' God – the text itself was omnipotent, all-seeing and wisdom personified. It is true that parallels to these ideas can be found in the rabbinic literature, however the connection between little Mark and Philo, and the specific Greek term used by both in their writings leads us to very provocative lines of inquiry.

There is a widespread tradition that acknowledges Philo not only as a Christian but nothing short of being the first 'bishop' of the Alexandrian Church. Did Philo have an influence on the composition of the first gospel? The subject has raged through academic journals for centuries. There has to be a relationship, but what kind of a relationship was it?

Whatever the truth of his standing as a Christian, to Philo divinity was seen as being present in blocks of text that had been deliberately hidden, and that could only be teased out by those who were extremely devout, absolutely meticulous and very bright. In many cases, the subject matter being discussed no longer had primary importance. What mattered was the 'shape' of the passage – its true but hidden linguistic significance and also the number values of the letters and words.

It was in the light of this realization, though long before Philo's time, that 'Gematria' was born. Gematria is a word that will be totally unknown to most Christians, but almost all Jews who know anything about the history and traditions of their own religion will be familiar with it. Gematria relates to a practice that was extremely important in a historical sense, even if most rational people these days may think it absurd.

Gematria is the study of words in their numerical context. It works like this: every letter of the alphabet, or sometimes sound, has historically been allotted a numerical value. It doesn't matter who first gave these numbers or sounds the value they are said to have, because that lies within the remit of the deity – in other words, in the conception of those who believe in Gematria, it is something divine.

Letters or sounds from a particular word are apportioned their numerical value, and all of these that relate to a particular word or sentence are added up to arrive at a specific total. The total is essentially the 'soul' of the word or sentence in question. This word or sentence will then have an automatic resonance with any other word or sentence that has the same numerical value.

As nonsensical as this sounds in the 21st century, it was once of supreme importance. We know for example that, as far back as the eleventh century BCE, the Babylonian King Sargon II was interested in and used Gematria. He was busy building a wall at Khorsabad, decreeing that it should be exactly 16,283 cubits long. This was exactly the same as the number value of his name, so we can take it as read that Sargon II actually had a very long name.

If the Babylonians were using Gematria so early, it wouldn't be at all strange to discover that the ancient Hebrews did the same thing. After all, in the sixth century BCE many thousands of Jews from Palestine were carried off into exile in Babylon, where they became slaves. Eventually they were allowed to return to their homes, but we know from some of the stories in the oldest part of the Old Testament that they absorbed a good deal from their Babylonian captors during their exile.

Not only did the Hebrews learn about Gematria while they were slaves in Babylon, but also they went on to make the subject into an art form. It turns out that the Children of Israel were fascinated by all manner of number puzzles, ciphers and codes, but Gematria is the best known and best understood. The word 'Gematria' likely comes from the same root source as the word 'geometry', and the theory underpinning the use of this form of numerology is that everything in the known world has a certain resonance with everything else, though in some cases the concordance is much greater and therefore highly significant. Of course everything is ultimately a reflection of God.

Philo knew, as did many of the earlier Jewish scholars, that one could not rely on a particular message imparted by a block of text to be the only thing of importance. On the contrary, specific stories, rules or observations probably meant something radically different from their apparent meaning. Once again we see that, to the Jewish mind, the 'true meaning' can be more important than the message that appears to be intended.

Were these Jewish scribes and scholars deluded or plain wrong in their belief that Gematria had been deliberately placed in their ancient texts? Probably neither. Certainly in the case of the Old Testament we have verification from a very significant source, Blaise Pascal. Pascal was a mathematician and physicist in the 17th century. He had a rational approach to mathematics and has been called 'the father of probability science'. If Pascal looked at a series of numbers or a block of text and said there was no pattern, you could bet next month's wages on the fact that he was correct. Pascal spent a great amount of time looking at the Old Testament but, at the end of it, he had only one sentence to utter. He said, 'The Old Testament is a Gematria.'

Pascal wasn't alone because Isaac Newton, the father of modern science, also spent far more time looking at the Old Testament than he ever expended on scientific endeavours. He was convinced that the whole truth of the universe was encapsulated in numbers derived from the description and size of King Solomon's Temple. He even learned Hebrew, the better to understand what he was looking at. Newton was nobody's fool and would quickly have abandoned anything that was irrational or absurd. He may not have been correct about the universe being a reflection of King Solomon's Temple, but he recognized a code when he saw one.

Jews had other codes and ciphers too, which Philo also understood. Philo had an earnest endeavour to reconcile Judaism with the sort of logic that had sprung up with the philosophers of ancient Greece. He loved Plato's view of the detached creative force and also held a complex view of the Godhead that mirrors many of the early heresies in the Church. Philo appears to have believed that Yahweh, the nationalist God of Israel, was actually not the Most High God, but rather a slightly lesser divine figure. This is made explicit in three separate places in the Torah, so Philo had only to read what was written there. What Philo sought in his lifetime was the *absolute source* of divinity – and he thought he could make the unknowable God of the Greek philosophers spring to life, if only he could fully understand what all the ancient texts were really saying.

He almost certainly wasn't alone in this. Since the days when Ptolemy had first ordered a Greek translation of the Torah, thinkers on both sides of the fence had been looking for commonality in all religions and in philosophy. What set Philo apart were his copious writings and the fact that, with his unique position in history, his wealth and his important relatives, he was able to take his ideas and help to put them into practice.

The comprehension that Marcus Agrippa acquired as an eight- or nine-year-old child can be seen only in terms of the influence that was being brought to bear on him. We can certainly see his mother as a significant factor, but she was, in the final analysis, a woman living in a man's world. When it came to Marcus' position as the promised Messiah, it is true that the actual events that took place in Judea and in the sky above it were important factors; but to bring a recognition of his position to the world at large he would need to travel elsewhere.

In Alexandria the Jews were open, urbane, intelligent and very cosmopolitan in their outlook. Many of them, like Philo, were rich and so therefore had free time in which to think, discuss and write. These men were not shocked by innovation in the way the Pharisees of Judea certainly would be, and they also had a vested interest in settling 'the Jewish question' once and for all.

The standing of the rich and influential Jews of Alexandria, and their continued wealth and power, depended entirely on Rome. They didn't want an independent Jewish state in Egypt; such a thing would have been totally out of the question. They probably didn't want an independent Jewish state in Judea either. What Philo and his contemporary Jewish intellectuals wanted was stability, and to establish a way of looking at life that could suit as many different believers as was possible. Certainly Rome was open to religious novelty – it had proved this time and again, and in any case, the Romans were not especially devout as a people. What they desired most was exactly what Philo sought: stability and peace.

So we can see that, on a balance of probabilities, it wasn't Marcus Agrippa or even his mother who paved the way to something quite revolutionary that would suit the sensibilities of both Jews and also their pagan neighbours. Rather, these plans were hatched first in Alexandria, most likely by Philo himself. This is why little Marcus, doubtless nervous and holding his mother's hand, made his way along the dusty and dangerous streets of Alexandria in the year 38 CE, in order to find the one man who was in a position to take the auspices of the previous year and make them into hard and fast realities. Philo may or may not have personally ordered and paid for the throne upon which Marcus would be crowned as the Messiah, but he is almost certain to have been the original power behind it.

CHAPTER 15

THE 'MARK' OF AUTHENTICITY

We don't know how long Marcus Agrippa remained in Alexandria when he went there to be proclaimed Messiah in 38 CE, but we do know that he went back to Alexandria time and again throughout the remainder of his life. As we shall presently see, his relative Philo probably lived to a ripe old age and there is evidence that he was still alive by the time Marcus reached manhood.

It would be no surprise to learn that Marcus probably felt happiest when in Alexandria; there he was a thinker in a city of thinkers. The importance of Alexandria to the eventual development of the world we live in today cannot be underestimated. It was in Alexandria that many of the early Greek concepts, both in philosophy and science, began to crystallize into accepted mindsets and where religious ideas could be examined, discussed and practised in freedom. Experts often look towards developments of Christianity taking place in Rome when Alexandria had far more to do with the beginnings of the faith. The city was filled with colleges, seminaries and meeting places, where the intellectual minds of the period could meet, talk and argue without fear of censure or interference.

Philo must have met everyone who was anyone in Alexandria, and readers who have followed the evidence so far may not be too surprised that amongst Philo's acquaintances in Alexandria was none other than the elusive St Mark. This strengthens even more the hypothesis that St Mark and Marcus Agrippa were one and the same person.

His Holiness Shenouda III, head of the Egyptian Coptic Church, though obviously constrained when it comes to lumping St Mark and Marcus Agrippa together, seems nevertheless aware of the connection. In his work *The Evangelist Mark* he even makes the suggestion that St Mark married a woman by the name of Berenice! He also has a great deal to say about St Mark's apparent connection with the same Philo of Alexandria whom we know to have been so important to Marcus Agrippa. On page 93 he acknowledges that:

> At the time St Mark came to Egypt, Alexandria was already an important centre for education in pagan worshipping. Through its library and school, many philosophers and scientists were well known. It was proper for the new Church to have a theological school to support the faith in the hearts of its believers. A school had to stand up against the idolatry. St Mark, who himself was fluent in Hebrew, Latin and Greek, noticed the danger of the idolatry on the faith. He established a Christian theological school and appointed Justus, a scholar, to manage it. The new school was based on the 'Catechism method', where education was received through questions and answers. Beside spiritual and religious subjects, medicine, engineering and music were taught. The pagan philosophers studied the Holy Bible, not to believe, but to be able to criticize and to fight it. It was also the responsibility of this school to be able to argue their claims and to respond to them … Justus was the first to manage the school and later became the sixth patriarch. Others who attended this school and were distinguished to have high calibre, were also selected to the seat of St Mark.

It is immediately obvious that, whether he realizes it or not, Shenouda is clearly talking here not about St Mark – the quite separate and totally mysterious man about whom nobody knows anything – but rather about Marcus Agrippa. The proof lies directly within what Shenouda already knows. He says that the theological school was founded by St Mark, but that it was run by a secretary named Justus. Surprise, surprise, throughout much of his adult life Marcus Agrippa had a secretary named Justus, a man of great intelligence, and a great thinker and writer. This Justus was an expert in pagan philosophy. The reader will doubtless realize, as I soon did, that a coincidence is just a coincidence, but there are some coincidences that are obviously nothing of the sort. When we learn from Shenouda that Justus not only became the principal of the new school but also later a patriarch in the Coptic tradition, it becomes abundantly clear that the two Justuses are the same man. At a stroke we have another verification that the St Mark of this tradition was actually Marcus Agrippa.

The Catechetic School created by Marcus was far from being a third-rate philosophical academy. If the Justus mentioned by Shenouda is indeed Agrippa's Justus (and it would be difficult to argue against that assumption) he was a world-renowned authority on Plato. His interpretation of the Greek master is cited in Diogenes Laertes' philosophical compendium. Here was a man eminently suited to the task he took on and he clearly became one of the foremost lieutenants of Marcus Agrippa's new religion. But Justus was famous for something else, mentioned by the Church Father Jerome and others: he was renowned for his ability to blend scripture and philosophy. If that sounds like Philo of Alexandria, it should, because both men were essentially serving the same cause and most probably knew each other very well.

Justus worked for Marcus Agrippa and the two had almost identical interests. The Acts of the Apostles cites Marcus Agrippa as being 'an authority of all the controversies of the Jews', whilst in Jewish rabbinic literature he is directly identified as being an expert in pagan philosophy. Who more than Marcus Agrippa would have had the incentive, the means and the opportunity to open the Catechetic School in Alexandria?

There will always be people who demand a degree of proof far greater than might normally be considered reasonable and, for their sake, it is worth looking at the similarities between the ideas and written material of Philo and another individual we have come across before. This is Marqe, the figure that was so influential in the development of Samaritan worship.

We have almost no biographical details for Marqe. We know he was critically important to the Samaritans, who certainly treated him as some sort of divinely inspired teacher and as an individual they thought of him as 'second only to Moses'.

Whilst we cannot say much about Marqe as a man, we do know a fair amount about what he thought. I am not the first to notice or point out the striking similarities between the teachings of Marqe and the written observations of Philo of Alexandria.

The writer Alexander Broadie goes into the similarities in great detail. In his book *A Samaritan Philosophy: A Study of the Hellenistic Cultural Ethos*, Broadie points out that Marqe, whom we might think of as being a distinctly Galilean individual, had a very Hellenistic (Greek) approach to his writing and his ideas. Broadie repeatedly suggests that Marqe's style bears a striking resemblance to that of Philo of Alexandria. As I pointed out earlier, some historians have placed Marqe in the fourth century, but for very tenuous and unlikely reasons. Broadie says that Marqe and Philo are almost identical in one especially surprising way: both deal in Greek philosophical arguments but do so only if they can prove to their own satisfaction that these arguments are paralleled in scripture. Broadie suggests: 'Neither Marqe nor Philo could accept a philosophical doctrine which they believed to be inconsistent with the Bible.'

Broadie points out that both writers also found similar philosophical meanings in Jewish writings that appeared to have no overtly philosophical intention. He says: 'The allegorical method in the hands of Philo or Marqah involves treating philosophy as if it were present in the Pentateuch [the first five books of the Old Testament] as the hidden meaning of the verses, and revealing the hidden meaning.' He adds: 'On numerous philosophical matters the ideas of the two thinkers coincide, and even their modes of expression bear, despite language differences, an undeniable similarity.'

One senses Broadie's surprise at this state of affairs, which is understandable since he still thinks of Marqe as being a character from the fourth century rather than the first.

Alexander Broadie may be surprised and shocked by what he inadvertently uncovered, but I am not. As I have demonstrated, there is plenty of evidence to assert that the character Marqe, complete with his name, was a Samaritan memory of Marcus Agrippa. Discovering that his writings and ideas are very similar to those of Philo of Alexandria is exactly what we would expect. After all, Philo was waiting in Alexandria for the child Marcus to arrive there in 38 CE. Both in his guise as the Messiah and later in his own writings, Marcus Agrippa was locked into Alexandrian Hellenistic doctrines. Marcus' chief mentor and the man who probably dreamed up the whole scenario in the first place was Philo. It would therefore be extremely odd if the two had enjoyed different thoughts or reached conclusions that were at odds, one with the other.

Philo and Marcus seem to have cooperated over a great many things. In addition to the Catechetic School they appear both to have been directly involved in setting up pseudo-monastic settlements dedicated to their developing religion, both in and around Alexandria and elsewhere.

Later Church Fathers, who clearly knew about these institutions, looked upon them with a great deal of enthusiasm and approval – probably because they looked so very Christian and came from an obviously very early date. The first recognized true Christian monk is St Anthony, who took to his desert retreat in Egypt at the start of the fourth century. The proto-monasteries most likely created by Marcus and Philo existed 300 years earlier. These institutions are described in detail, and though they may owe something to Jewish thinking, they are, in most senses, distinctly un-Jewish.

The groups of men and women involved with these settlements have become known to history as the *Therapeutæ* in the case of the men, and *Therapeutrides* for the women. In Alexandria they were to be found outside the city on a low hill by Lake Mareotis. There they lived a contemplative and simple life, which sounds so much like Christian monasticism that it is virtually identical. Philo describes them as 'the best' and of a kind 'given to perfect goodness'. He suggests that their name probably means 'physicians of souls'.

Throughout six days of every week the Therapeutæ indulged in spiritual activities such as reading the gospel, praying, fasting and studying the scriptures in the seclusion of their own individual cells. Philo reports:

The entire interval from dawn to evening is given up by them to spiritual exercises. For they read the holy scriptures and draw out in thought and allegory their ancestral philosophy, since they regard the literal meanings as symbols of an inner and hidden nature revealing itself in covert ideas.

On the seventh day of each week the Therapeutæ gathered together in order to hear what Philo called 'discourses' and every seven weeks they held an all-night vigil after a meal which they served, one to another.

Everything about the Therapeutæ smacks of a much later form of Christian monasticism, of the sort first instituted by Pachomius in the fourth century, but which only really gained ground after St Benedict in the sixth century. Actually this is quite strange, because the early Church Fathers tell us that St Mark initiated no less than three monasteries in Egypt, though any knowledge of them is lost to history – unless of course they were communities of Therapeutæ like the one by Lake Mareotis.

Philo points out that there were Therapeutæ in other places too, even in the land of the barbarians. This is borne out by other commentators who point to communities identical with the Therapeutæ as far away as the south of France.

Later commentators were aware of the Therapeutæ and also of Philo's association with them. Eusebius of Caesarea, the so-called 'father of Church history' writes about them in the fourth century, though in his conception they were clearly Christian monks and nuns. But that left him with something of a problem because, knowing how much Philo admired the Therapeutæ, he had to make Philo into a Christian too. This assumption, even to the extent that Philo was retrospectively granted the title of 'bishop', continued right through to the end of the 18th century, by which time Philo's true religious affiliations and the genuine period of his life became more widely known.

The truth of the situation is undoubtedly that Philo and Marcus cooperated over the creation of the Therapeutæ and that the Therapeutæ probably sprang out of the Catechetic School that Marcus Agrippa had created and which was first run by his secretary Justus.

During a period of history for which we have little independent written evidence, the various communities of the Therapeutæ remain virtually unknown. This state of affairs is compounded by the fact that later, Catholic writers who do mention them maintain their Catholic Christian credentials, even though such a thing could not have been possible at the time. Yet at the same time we have reports that St Mark created monasteries in and around Alexandria, about which we have no hard and fast evidence either.

What seems most likely to have happened is that, after the unrest in Alexandria was quelled around the year 38 CE, the city was made the headquarters of Marcus' and Philo's new religion. In addition to the Catechetic School that was founded once Marcus reached manhood, communities of Markan 'monks and nuns' were established, not simply in Alexandria but also in other places, some at a great distance from Egypt.

What is of particular interest with regard to the Therapeutæ is how much they parallel what we are beginning to realize about the nature of Marcus' religious adventure. We have seen, for example, how absolutely fascinated Philo was by the laws and scriptures of Judaism, and how he viewed these in very specific ways – in order to establish the 'hidden truth' that lay within them. Is it surprising then that we find the Therapeutæ reported as doing the self same thing? What else could we take from the following sentence about their scriptural obsession that tells us this? '… they regard the literal meanings as symbols of an inner and hidden nature revealing itself in covert ideas.'

It becomes clearer and clearer that there was something deeply secretive and mystical about Marcus' revolutionary religion. True, it was based on Jewish documents and basic beliefs, but it had at its heart something quite different, something deliberately hidden that could only be coaxed out through intelligence and persistence. Markan Christianity relied heavily on codes and ciphers that were already of the most tremendous importance to many Judaic scholars. We should therefore not be surprised to realize that, when Marcus Agrippa wrote his own gospel, much of what he genuinely had to reveal lay *beneath* the apparent text of his work. As I have shown to be the case time and again, it isn't so much the story that St Mark's Gospel tells that is important, but rather the *way* it is told that was of the greatest significance to those who understood what they should be looking for.

To this end, the Throne of St Mark turns out to be of critical importance because it demonstrates the inner secrets of Markan Christianity in many ways. Once we understand what the throne is trying to tell us, our picture of Marcus Agrippa and his ultimate intentions become so much clearer.

CHAPTER 16

HERETICS AND GNOSTICS

When any Christian commentator such as Irenaeus was levelling accusations at early or indeed contemporary Christian sects who were at odds with his own cherished beliefs, there were two words that he used time and again. The first of these was 'heretic' and the second was 'gnostic'.

'Heretic' is a word that is generally understood these days to mean anything that deviates from a standard, accepted form. In a strictly Christian sense we know that anyone whose views differed from those of the Roman Catholic Church in earlier centuries could be accused of heresy, and would be subject to the worst imaginable forms of torture and execution. The horrible institution known as the Inquisition existed primarily to discover heresy and stamp it out with all the hatred and force it could muster.

The word 'heresy' has so much dread for most of us, even in these enlightened days, that it is usually viewed in a negative sense. We might be left with the impression that it was coined with its present usage in mind, but this is far from the truth.

Heresy derives from the Greek word *haireomai* which means simply 'to choose'. In its earliest use it merely referred to philosophical beliefs; there was no negative connotation to the word. One might choose to follow the beliefs of Plato, Aristotle or any other philosopher. So to a group of believers in the ideas of Plato, anyone who did not hold to Platonic notions might be termed a heretic, but only to differentiate them – to suggest that they believed something different. To be a heretic in this sense carried no inference of 'being wrong' and certainly did not imply that the heretic was either possessed by or a servant of the Devil, as the Catholic Church came to believe.

The word 'heretic' first begins to appropriate something like its present meaning with the writings of our old friend Irenaeus, but even he did not use it entirely in its modern sense. In the late second century there was a backlash in certain parts of the Church against the proliferation of Greek philosophical ideas, seen to be creeping into the faith. This is what Irenaeus is addressing when he uses the word 'heretic' against those he disapproves of, in terms of their religious beliefs. Irenaeus, and many who followed him, were of the opinion that the Church should go back to its 'primitive' roots and that it should not bother itself with philosophical ideas or discussions.

Irenaeus was wholly committed to scripture and to doctrines and teachings he saw as being entirely orthodox. Gradually the Church was becoming more organized: it was gaining more priests and bishops – professionals if you will; a power base was forming; and people with even slightly different ideas were increasingly unwelcome to those who jealously guarded their flocks. Irenaeus wanted things done literally 'by the book', and since he had as good as created the book – or rather, in his case, four books – he knew exactly what should be in it and what should not.

What Irenaeus particularly disliked was the tradition of passing on Christian beliefs by word of mouth. In his defence, the reasoning behind this was that oral traditions are likely to give way to wrong interpretations or even to change certain teachings altogether. If we are to be less charitable we can see that a wholly *written canon* is restricted to those who hold the accepted books and to those who can read them, or even change them to suit their own purposes. Irenaeus might say, 'If you want a cabbage go to the market, but if you want to know about Christianity go to an ordained and educated priest.'

It is clear that when Irenaeus talks about a heretic he actually means someone whose version of Christianity is subject to philosophical scrutiny, as opposed to someone who holds to an argument purely because it is an act of faith to do so.

Of necessity then, anyone who held to the sort of beliefs espoused by Marcus Agrippa or Philo of Alexandria was, in the conception of Irenaeus and many who followed him, a heretic. Marcus and Philo had lived in a Greek-dominated world and Platonism in particular formed an important part of the philosophy that underpinned their religious beliefs. However, Irenaeus went further. He also accused such people of being Gnostics, which is yet another word that means something far different now than it originally did.

The term 'Gnostic', when applied to religion, has become rather woolly and over-used during the last 2,000 years. Modern interpretations of the word infer that it relates to specifically Christian sects that took a more or less different approach to matters spiritual than later Catholic Christianity. We are told that Gnostics believed in the existence of the human soul and considered it to be caged inside a material world, necessarily divorcing it from its true and divine origins. Gnostics, we are told, invariably identified the force that had trapped their souls as being the 'demiurge' which, to some groups, was equated with the original God of Judaism.

It can be seen immediately that such beliefs would be in direct competition with those of accepted Christianity, which elevates the God of Abraham and sees him as an unequivocal source of goodness. Gnostics have also been accused of being dualistic, in that they have suggested 'levels of divinity', sometimes inferring that the God they expected to free them from their earthbound state of spiritual ignorance was not the same divinity as that represented by the demiurge. Today the subject of Gnosticism has become an absolute minefield – to the extent that modern commentators spoil reams of paper simply deciding whether this sect or that group actually was Gnostic or not.

Definitions of *gnosis* today generally limit themselves to suggesting that the word means 'knowledge', though of a very specific sort. The *Oxford English Dictionary* defines gnosis specifically as 'a knowledge of spiritual mysteries', but it is also seen as that illuminating spiritual spark that might be possessed by a saint or some other elevated and enlightened soul. With regard to Plato, who seems to have been the first to use the term, we are told these days that he intended it to mean 'specific knowledge that allows one to influence and control'. In this regard it has no spiritual context whatsoever. Beyond Plato, Greek philosophy went on using 'gnosis' to indicate knowledge through experience.

Irenaeus might not have been the first Christian apologist to use the word 'Gnosticism', but he can be tied to a tradition that was certainly the first to make it into a negative term. But before we look at some of the accusations Irenaeus hurled at Marcus Agrippa and his beliefs, it is first necessary to deal more fully with this word 'gnostic', in order truly to understand what Plato, the man who first used it, intended it should mean.

Plato refers to *gnostike techne*, which could reasonably be translated as 'the art of knowing', or perhaps even 'the art of managing things that are known'. He is very specific about this term because he suggests that any king or ruler who had this quality would be 'like a god come down to rule mankind'. To illustrate this Plato created a fictitious dialogue between the young philosopher Socrates and a stranger. In this long conversation Plato makes Socrates expound on the virtues of the political ruler who has true gnosis. The modern commentator Morton Smith, in his book *Studies in the Cult of Yahweh* (p 186), sums up the meaning of this long passage and Plato's ideas about the king who has *gnostike techne* by saying:

> [In Plato] this individual would be the ideal king, the only man capable of knowing God, who would therefore act as the mediator between God and man; he would be, in effect, the *nous* [the divine intellect] of his subjects in whom he would restore their lost contact with the heavenly world from which he came.

This is very important because, in his persona as Messiah, this description fits Marcus Agrippa perfectly – or at least, it fits what the Messiah was claimed to be in Old Testament scripture. So when Irenaeus speaks of Marcus and his followers being Gnostics he is actually telling the truth, not so much as an insult but to differentiate their beliefs from his. Certainly they are to be despised, and of course they must be eradicated. This is especially important to Irenaeus because many of the Gnostics of his day were functioning not outside but within the Orthodox Church.

Clement of Alexandria, a contemporary of Irenaeus, was harassed, persecuted and driven from office by forces aligned with the Roman emperor Septimius Severus, even though Roman Christians in Alexandria were left unmolested. This is certainly a reflection of the fact that Clement not only accepted the significance of Christian *gnosis*, but quite openly confessed himself to be a Gnostic Christian. Clement was more than familiar with the works and ideas of Plato, and he accepted that these were not at odds with Christianity as he understood it. This demonstrates a deep divide between the Christians of Alexandria and those who responded to Rome as early as the second century.

Irenaeus was very specific in his criticisms of people he thought were deviating from the correct form of Christianity. He never directed these specifically at Marcus Agrippa – either because he was confused as to Marcus' identity or because he had reason to hide such knowledge. Nevertheless the enlightened reader is left in no doubt as to the intended target of Irenaeus' fury. Some of his greatest venom was turned against a character about whom we know little or nothing, except by way of Irenaeus. By now the reader may not be unduly surprised to learn that the name of this particular individual was Marcus!

So, Plato invented a term that described the ideal king as a mediator between God and man, and Irenaeus identified a certain 'Marcus' as ruling over a community in which '… men and women join themselves to him, as to one who is possessed of the greatest knowledge and perfection, and who has received the highest power from the invisible and ineffable regions above'. Morton Smith emphasizes that this sect of Marcus appears to be source of Irenaeus' attack against all Gnostics.[91] Irenaeus accused the character Marcus of all manner of evils, yet a careful examination of almost every accusation draws us ever closer to what we have established so far regarding the original evangelist Mark.

According to Irenaeus, Marcus the Gnostic promoted a fuller gospel. Marcus also claimed to be the 'only born' of God – a term that we have already seen ultimately comes from the account of the binding of Isaac.[92] This Marcus was also certainly the Christ of his Christian community, the messianic bridegroom to whom his various 'brides' cleaved in order to receive redemption.[93] The Marcus at whom Irenaeus hurls so many insults clearly believed in a God higher than that of the Jews and he most definitely considered Jesus and Christ to be two separate individuals.

This Marcus, 'the Magician' as Irenaeus refers to him, was also said to be addicted to astrology and the power of the letters of the alphabet. Marcus the Magician sounds like the quintessential Jew in many respects and his interpretation of the Old Testament was one directly allied to mystical Judaism; even his liturgy was preserved in Aramaic. One can even discern an original interest in two thrones of different sizes – one smaller than the other – by which the community was said to prophesy. We will speak about this at more length in subsequent chapters.

Between the lines of Irenaeus' venom, one can feel that the Marcus in question had built up a tremendous following. Women in particular were drawn towards him and his teachings – especially those of high birth. This seems to infuriate Irenaeus more than anything else. Bearing in mind his pro-Roman stance, Irenaeus is particularly scathing in his assertion that the followers of Marcus associate their beliefs with kingship and proclaim themselves to be kings of a greater rank than Caesar – which might explain more fully why Clement of Alexandria and his immediate followers were vilified and punished by Rome.

All of these details are well known to scholars. We can however take matters one stage further. What we need to do is to look at passages written by Clement of Alexandria, in which he described the beliefs of the Alexandrian Gnostic community of St Mark. We then need to compare these with Irenaeus' accounts regarding the beliefs of the followers of Marcus the Magician. When we lay passages dealing with the numerological mysticism described in the pages of Clement alongside similar passages in Irenaeus (see Appendix C), the two accounts match perfectly – word for word! The system of allegory used by Marcus and his followers was identical with that familiar to the contemporary Alexandrian community of Mark the Evangelist.

Irenaeus' attacks were directed against a worldwide Markan tradition that had only recently become unacceptable to Rome. Marcus the Gnostic represented a spiritual degeneration of the original messianic mysticism associated with Marcus Agrippa, and this was systematically persecuted throughout the next 100 years of history. Members of the tradition were offered one of two choices: death, or the acceptance of Irenaeus' formulation of orthodoxy – and this included as its centrepiece a 'fourfold' gospel truth.[94]

Irenaeus made it plain that his work *Against the Gnostics Falsely So Called* was created to help the bishops all over the Christian world to identify and catch the various heretics lurking within their congregations. The analogy he used at the end of the first book was that of endeavouring to kill a fox that has run onto one's property. He suggested that his description of the heretics would allow bishops to, '… not only expose the wild beast to view, but to inflict wounds upon it from every side', and ultimately to slay it.

All of this leaves us with big questions regarding the true position of the Coptic Church today. As we have seen, the present patriarch of the Coptic Church, Shenouda III, comes very close to revealing the true identity of St Mark, upon whom Coptic Christianity relies so heavily. Is it possible that, to this very day, there are Copts who know full well that St Mark and Marcus Agrippa were one and the same person? If so, they might be no more inclined to admit it now than they were nearly two millennia ago.

Is it conceivable that the true Markan tradition still flourishes in secret and that somewhere in or around Alexandria the original gospel written by Marcus Agrippa is being secretly and reverently safeguarded? It is clear that even in these more enlightened times neither Rome nor the headquarters of the Eastern Orthodox Church would take kindly to irrefutable proof that the 'real' St Mark was actually Marcus Julius Agrippa, the last of the Jewish kings.

It must be emphasized that Alexandria is repeatedly identified as the breeding ground of Gnosticism. Clement, the first Catholic representative in the city, appeared only at the end of the second century and, as we have already demonstrated earlier in this book, his orthodoxy was suspect – so questionable that he was actually excommunicated posthumously in the 16th century!

It is Clement who openly identified the Alexandrian tradition as Gnostic and then hinted that the 'mystagogue' St Mark was behind all its secret teachings. But there was at least a century and half of Christian history in Alexandria before Clement's conversion, of which we have no information whatsoever, other than the knowledge that it was directly responsive to this Gnostic St Mark.

Many scholars agree that the lost history of Alexandria was based on

Gnosticism, though of course these academics don't use the term in the way Plato intended. They look at the common pattern among all those sects Irenaeus identified as Gnostic and notice that they all preached about 'another god', who was more elevated and important than the God of the Jews. Irenaeus, perhaps understandably, placed 'Marcus the Gnostic' into this group of heretics. But can Marcus Agrippa really be seen as the ultimate historical source for these Gnostic teachings?

The tractate Abodah Zarah, folio 55a, in the Talmud, helps us fill in many of the gaps here. It tells the story of the historical summoning of the four principal rabbinic authorities of the Jews to Rome at the end of the first century, presumably to face charges that they were continuing to persist in the 'Jewish error' of their ancestors – circumcision and the other commandments of the Mosaic revelation had by now been forbidden by imperial decree.

The story is very interesting because it is said that the rabbis were immediately confronted by a group of philosophers who heaped abuse upon the Jewish religion. One philosopher asks why the Jews don't worship the sun. Another philosopher wonders why they oppose idolatry. This is typical of other passages in the Talmud. However something unusual happens as the narrative continues.

Out from this assembly of otherwise anonymous philosophers appears Marcus Agrippa. In other sources where this story appears, his name continues to remain hidden and he is just another philosopher in the crowd. Yet in the Talmud and other earlier sources it is Agrippa who helps the Roman philosophers refine their attack against Judaism. His expertise in Biblical matters is amply displayed when he tells one of the elders:

> It is written in your Torah, 'For the Lord thy God is a devouring fire, a jealous God.' Is a wise man jealous of any but another wise man, a warrior of any but another warrior, a rich man of any but another rich man?' He replied, 'I will give you a parable. To what is the matter like? To a man who marries an additional wife. If the second wife is her superior, the first will not be jealous of her, but if she is her inferior, the first wife will be jealous of her.'[95]

We should pay special attention to the deliberate emphasis in this story that there were two Torahs in Israel at the time. The idea is repeated

155

throughout the Jewish writings, as is Agrippa's status as an 'outsider' to the original Torah of Moses.

Agrippa's point is clear – he knows of another, 'better' Torah and another, 'better' God than the God of Israel. In this way he is perfectly suited to being the historical source for all the so-called Gnostic literature identified by contemporary scholars. He is the Gnostic before what is now called Gnosticism. What is more, he perfectly fits Plato's description in the *Politicus*. This appellation would only have been natural for the 'philosopher' Agrippa described in the tractate of the Talmud.

It might be reasonably suggested that, if we take the word 'heresy' as it is used today, it is not the Gnostics who stand 'guilty as charged', but rather the Fathers of the modern Christian Church, because it was they who distorted the original faith to suit their own purposes.

Once we acknowledge Marcus Agrippa's role in Christianity, our understanding of the gospel necessarily changes too. We would have to abandon once and for all the notion that it is a simple history – a literal account of what happened to Jesus leading up to his crucifixion. With the realization that the original author was Marcus Agrippa, a man who was himself acknowledged to be the Messiah, the text reveals itself as *his* mystery. Jesus becomes little more than an 'opening act', a distraction to divert our attention from the little boy at the margins of the text, a child accompanying Jesus everywhere he went and ultimately emerging from the tomb in Jerusalem.

It now becomes clear that Agrippa was the Gnostic envisioned by Plato. He is identified by pagan critics as having '... misunderstood the words of Plato [and] loudly boasted of a "super-celestial" God, thus ascending beyond the heaven of the Jews'. If we can accept Marcus Agrippa as 'the' Gnostic then it follows that he must also have appeared in Alexandria in order to reveal some new understanding of God to his subjects. I believe that, if we study the Throne of St Mark closely, we can for the first time discover what that 'secret gnosis' was.

CHAPTER 17

THE LOST PAST

In the preceding chapters I have built up a picture of the distant past that might be surprising and even shocking to many readers. Impressions that many of us have been brought up to believe will have to be significantly modified in order to take account of evidence that 'experts' have generally ignored. The time has now come to draw the strings together and to look at Marcus Julius Agrippa in the context of his historical setting. We need to face up to a few unpalatable truths regarding our common heritage.

It is clear that Marcus did not 'come from nowhere'. This was not a case of a man who just happened to find himself in a position from which he could reorder Judaism and, on a whim, create a brand new religion and a new covenant with God, as promised by the Old Testament prophets. The mechanisms for Marcus' actions in life were already set in place when he was born. The Throne of St Mark, which we will begin to look at specifically in the next chapter, shows that practically everything Marcus did and believed in his later life was already in place by the time he was a small child of only eight. This tends to indicate that someone, or more likely a group of people, had been waiting patiently, maybe for generations, for the right individual to come along, who could take a set of preconceived ideas and make them work in the real world.

One representative of this way of thinking was clearly Philo of Alexandria. It was to Philo's house that Marcus went on his first trip to Alexandria. It was Philo who had already been writing for years about the unique synthesis of Platonic philosophical ideals and Judaism that proliferated amongst the Jewish thinkers of Alexandria. Theirs was a strange world because although history and tradition pervaded the Jewish community of the city, these people found themselves immersed in a heady blend of religious and philosophical concepts that stood outside of Jewish history in its homeland.

They were Jews – but of a very different complexion to their compatriots in the stuffier and much more conservative surroundings of Jerusalem. Men such as Philo were rich, and he most certainly had slaves and servants, which gave him time to think and ponder on aspects of life that might have never occurred to him had he been committed to physical work in the fields or endless days ducking and diving in the commercial world of Alexandria.

What came out of all this leisure time was a series of realizations regarding the one thing that he and his fellow Jews in Alexandria lacked – power. Despite their wealth and influence they were still relegated to being second-class citizens in this all-too-Greek city. Yet the Jews weren't alone in this camp – the native Egyptians had also grown tired of being kept down by the unwanted 'foreigners'. In many ways the story of Moses and the Exodus must have had great resonance to even these traditional enemies of all things Hebrew. It was the Greeks who were now the embodiment of all things evil.

With the arrival of Marcus Agrippa everything suddenly changed for these people, thitherto excluded from any real power in their native land. Here was a living symbol of triumph over adversity. This little boy defied the odds, managing to rise to a position of authority from the lowest rungs of human despair. He was a natural inspiration to those who felt similar bonds of oppression. All that was needed now was a mystery, a system of indoctrinating large numbers of outsiders into a secret inner doctrine that might transform their lives in the near future.

Philo and his fellow Jewish thinkers must have been convinced that something incredible was about to happen in the period leading up to Marcus Agrippa's arrival. The Jubilee was imminent and the skies were positively shouting that the promised Messiah was at hand. And then, in 37 CE, their prayers were answered. Everything came together at the same time to tell them without any ambiguity who the Messiah was. What was more, it turned out to be one of Philo's own relatives.

Philo would have received the news that Tiberius was dead and that his successor, Caligula, had raised little Mark in Judea to the rank of a rich and powerful king quite quickly. What was more, this elevation had occurred at the time of the spring equinox whilst the Sun and Venus were doing their magical dance in the eastern sky at dawn. What more proof could be demanded? There was no need for a protracted search, such as that which takes place in Buddhism when the Dalai Lama dies and his successor is sought. Israel's God of Ages had left the matter in no doubt. Marcus Julius Agrippa was the promised Messiah and it only remained to let everyone know that this was the case.

Nearly a year passed before Marcus travelled to Alexandria. This isn't surprising as there was much to be done in preparation, including the creation of the very special throne upon which the child would sit and receive the adoration of the Jews of Alexandria. Further proof of God's intentions was forthcoming when Flaccus, the Roman governor of Egypt, apparently lost his mind and allowed a massive pogrom to take place. This might not have started until Marcus arrived, but it is equally possible that some other factor had put a light to the fuse. Jews were soon dying in their hundreds, and yet when the child Messiah was enthroned and had contacted his friend the emperor, the killing stopped immediately and the transgressor was removed from their midst.

If there had been any doubters in the Jewish community regarding Marcus' true position, they must have become convinced of the truth almost immediately. One is reminded of the words of Elizabeth I of England who, on hearing that she had suddenly and unexpectedly become queen instead of being executed as a traitor, uttered a sentence from the Old Testament. This may well have been the same sentence Philo spoke when the child Messiah lifted his hand and the storm ceased: 'This is the Lord's doing; it is marvellous in our eyes', from Psalms 118:23.

Marcus' mother Salome had been working feverishly on behalf of her son, whom she almost certainly saw as some sort of reincarnation of his father. As we have seen, she appears to have been a devotee of the Egyptian-Greek Horus cult, seeing herself as Isis in the story. Living one's dreams and even one's fantasies through one's children is not just a modern-day phenomenon!

Marcus was soon betrothed to his sister Berenice, the better to play out the Horus myth and also to consolidate power within the family. All the while he consulted with Philo and no doubt a whole series of other advisers in Alexandria who are unknown to us by name.

How long Philo lived we have no way of knowing, but it was certainly long enough to school Marcus in his expected role. It probably wasn't hard. We know Marcus Agrippa to have been extremely intelligent – a natural thinker and linguist. The remainder of his life proves conclusively that he had a very good handle on what Philo and his Jewish associates in Alexandria had expected. History shows that he would not have disappointed them. Philo would have told Marcus that he was not only the Messiah of Jewish prophecy but that he was much more. Marcus would be a herald to a new age, the holder and imparter of a new covenant with God – no less than the *gnostikos* of Plato's *Politicus* – the divinely inspired king whose authority and wisdom came straight from God.

Nevertheless, Marcus Agrippa was a king in name only. From the beginning it was considered by most people that he was another puppet of the Roman Empire. He may have taken some day-to-day decisions about the people who fell under his sway, but all the real instructions came from Rome. It was Roman officials who collected the taxes, but there was enough money left over to make Marcus fabulously rich. Everything about Marcus and his life demonstrates that, in addition to being extremely bright and utterly charming, he could also be quite duplicitous. Being a puppet king with little to do but indulge himself was fine, because he had plans. He didn't simply accept the presence of the Romans – he used them to his own ends.

It is clear that Marcus was not only a king and a self-confessed Messiah, he was also a mystagogue. He undoubtedly built on the extensive work of Philo, spending years teasing from the Torah and the sacred scriptures the *real* meaning that had been placed in them by the scribes centuries before. All the time he patiently chipped away at the conservative agencies within Judea. He spent years trying to reconcile a stubborn population to the certain changes that the new covenant would necessarily bring. In Alexandria there was no problem; people there remembered what he had done for them. Had he not wrought a miracle that could have been possible only in the case of a genuine Messiah? But his own countrymen hated him and refused to accept his claims of Messiahhood. To the most conservative he wasn't even a 'real' Jew, but merely the latest representative of a clan of greedy interlopers and sycophants that accepted Roman domination of Judea and lived in absolute splendour at the expense of true believers.

In Marcus' conception the Jews around him had been given ample chance to realize what was truly happening. Marcus was a believer — and he believed primarily in his own position, though he was also a philosophically trained realist. If Judea didn't change its attitude it was heading for disaster, and he was not prepared to go down with the ship. He knew, through his mystical appreciation of the true worth of scripture, that something massive was coming, nothing less than the fulfilment of prophecy regarding his own position as Messiah. In years of arguments with the Pharisees and the Zealots he must have realized only too well that the past was so deeply embedded in the breast of Judea that it could only be rooted out at the point of a sword.

The impending war coincided with Marcus' completion of his gospel — a definitive work that was part truth, part allegory and part deep mystery that was to serve as a beacon to future generations. It was a work that was deliberately coded with neo-Platonic and Pythagorean codes. It was also heavily influenced by the kind of ciphers that had been popular in mystical Judaism since Babylonian times. The new gospel was available to anyone who could read, but that did not mean it would be fully understood by all who read it. It was and remained essentially a closed and secret book, except to those with the *gnosis* and the *nous* to really understand it. As we have seen to be the case from the mists of Jewish history, it wasn't so much the stories or accounts of Marcus' gospel that really mattered. It was the shape, the numbers, the substitutions and everything that existed between the lines. Marcus was a Gnostic philosopher-king and this work of his own creation proved the fact beyond doubt.

By 66 CE, in Alexandria and much further away, there were communities already living lives of devout service and prayer, committed absolutely to his ideals for the 'new world'. But in Marcus' own home, greed and insurrection reigned supreme. He was called back from Alexandria at a moment's notice when the powder keg exploded. But he was well prepared and he used the Roman legions to do what he could not do himself – to get rid of the old covenant once and for all and to replace it with a new God-given world – given not just to Jews but to the whole of humankind.

The slaughter was terrible and doubtless Marcus wept at the death of innocents, but he knew, as do all men who are essentially dictators, temporal or spiritual, that 'the end justifies the means'. In any case this wasn't his doing: it was quite clearly the work of God.

The very Temple itself, a symbol of everything that had gone before and a mark of the influence of Moses on his people, was utterly destroyed. With it went the last vestiges of power of a sub-god, the deity of Moses and the Israelites but not the true God, certainly not the Most High, who stood far beyond any one nation or its wishes. The Zealots were dead and the Pharisees were destroyed, Jerusalem lay in ruins and everything was right for the new start that Marcus had been promising since childhood.

For those who encompassed his beliefs it was indeed a golden time. The Samaritans took on his message, in the guise of Marqe, and they prospered. Alexandria had its ups and downs but in the main its Jewish and Samaritan population continued to keep faith with the Messiah. Successive emperors fell victim, as they previously had done, to the charm, charisma and, from their perspective, downright common sense of Marcus Agrippa. He had kept faith with them, so they rewarded him, giving him the time he needed to instigate his changes. Nowhere in the scriptures did it suggest that the new world would arrive overnight – it was simply a matter of patience.

As far as his 'new way' was concerned, Marcus believed that only the original Ten Commandments had come from God. For all we know he may have considered that even these rules were established at the behest of the 'lower deity' that had guided the Children of Israel. Rabbinic tradition shows clearly that Marcus Agrippa held to the absolute belief that the God of the Jews had always been jealous of the greater God. Marcus Agrippa was remembered in Jewish circles as one who regularly turned around passages from the Law and the Prophets to prove that there was a better Father Divinity in heaven than the old God of the Hebrews. It was the new Father Divinity's revelation that had ushered in the messianic age.

There can be no doubt that Marcus Julius Agrippa was also the St Mark of Christian tradition. He was given this rather unconvincing alias after his death. The reasons for this state of affairs are really quite straightforward, though exactly *why* Marcus had to be forgotten as the creator of Christianity is a more complex issue. Once the decision was made, St Mark, and a host of other fictitious characters that stood as substitutes for Marcus, were absolutely vital. What Marcus Agrippa had achieved was far too massive and all-pervading to be totally wiped from history. It would have been ridiculous to try to eradicate him altogether because everything the Christian Church had become was modelled on his original conceptions. For reasons I will discuss more fully when I talk about the Throne of St Mark, it became necessary for Jesus to take the role of the central character in the developing religion. Marcus then became merely one of his disciples, and a rather flimsy biography was invented for St Mark – the man who never really was.

It was a long, hard struggle for Roman Christianity. Time and again, the most Gnostic elements of Mark's original Christianity began to break out, especially in the East. Ever greater punishments and penalties became necessary in order to force recalcitrant Gnostics and Markan Christians back onto the Roman path. We see this struggle at its height around the time of Clement of Alexandria and Irenaeus of Lyons. Clement was *in* Alexandria, where knowledge of Marcus, his life and his teachings were still remembered. Clement declared himself to be a Gnostic Christian and, though we have no way of knowing how deep his allegiance to Marcus ran, it was deep enough to infuriate Rome. It is quite conceivable that one of the reasons Christianity had to change was because Marcus' supporters eventually declared themselves to be more powerful than the emperors of Rome. Marcus himself would clearly never have made such a statement, since his life would most likely have been instantly forfeit. However, others undoubtedly did make it on his behalf.

Right back in the early days of Marcus' kingship Caligula had travelled to Alexandria. Whilst there he had visited the Jewish part of the city where he noticed that there were statues in the synagogues which he knew only too well represented Marcus Agrippa. (Effigies of any sort are anathema to Judaism, which itself is indicative of how much Marcus changed the old religion.) Caligula was both puzzled and furious. 'Why,' he wanted to know, 'do the usually idol-hating Jews allow statues of Marcus in their holiest buildings, but not statues of Caligula himself?' We don't know what answer he received. Doubtless little Marcus, with his usual charm, had a way of defusing the situation. But the story does go to prove that emperors were jealous people and, perhaps as Marcus' following grew immediately after his death, the emperors became more jealous still. Here was a religion that threatened to run out of control. Together with Church Fathers who saw survival as more important than the original truth, the emperors found a way to capture and tame Christianity.

But there are undoubtedly other reasons why Marcus had to cease being the central character of Christianity. These were closely related to the fact that the hope of a new order and a salvation for humanity had to be shifted from the material world to the conception of a spiritual afterlife. The New Jerusalem on Earth was deferred: it could only take place with the second coming of Jesus, who himself had been elevated from herald to Messiah. When this might happen nobody knew, but at the very least it kept believers on their toes, attentive to whatever new imposition the Church authorities wished to heap upon the devout.

So there we have it, the story of a man who is now largely forgotten by history and religion. True, he survives in the Coptic Church in something like his true and original form, but even there adherents have fought shy of facing up to the real implications of a Messiah who is now forgotten by the rest of Christianity.

Almost everything that has appeared in the last 17 chapters came out of 20 years of diligent research, supported by much deeper and more specific references for those who wish to explore my findings more thoroughly. I decided a long time ago that, though every part of my thesis is open to scrutiny and is bolstered by documents and first-hand accounts, it might all be too much for the average reader to accept. The alterations made to Christianity took place so long ago and people are generally so conditioned to accept what they were brought up to believe that such radical departures seem incomprehensible.

Then, one day in sunny Venice, I first saw the Throne of St Mark and gradually began to realize that, here, with this ancient alabaster seat, is a series of absolute proofs that Marcus Agrippa was indeed once revered as the Messiah. The throne confirms that he did start a religion that, albeit in a much altered sense, has become one of the world's most influential faiths. With a full knowledge of the throne and what it tells us about those far-off days, it is possible to give a physical reality to a strange and even dangerous view of our own past.

To speak truth is never wrong. This is a principle that lies at the heart of Christianity. With the knowledge to be gained from the Throne of St Mark, will it now be possible to coax the Church into revealing the truth about itself? We shall see.

CHAPTER 18

ST MARK'S THRONE

The treasury of St Mark's Basilica in Venice houses many precious objects, most of which might be considered by the casual observer to be of greater worth than the little throne of calcareous alabaster. This may indeed be the case, but looks can be deceptive.

The alabaster comprising the throne undoubtedly came from further south in Egypt, where it was and is found extensively around the plain of Tell el Armana, about 521 km (just under 324 miles) south of Alexandria. This sounds like a fair distance to bring such material but it would have been relatively easy to transport large blocks of stone straight down the Nile on barges specifically made for the task.

The throne was certainly carved in Alexandria, but of its location for about 500 years after its completion it is impossible to be specific. It is said that the throne came to Venice from Grado, near Trieste, and that it was given to the city of Venice by the Patriarch Primigenio. When this happened is impossible to say, but it is almost certain that the throne had originally been in Aquileia. This city was not far from present-day Venice, originally founded in around 181 BCE along the Natissa River. Aquileia eventually became a thriving community and acted as a protection to the people known as the Veniti, who had been staunch allies of the Romans for centuries.

Aquileia gradually became rich and prosperous, partly thanks to reserves of gold that were found nearby. The population of the city was cosmopolitan and included many Jews who, it is suggested, may have become the city's first Christians. The Christians of Aquileia had a special veneration for St Mark. In popular tradition he is supposed to have travelled there and to have brought Christianity to the city, where it flourished from a very early period.

After 400 CE Aquileia was attacked by a succession of invaders. Many, if not most, of the citizens fled and took refuge around the nearby lagoons. Some of them went to the safer community of Grado, and we know that in 452 these included Nicetas, the bishop of Aquileia. Presumably he would have brought the treasures of his cathedral with him for safety, and it is possible that included amongst the precious objects was the Throne of St Mark.

It is also suggested in popular fable that the throne had originally been given to the Patriarchs of Grado by Emperor Heraclius (c.575–641) in 630, although this version of events could have come about due to a misunderstanding because Grado was originally a settlement belonging to the emperors of Rome.

Whatever association Heraclius may or may not have had with the throne, we can be quite certain that it was the Patriarchs of Grado who handed the throne over to the newly created city of Venice, though the date at which this took place is uncertain. It was most probably in the early ninth century CE.

The throne is clearly an impressive work of art in its own right. It carries carvings on all its various surfaces. These can be seen in detail in the plate section. The dimensions of the throne are such that it would be an ideal size for a child of about eight to ten years, and any fair-sized adult might find it somewhat uncomfortable, at least in terms of the width of the seat. It measures 147 cm at its highest point, whilst it is 55 cm wide and 53 cm deep (57.8 x 21.6 x 20.8 in).

Around the sides are carvings which many of those studying the throne have taken to be representations of the four creatures mentioned by Ezekiel in his vision of the Throne of God. This is what Ezekiel claims to have witnessed:

Also out of the midst there came the likeness of four living creatures …
As for the likeness of their faces they four had the face of a man, and the

face of a lion, on the right side, and they four had the face of an ox on the left side and they four also had the face of an eagle. (Book of Ezekiel, 1:5 and 10)

These carvings have also been associated with the Book of Isaiah and with the Book of Revelation, an apocalyptic book in the New Testament.

Many of the scholars that have viewed the throne and its carvings report it as having a distinctly 'Semitic' feel which, bearing in mind the subject matter, is not surprising. Plenty has been written about the throne over the last century or more, though it has to be admitted that most of the reports have been by those who were specialists in ancient religious art, as opposed to experts in ancient symbolism or religion. Almost everyone who has studied the throne is agreed that the 'medallion' (the circular part at the very top of the back of the throne) was made separately from the throne itself, and some speculate that it was a later or alternative addition.

One of the most frequently accessed studies of the throne was that undertaken by a naturalized Frenchman, originally of Ukrainian origin, named André Grabar (1898–1990). Grabar was an internationally known expert in Byzantine art. He set out to interpret the throne as if it naturally fitted into the Byzantine period – even though in many respects the carvings are quite unlike much else to be found amongst Byzantine art. Grabar's was one of only very few reports on the throne that were translated into a number of different languages and it may be partly for this reason that he is so studied and quoted on the subject.

As Grabar sees it, the Throne of St Mark was a reliquary, a purely ornamental piece that was used to store something of great religious worth in the hole that can be seen on the throne's side and back. Reliquaries were common throughout Christendom and many still exist. They often carried the bones of departed saints, pieces of the True Cross, the blood of Christ and a host of other strange and macabre relics.

Grabar claims that this particular reliquary is derived from a tradition of representing enthroned martyrs going back to a relatively early date in Christian tradition. In this regard St Mark would be seen as only one of a number of such saints who would hold a 'seat of honour' at the Last Judgment. Grabar associates the images of the four creatures on the throne with the four Evangelists, Matthew, Mark, Luke and John. This is linked to a long-standing notion that each of the Evangelists can be equated to one of the creatures surrounding the Throne of God, mentioned by Ezekiel and also appearing in the Book of Revelation.

Unfortunately Grabar paid little attention to the strange Hebrew 'mirror writing' that appears on the front of the seat of the throne. He relegated its significance to a footnote in his article. In this footnote he explained that he walked across the hall of his university to a certain Professor Février in order to get him to translate its meaning. Février was equally dismissive and argued that the Hebrew inscription was an intentionally meaningless effort on the part of later Italian Jews in the 14th century to give the object a mysterious origin. Why *Jews* would want to do such a thing to an essentially Christian item is something of a puzzle. In any case, why would the true owners of the throne allow them to do so? Février agreed with most of his predecessors that the Hebrew writing had something to do with the Throne of St Mark. However it is plain that he attached little significance to the inscription and so, as a result, Grabar treated it with the same contempt.

It is unfortunate that Grabar's work was so influential. Almost every writer on the subject of the throne since then has alluded to Février's appalling attempts at translating the Hebrew letters. Few of those who referenced Grabar's paper in their own work seem to have realized that Février wasn't even an expert in Hebrew. His area of speciality was in transcribing Punic inscriptions. Partly as a result, every successive attempt to develop an understanding of the throne has hit a brick wall whenever it came to the most important piece of evidence – the Hebrew inscription.

Another example of dubious scholarship regarding the throne comes from Mab van Lohuizen-Mulder of the Cathedral of St Mark in Venice. It is clear from her work that epigraphy is way down on the list of priorities for at least some art historians.

Lohuizen-Mulder contributed to the study of the throne by emphasizing that its iconography is Egyptian and Coptic rather than classical. Her work elsewhere on the few remaining fragments from fourth-century church ornamentation in Alexandria convinced her that, stylistically, the throne dates back to at least this period.

With regards to the Hebrew inscription she cites Grabar's disastrous work, noting that: '… the inscription on the front, just underneath the seat, also indicates Egypt, although it seems that the language is Hebrew. There exists a consensus about the translation of the first part of the inscription.'

She suggests that the inscription may have been chiselled into the throne by a Coptic Egyptian Christian, at a later date than the creation of the throne. She further asserts that this was done to give the throne a greater air of authenticity. Lohuizen-Mulder believes the inscription is written in mirror writing because the person responsible didn't know better. However, this same individual was clearly aware that St Mark was associated with Jews and not Greeks. This is why they chose Hebrew for the inscription, once again trying to give the throne an air of authenticity. A Greek inscription would not have been so convincing in the known historical context. She finishes by surmising that this would have been quite in step with the thinking and practice of Christian Egyptians.

Apparently Lohuizen-Mulder was not aware that this type of Hebrew mirror writing was actually a very Jewish practice, and from an early period. It is especially common in texts from Qumran dating from the Herodian period.

Lohuizen-Mulder acknowledged getting the assistance of a Prof Avraham Ronen of Tel Aviv University to help with her translation of the inscription. Presumably she assumed that all Jews speak Hebrew and that professors are generally very smart people. Unfortunately Avraham Ronen had no expertise in any field remotely related to the complexity of ancient Hebrew inscriptions. He is a Jewish art historian, though it is probable that he does speak Hebrew. Avraham Ronen was of the opinion that the inscription must have been put onto the throne in Alexandria by someone who was not Jewish. He assumes this must have taken place after or even at the same time as it was made. Unlike Grabar, he doesn't consider it likely that the inscription was added in Italy during the Middle Ages by an Italian Hebrew.

Avraham Ronen was apparently puzzled by the casual way the inscription was written, or more properly scribbled, onto the throne. However, anyone who has any familiarity whatsoever with ancient

Hebrew inscriptions knows full well that the script used for inscriptions was never duplicated. Lohuizen-Mulder does provide us with some useful information when she notes that:

> An inscription in such a visible place on the front of a throne is not unique or even unusual, as ancient Egyptian thrones had hieroglyphs inscribed on prominent places too. The chair from Saqqara also has an inscription on the front.

Lohuizen-Mulder was at least the first expert I have come across to develop a systematic understanding of the important relationship between the images on the throne and the Bible. In her opinion the images on the sides of the throne correspond better to the Book of Revelations than they do to the accounts of Ezekiel. However, the most insightful work on this subject comes from Rory Boid, someone who truly understands Biblical material and ancient Hebrew.

Boid also noticed that almost all the images appearing on the throne could be connected to passages from the Book of Revelations. He contends that once we take a critical look at a few important passages from the Revelation of St John, '... it is immediately obvious that almost every piece of symbolism on the throne is a symbolic equivalent of them.'

Boid suggests that the Book of Revelation is first and foremost a 'throne vision'. It might be suggested that the carvings on the throne bear a striking similarity to descriptions in the Book of Revelation because whoever carved the throne was already familiar with the book. However, Boid thinks the connection is the other way round. In other words he is convinced that the descriptions in the Book of Revelation came from the pen of an author who had *seen* the throne.

Boid starts at the very beginning of the text of the Book of Revelation, pointing out that John, its author, emphasizes that his own vision has come from 'Jesus Christ ... the ruler of kings on earth'. Almost immediately John offers a description of the human Seraph on the left side of the throne, where we see an image of two angels blowing shofars:

> I was in the spirit on the Lord's day, and I heard behind me a voice like a trumpet ... Then I turned to see the voice that was speaking to me, and

on turning I saw ... one like a son of man clothed with a long white robe and with a golden girdle round his breast; his head and his hair were white as white wool, white as snow; his eyes were like a flame of fire, his feet were like burnished bronze, refined as in a furnace, and his voice was like the sound of many waters ... and his face was like the sun shining in full strength.

As John falls to the ground 'as if dead', the man lays his hand on John gently and says:

Fear not, I am the first and the last and the living one; I died, and behold I live for evermore and I have the keys of Death and Hell. Now write what you see, what is and what is to take place hereafter. (Rev 1:11–19)

If we assume that the images John relates came from his knowledge of the Throne of St Mark, we might imagine that the figure at the left side of the throne is developed into the person of Jesus Christ – who has come to guide John to the proper understanding of the meaning of the Holy Throne. At this point there is a transformation and John declares that:

At once I was in the spirit, and lo!, a throne was set in heaven, with one seated on the throne ... And round the throne, on each side of the throne, are four living creatures, full of eyes in front and behind; the first living creature like a lion, the second living creature like a bull, the third living creature with a human face, and the fourth living creature like a flying eagle. And the four living creatures, each of them with six wings, are full of eyes all round and within, and day and night they never cease to sing 'Holy, holy, holy, is the Lord God Almighty, who is what has existed and what exists and what will exist! (Rev 4:2, 6B, 7–8)

Whoever underwent the vision described in the Book of Revelation was almost certainly looking at this Throne of St Mark for his inspiration. But it is also clear that the writer set out to impose his own particular understanding on the object. This is because, although the seat is known as the Throne of St Mark, the writer of Revelation places Jesus, rather than St Mark, as the central theme of his vision.

As the narrative continues, the writer is now once again in front of the throne where he receives another vision. He tells us that:

> Then I saw a great white throne and him who sat upon it … And he who sat upon the throne said, 'Behold, I make everything (*panta*) new' … And he said to me, 'It is done! I am the Alpha and the Omega, the beginning and the end'. (Rev 20:11; 21:5A, 6A)

The writer of *Revelation* asserts here that the throne is for Jesus Christ, despite the fact that we know full well, as the Hebrew inscription clearly demonstrates, that this is the Throne of St Mark. The narrative continues and the writer tells us:

> Then he showed me the river of the water of life, bright as crystal, flowing from the Throne of God and of the Lamb through the middle of the street of the city; also, on both sides of the of the river [sic], the Tree of Life with its twelve kinds of fruit, yielding its fruit each month; and the leaves of the tree were for the healing of the nations. There shall no more be anything accursed, but the Throne of God and of the Lamb shall be in it, and his servants shall worship him; they shall see his face, and his name shall be on their foreheads. (Rev 22:1–4)

It is clear that at this point the writer of Revelation has lifted his gaze to the backrest of the throne, where the images he has described here can be clearly seen.

Okay, we might say, there is a definite similarity, but isn't it just as likely that the carver of the throne was reading the Book of Revelation? However, it is at this point that a little detective work by Rory Boid proves beyond doubt that the throne must have come first. A close and careful examination of the throne shows conclusively that the animal depicted on the backrest is not a lamb at all. It is in fact a ram, and its horns are clearly visible if anyone takes the trouble to look closely. How could the sculptor have been *following* the Book of Revelations when he gets basic details so fundamentally wrong – such as whether or not it is a *lamb* or a *ram* that is depicted? Rams have definite, curved horns, which lambs do not. A much more likely scenario is that this depiction is that of a ram with its horns caught in a bush, as in the case of the ram in the Old Testament story of Abraham and Isaac.

As I pointed out earlier, for the sake of those who might ask why Isaac himself is not depicted on the chair, it is plain that the counterpart of Isaac did not need to be depicted on the carvings because *he* was sitting on the throne.

Other images in the Revelation of John conform closely to the iconography of the throne but, in true Agatha Christie style, the writer has already given himself away. There can be no doubt that the throne came first and that the visions are based upon it.

It is interesting to note that the Book of Revelation was far from being accepted as either valid or genuine until at least the fourth century. What is more, early commentators who cast doubt upon Revelations were invariably related to the Markan tradition of Christianity in one way or another.

Dionysius, a second-century bishop of Alexandria who was a student of Origen and the Catechetic School established by Mark, is a good example. Like many Alexandrian clerics of his time, he had to learn that discretion is the better part of valour, or else one could be persecuted by the developing Roman Church. As a result, instead of openly repudiating the genuine nature of the Book of Revelations he noted that:

> Some before us have set aside and rejected the book altogether, criticizing it chapter by chapter, and pronouncing it without sense or argument, and maintaining that the title is fraudulent. For they say that it is not the work of John, nor is it a revelation, because it is covered thickly and densely by a veil of obscurity. And they affirm that none of the apostles, and none of the saints, nor any one in the Church is its author, but [a heretic] … desiring reputable authority for his fiction, prefixed the name. (Eusebius, *Church History*, Book 7, Ch 25)

As Dionysius continues, we can see by the twists and turns of his argument that it is not simply the Book of Revelations that he rejects. Like other luminaries of his period, and especially those from Alexandria, Dionysius is dubious about most if not all of the material in the New Testament that is associated with this particular John. As far as Dionysius is concerned it all has a spurious origin.

The 'John' who wrote the Book of Revelation has historically been connected directly with the same John who supposedly wrote the

Gospel of John. However the early Church scholars such as Dionysius of Alexandria and those who immediately followed him are sceptical about both works. The wealth of surviving hostile references to the Revelation of John from the late second and the third century quite clearly focus on sections of the text dealing with scenes that do not appear on the existing Throne of St Mark. In other words, their point seems to be that the author of Revelation and possibly also St John's Gospel had quite definitely seen the Throne of St Mark but that, either in ignorance or deliberately, he misrepresented what he had seen. What pointedly annoyed Dionysus of Alexandria and others of his ilk was that whoever this 'John' might actually be, he clearly had no idea as to the genuine secrets of St Mark's Throne.

CHAPTER 19

DECODING THE THRONE

It is quite natural that people brought up in a Christian society should accept the doctrines that they are raised to respect and follow. After all, everything about Christianity seems to be so old and so 'fixed' that one gets the impression it has been the way it is now for the last 2,000 years. But it doesn't take much investigation to realize that this is not the case at all.

Almost every aspect of Christianity has been debated, fought over, accepted, rejected, revised and revisited by theologians and the Church hierarchy at some stage down the long road, from the start right through to the modern era. If we were to go back in time 1,800 years or so and visit almost any Christian community of the period we would be surprised at just how different the whole business was in comparison with Christian worship today. We would also be astonished by how much Christianity differed from place to place.

Great controversies took place as the new religion began to shake itself down, developing the sort of rules and regulations that would ensure its survival. Arguments occurred between various scholars, especially with regard to which books should or should not be included in the ultimate Christian canon. As we have seen in the case of Irenaeus, this sometimes extended even to *creating* the necessary books to support the developing religion, if such proved necessary. After all, as the famous newspaper adage goes, 'Why let the truth get in the way of a good story?'

But this didn't mean that those developing and running the Church in Rome had everything their own way – at least, not for a couple of centuries. Nowhere is this more evident than in the controversy regarding the work of the mysterious John, the supposed writer of the Gospel of St John and also the Book or Revelation.

If we look carefully at the writings of Clement of Alexandria, Dionysus of Alexandria and a number of other early Eastern Church Fathers, we can see that these men were desperately trying to hold their own against a tidal wave of invective, slander and even persecution, coming from the direction of Rome. Considering that most of them were in fear for their very lives, it isn't hard to see why their arguments were guarded and also why they so often appeared to favour the 'Jesus-centred' development, even though between the lines they inferred something quite different.

To this end, the Revelation of John was one of the most bitterly disputed texts that ever made its way into the New Testament. It was quite pointedly rejected by those remnants of the original Markan tradition that had reluctantly joined the Roman Church, quite obviously as a way of escaping imperial sanctioned pressures and punishments. But there were also occasions when it was better and far less dangerous to bite one's tongue. One is reminded of the Italian scientist Galileo, forced by the Church on pain of death to state publicly that the Earth did not go around the Sun. This he did, with very bad grace, but on standing down from the lectern he was heard to say, 'And yet it does.'

As far as Clement of Alexandria is concerned, in his whole corpus of written works he made only one apparent reference to the Book of Revelation. Clement acknowledges that Christ is the 'Alpha and the Omega'. This reference is generally understood to have originated with the surviving canonical text of the Revelation of John. Supporters of the Book of Revelation might therefore surmise that Clement sanctioned its authenticity.

Interestingly, a reference to the Alpha and the Omega also figures prominently in Irenaeus' report on the heretical followers of the 'Gnostic Marcus'. Irenaeus, it will be remembered, argued forcefully for what he would have seen as being orthodox Christianity, as opposed to the Eastern Orthodox sort, which to him was pure heresy. Irenaeus often tells us a great deal about the Markan Christians of the East because, in order to repudiate their beliefs and practices, he first had to explain them. In this instance he tells us that 'Mark' suggested that the name of Christ '… is formed of all [letters and] numbers; and on this account Jesus is called Alpha and Omega' – because alpha and omega are the first and last letters of the Greek alphabet. It seems therefore as if Irenaeus agreed with the one statement Clement of Alexandria made on the same topic. However, the ultimate question is whether Clement and the followers of St Mark were really *quoting* from the Book of Revelations at all. Did the reference to alpha and omega actually derive from the Throne of St Mark?

It is commonly accepted by scholars today that the reference to alpha and omega to be found in the Book of Revelation was clearly and unequivocally borrowed from Jewish mysticism, with its love of codes, ciphers and word games. It is quite common even for early Jewish writings to identify the first and last letters of the Hebrew alphabet in an identical manner. Take for example the word 'truth', which in Hebrew is *Emeth* or *Emet*. Emeth is repeatedly identified in rabbinical literature as representing the first, middle and last letters of the alphabet. It is also a word consistently identified as having a numerological value of nine. This is just one example, but anyone who conducts sufficient research will discover that witnesses both ancient and modern have recognized that the Revelation of John borrowed many of its ideas from Jewish sources. What we need to ascertain is whether these came almost exclusively from the Throne of St Mark.

It is clear from early writings that the Alexandrian tradition was reluctant to accept the 'throne revelation' of St John. Clement wasn't alone in this regard. Dionysius, a third-century head of the Alexandrian community and the man who occupied St Mark's Throne (in a figurative sense at least), was one of the leading critics of the Revelation of John.

In his subtle attack against Revelation Dionysius acknowledged that the 'Alpha and Omega' statement is a borrowing from 'barbarous' (i.e. non-Greek) sources. Dionysius openly ridiculed the notion that it could possibly be the same John that wrote the Gospel of John and the

Apocalypse. He emphasized that the gospel was written not only without error, in terms of its Greek language, but also with elegance of expression and sound reasoning throughout its entire structure, and that it was 'far from betraying any barbarism or solecism, or any vulgarism whatever'. By contrast, he notes that in the case of the Book of Revelation, the author's '… dialect and language are not accurate Greek'. Further to this, Dionysius tells us that the author used '… barbarous idioms and, in some places, solecisms'.

Dionysius definitely showed great scepticism regarding the authenticity of the Book of Revelation, most likely because he was a follower of the Markan tradition. As such he knew that John's Revelation had to be a later fake and of no religious worth. But, stuck as he was between a rock and a hard place, he could not actually say in as many words that he rejected the text on religious grounds, particularly since the Book of Revelation was accepted in Rome.

Whenever a discussion arises regarding the historical authorship of the Book of Revelation, the name of a man called Cerinthus of Alexandria invariably surfaces. Cerinthus has been described as a mystical Gnostic. He is universally acknowledged to have been a Jew and thus would almost certainly have been able to read Hebrew. He could also have passed on Jewish mystical ideas such as that of Christ being 'the Alpha and the Omega'. As his name implies, Cerinthus came from Alexandria and quite likely got his ideas whilst looking at the little Throne of St Mark, still in the city during his life. The difference between him and people such as Dionysius is that Cerinthus is clearly *not* a follower of the Markan tradition.

Interestingly, amongst the earliest Coptic writers in and around Alexandria, there was a consistent understanding that the term 'throne' represented a heavenly female figure that was, herself, connected to the letters alpha and omega.

Meanwhile, amongst advocates of Egyptian religion, the name 'Isis' literally meant 'she of the throne'. As late as the 10th century, the Coptic Church Father St Severus speaks of the Throne of St Mark as '… the elect Lady of the first and the last', and of Mary as '… the throne of him who is Lord of the first and the last, without division or change, of him whom no space can enclose, and no time contain'. It would be very easy to assume that this concept is indeed rooted in the much older association of Isis in her representation as the throne on which successive pharaohs sat, but there is a much more recent context that is worth exploring.

The very same idea, regarding a 'throne', is present in Irenaeus' description of the Markan heretics. Not only does Irenaeus identify this community as prophesying by means of a small and large *kisse* (which means 'throne' in Hebrew) but he reports that Marcus himself is remembered for having brought down from heaven a female object called 'truth' (Hebrew *emeth*) which had the symbols of 'alpha and omega' on its face. Irenaeus says that Marcus instructed his followers that this object could 'speak' to those who beheld her and bestow great wisdom upon them. This could easily allude to the Throne of St Mark which, as we shall see, can speak volumes to those who understand its language.

To this end it seems reasonable at least to consider the possibility that Clement, Dionysius and various other surviving members of the Markan tradition *knew* that Cerinthus got his idea from their throne. Either knowingly or not, he was promoting an incorrect interpretation of its symbolism.

For the moment we will have to leave this matter aside, and just acknowledge that there are indeed secret codes in the images and letters appearing on the surface of the throne. This understanding has long been established in the literature associated with the throne. In his fairly recent article on the throne, Wladimiro Dorigo, former professor of Medieval Art History at the University of Venice, argues that the object was specifically constructed according to deliberate mystical symbolic measurements. Dorigo examined the dimensions of the throne very carefully, coming up with a surprising discovery. Presumably his starting point was to try to establish what measuring system might have been used in the throne's construction, the better to date it. He became certain that it responds to an 'inch' and a 'foot', which are known to have existed in ancient times in Beirut. The same measurement seems to have been used extensively across the Near East at a very early date, as an alternative to the more familiar cubit. In the case of the throne, the inch is around 2.82 cm in length, leading to a foot measuring between 33 cm and 34 cm.

There might not be anything too surprising about this discovery, but Dorigo noticed that a definite pattern began to emerge in which all the measurements of the throne represented even numbers of inches. These he quotes as being 12, 52, 40, 12, 20, 18, 20 and 18. This state of affairs would be extremely unlikely by chance and, as a result, Dorigo wondered if there was a code involved in the throne's dimensions. He could not be specific and suggested further investigation. I concur and, bearing in mind everything else that is now coming to light regarding the throne, the possibility seems more likely than ever. It is too early to say for certain what the message might be, but this is another area of research for the future.

For the moment it is enough to say that it would be hard for any serious scholar to *deny* that the Throne of St Mark was constructed with a very specific mystical function in mind. There is a series of great Gnostic secrets contained within its images and perhaps even its dimensions. Of course, most scholars are more comfortable dealing with knowable quantities. Almost every paper ever written on the Throne of St Mark merely compares the throne with other known historical artefacts. Experts point out that there are reports of other thrones of apostles having existed in various cities, and there are also many examples of the four strange creatures from Ezekiel's vision.

Nevertheless it is becoming more obvious that the Throne of St Mark is very different from any other ancient Christian relic. I use the word 'Christian' cautiously because the throne carries an almost complete lack of Christian symbolism anywhere on its surface! There is no overt reference to Jesus, the apostles (except on the medallion, which by almost everyone's assessment is a later addition) or familiar scenes from the gospel. In fact, the scenes carved onto the throne are all unmistakably Jewish or Samaritan.

Rory Boid is the first Hebraist to ever look at the inscription on the throne and, in a matter of hours, he realized its significance. When one goes through the laborious process of applying a mirror to each letter and copying out the new character one gets the following:

The Coronation of Mark and Evangelist (of) Alexandria.

Most readers will now think it quite reasonable for me to put forward the assertion that the Throne of St Mark exists as the commemoration of a specific event in the life of St Mark of the Alexandrian community, who of course is also Marcus Agrippa. The throne has little or nothing to do with Jesus Christ. It is in fact the last surviving material evidence of a real event from history that has remained unknown to Christianity for almost 2,000 years.

As far as the date of this important event is concerned, which was of course the enthronement of the Messiah, the throne itself tells us that it must have taken place during a Jubilee. This doesn't entirely depend on my original identification of the phrase 'year' or 'year one' in Samaritan letters on the inscription; a careful examination of other details on the face of the throne also confirms this. The most obvious expression of the coronation occurring during a Jubilee is the presence of fifty stars on the back and sides of the object. This relates to the fact that, although the operative number in Judaism was seven multiplied by seven, which of course equals 49 years, the Jubilee itself was held in the 50th year.

It is also worth pointing out that, if the observer looks just below the image of the ram and the bush on the backrest, there is the strange but undoubted image of the four rivers of Paradise. In the depiction, they are emerging from what is clearly a cube. The symbolism of the cube representing the Jubilee year was well known to early members of the Alexandrian tradition. Clement of Alexandria writes that, '… eight is the first cube, counting the fixed sphere along with the seven revolving ones, by which is produced the "great year", as a "period of recompense of what has been promised"'.

The presence of the four rivers of Paradise on the front of the throne's backrest is clearly intended to mean that Mark's enthronement in the year of Jubilee was expected to transform the world and to bring humanity back to the Garden of Eden. The ram on the throne's backrest, ready for sacrifice, is meant to represent Jesus, whose willing sacrifice made it possible for humanity to receive Marcus Agrippa, its awaited Messiah. Bearing in mind the composition of the text, we can be certain that the author of the Book of Revelations saw not only the ram and the bush on the throne but also the cube, because this too is mentioned in Revelations. Yet for him the cube is transformed into a symbol of the New Jerusalem 'coming down from heaven' to renew the world.

Whoever John actually was, it is certain that he saw the Throne of St Mark and that it impressed him significantly. Maybe he viewed it at a time of celebration or mystery, raised up on a plinth and surrounded by the heady smoke of incense. Perhaps he felt himself to be intoxicated or 'possessed' but, for whatever reason, he misrepresented what he had seen – or, more likely, misunderstood its significance. His ultimate conclusions and the strange book he wrote have obscured for many centuries what the carvers of this most remarkable piece of sculpture intended.

CHAPTER 20

APOCALYPSE THEN

I hope I have already proven to the satisfaction of most readers that I have identified much more than a mere series of coincidences regarding the life of Marcus Agrippa and his role as the Messiah of the Jews. But I still face the daunting task of reconciling my theories with the few, but nevertheless well accepted, theories about this particular period of history that seem to contradict some of my basic assumptions.

For example, it is a central supporting column of this book that Marcus Agrippa had to have been an eight- or nine-year-old boy when he came to Alexandria in 38 CE. Directly confronting this assertion are the surviving texts of Josephus, which make clear he was closer to 50 years of age.

Why should I consider that my opinion is correct, when it flies in the face of one of the most fundamental texts dealing with this period of history? Well, first of all there can be no doubt that the throne is too small for an adult to sit on comfortably. To counter this, there is a body of scholarly literature that claims the throne was not designed to be sat upon at all. Such commentators suggest that the Throne of St Mark was solely intended to be a reliquary. After all, doesn't it have a large hole near its base that was clearly intended to be a receptacle for something? Perhaps all this business about secret codes is just a product of my having too little understanding and too much imagination?

I have to admit there were many times that I doubted my own theory about Marcus Agrippa's central place in Christianity. This is the reason why I never sought publication before I became familiar with St Mark's Throne. But all of my doubts gradually evaporated as I looked more closely at the iconography on the throne, even though, for some time, I knew there was a great deal more to do before I could claim I had proved my case.

I suspected from the outset that there was an ancient Alexandrian oral tradition relating to the images on the throne. I have already demonstrated that Clement and Dionysius seemed to reject the claims made in the pages of the Revelation of John. Their attitude towards this extraordinary book seemed to suggest that they knew better. Origen similarly recognized certain mysteries related to the divine throne. However, he stopped short of revealing what these Alexandrian secret teachings about the throne might actually be.

In my search for this lost oral tradition I went as far as visiting Coptic churches and seminaries all across America, armed with pictures of the throne and hoping that somehow, somewhere, some light might be thrown on the problem. After thousands of miles of travel and countless questions asked, I eventually had to admit that nothing was forthcoming. It wasn't that I considered there to be some secret cabal amongst Copts trying to prevent me from getting at the truth. Rather, I suspect that, once the throne was stolen from Alexandria, the Alexandrian Christian tradition gradually forgot about the throne and its secret codes.

I had already discovered so much about the throne, yet I knew there was something else – something even bigger and more unequivocal. I had obtained as many pictures of the throne as I could, taken from as many different angles as possible, though despite my searches I had no text or surviving oral tradition to guide me when it came to figuring out what the carvings actually meant. Almost a month had passed since my first realizations regarding the throne, and I can still remember standing in the kitchen of my home, looking carefully at the pictures of the throne's backrest. There was the ram, the bush, the rivers flowing out of the cube ... and then, suddenly, I was struck with what I can only describe as a sudden insight. Something about the fruit or leaves that appeared on the bush seemed to attract my interest and I studied them more closely. Whether these are meant to be leaves or fruit I still do not know, but it was their presence that seemed odd, because they are very stylized and somehow far from being a simple embellishment.

I could account for every other part of this particular image in terms of the text of the Book of Revelation but the number of fruits or leaves was not mentioned anywhere. Nevertheless they had been so carefully executed and so deliberately placed in the scene that I was sure that they were significant in some way. I counted them several times and always came up with the same number – 35. Thirty-five was a number that did not seem to figure at all in either Jewish or Egyptian symbolism. Why would the craftsmen have spent so much time on the throne establishing six wings here and four rivers there, and then to come up with some arbitrary number regarding the fruits or leaves on the bush?

I then looked more carefully at the way the fruits or leaves had been carved. In one instance I could see that the artisan had quite obviously chiselled a small section out of the natural line of a branch in order to fit in an extra fruit or leaf. As I spent the greater part of an afternoon looking at the picture from different angles I began to wonder … maybe it wasn't the total number of fruits that was significant, but how they were grouped onto each branch?

I looked at the bush once again. There were five main branches emanating from its trunk. Bearing in mind the codes and ciphers I had already recognized, I began to wonder if the numbers of fruits or leaves on each branch might have been meant to represent letters. Reading left to right there were eight, seven, six, five and then nine fruit on each branch. At first I doubted my original hypothesis. Maybe the arrangement was just an expression of artistic symmetry? But, as the reader should discover, the bush isn't really all that symmetrical at all.

I decided to render each number to its equivalent letter in the Hebrew alphabet, using the known and established number letter sequence. 8 7 6 5 9 would be naturally read HZVET (using here the Roman letters historically equivalent to the Hebrew ones, which are only partly the phonetic equivalents). I am far from being an expert in Hebrew or Aramaic, but I knew that this wasn't a word. Nevertheless, I couldn't help but think that the first three letters formed the beginnings of various tenses of the Hebrew word *haza*, which means 'to see' or 'to envision'. But apart from that, for the moment I was puzzled.

I wondered whether the last number, which didn't seem to fit at all, had been intended to represent exactly what it was – a number. It was just possible that, if this was the case, the remainder might make sense in some bizarre dialect of Aramaic. I sent an email to Rory Boid asking if HZVE 9 meant anything. He replied that it did, though at the time he had no idea why I had asked the question. He said that, in total, the letters and the number would be pronounced *h.ezwa tish'ana* and that they meant 'the ninth vision', though not in Hebrew, in Aramaic.[96]

When I explained why I wanted this information, neither he nor I were sure whether this was going to lead to something important. Referring to the Bible I counted the number of revelations or 'visions' detailed in the Book of Revelations, but that didn't reveal anything. Rory Boid at first thought that the Book of Daniel might yield an answer to the problem, but I wasn't convinced. I spoke to other scholars I knew and asked whether there was any established tradition which divided Daniel into nine visions. Most said no, but one or two did point out that the Book of Zechariah was definitely divided in such a way.

Shortly after, Rory Boid came up with another solution. He counted the number of 'visions' in the Book of Genesis and found that the 'binding of Isaac' was the ninth. This seemed to solve the problem, as the ram and the bush framed the scene in the carving on the backrest of the throne, where the encoded message appeared. The only problem was that I had never heard of a tradition of counting the number of visions in the Book of Genesis.

I was unconvinced by the Genesis explanation and so I decided to revisit some of the leads I had developed along the way. I had by now realized that Agrippa was undoubtedly nine years of age when he sat on this throne in Alexandria. I also knew that nine was the original age that ancient Jews thought that a boy reached manhood. As such the 'vision of nine' might well be related to Agrippa becoming a 'new man' in Christ (Eph 2:15). I was also drawn to the ancient kabbalistic understanding associated with the number nine – that it represents the value of *emeth*, the alpha and omega which we have already spoken of.

Yet even with all these intriguing explanations I remained unsatisfied. There had to be some hidden Gnostic understanding that could reconcile together all these loose ends into one powerful messianic statement.

I took up the advice of a professor from Columbia University and read what the 'ninth vision' of Zechariah was all about. When I read the Alexandrian Greek translation of the original Hebrew text, I was stunned by what I found! I read a clear testimonial of a future messianic enthronement – exactly that which we see on the Throne of St Mark:

> Thus saith the Lord Almighty; behold the man whose name is the Rising Sun; and he shall spring up from his stem, and build the house of the Lord. And he shall receive power, and shall sit and rule upon his throne; and there shall be a priest on his right hand, and a peaceable counsel shall be between [them] both … and they [that are] far from them shall come and build in the house of the Lord, and ye shall know that the Lord Almighty has sent me to you. (Zechariah 6:12–15)

I knew immediately that this was the passage intended by the code on the throne. However, there was so much misunderstanding in scholarly literature regarding this extract that I had to sort out why the English translations of the Greek and Hebrew texts looked so different from one another.

When opening most Bibles we find the Hebrew word *tsemah*, which is directly translated into Greek as 'the rising [sun]', rendered as 'the branch', or something to that effect. Nevertheless, any expert in ancient Hebrew would suggest that this is a bad rendering. The sense of the sentence in Hebrew and Greek is 'There will be a man called the Risen Sun, who will dawn from down below' – from the underworld. The words are carefully chosen and deliberately emphasize that this newly risen sun is not as bright or hot as the sun at midday.

There are two main groups of meanings of *tsemah* in Hebrew and *anatolê* in Greek. They can mean 'sprouting' and 'first appearing over the horizon'.[97] The two verbs *tsemah* and *anatellein* have the same range of meaning as the noun. Both words apply, for example, to the growth of vines or eyes of potatoes. It seems almost comical if taken out of context – 'behold a man whose name is Sprout'. However, that is what the text actually says.

It might help to look at some of the different ways the word *tsemah* is rendered in Greek, before we directly connect it to the little nine-year-old 'sprout' Marcus Agrippa, for whom the throne was made.

It is possible to ascertain that Aquila and Symmachus, the ancient Greek translators of the Bible, render the term correctly. The *Bible de Jérusalem* and the *Traduction Ecuménique de la Bible* also both translate correctly as '*germe*' in French. It is our standard NRSV and NEB texts with their translation 'branch' or 'branch out' that would naturally lead most people away from the true meaning of the passage. It shows an absence of feeling for Hebrew. Any branching out would have to come after the sprouting.

It looks then as if the ninth vision of Zechariah is part of the secret built into the throne of Marcus Agrippa. As a nine-year-old boy who was on his way to Palestine to receive his grandfather's kingdom, it would have been inappropriate to suggest that Marcus was already the awesome figure the Messiah was envisioned to be by the prophets of the Jewish writings. The Hebrew can be translated as 'and he will appear over the horizon or show the first sprout',[98] or more literally still, 'he will rise from where he is'.[99]

The best sense of the passage comes when it is rendered into Aramaic by the Targum. Verses 12 and 13 read, 'And you shall say ... Behold a man whose name is *Meshiha* [the Anointed]. He will be revealed. He will become great and will build the Temple of the Lord. He will build the Temple of the Lord and will bloom. He will sit and rule on his throne.' The point is that the translator stresses that the figure who sits on the throne will only become great – not 'will initially be great' – and his 'blooming' is not the first event in his rise to greatness. For the moment he is merely a 'sprout' – a child – exactly as Marcus Agrippa was when he came to Alexandria in 38 CE, in the year of the Samaritan Jubilee.

The true meaning of this throne 'secret' is now quite clear. Marcus Agrippa was seen as nothing short of a messianic 'sun god', the perfect embodiment of the Gnostic or, in the words of Morton Smith, taken from Plato: 'the ideal king, the only man capable of knowing God, who would therefore act as the mediator between God and man; he would be, in effect, the *nous* [the divine intellect] of his subjects, in whom he would restore their lost contact with the heavenly world from which he came.'

We don't have to rely on the work of a recent scholar to prove this to us. All we have to do is to pay careful attention to what Philo of

Alexandria – Marcus Agrippa's relative and his host when he first sat upon the alabaster throne – had to say. Not surprisingly, Philo connects the rising sun with the east because this is where the solar disc rises each morning. Philo uses solar allegory when he speaks of how divine revelation 'dawns on the soul' of initiates into the religious mysteries, of which he is himself a part. It occurs when:

> ... the light of the virtues shines forth like the beams of the sun ... [which is embodied in the saying] 'And God planted a paradise in Eden, toward the east', [Genesis 2:8], not of terrestrial but of celestial plants, which the planter caused to spring up from the incorporeal light which exists around him, in such a way as to be for ever inextinguishable. (Philo, *On the Confusion of Languages*, 14)

Philo immediately adds that he has heard from 'one of the companions of Moses' – Zechariah – the very saying 'Behold, a man whose name is the Rising [Sun]!' (Zechariah 6:12). Philo explains that this is:

> ... a very novel appellation indeed, if you consider it as spoken of a man who is compounded of body and soul; but if you look upon it as applied to that incorporeal being who in no respect differs from the divine image, you will then agree that the name of the Rising has been given to him with great felicity. For the Father of the universe has caused him to spring up as the eldest son whom, in another passage, he calls the firstborn; and he who is thus born, imitating the ways of his Father, has formed such and such species, looking to his archetypal patterns. (Ibid)

Bearing these extracts in mind, Philo had quite understandably believed that the Jewish Messiah would come as a solar god, exactly as we see depicted on the throne. He would therefore be someone close to the 'dawn' of his life. This is hardly surprising, since Philo undoubtedly had a hand in creating it!

It is becoming apparent that there is an unmistakable consistency to all aspects of the throne. The reason it was made with such a small seat, and with the seat so close to the ground, was because it was designed for a child. The image that appears on the backrest, displaying the story of Isaac and the way he was spared by God from being sacrificed, is extremely important. Not only does it show Jesus – the ram that was ultimately sacrificed – but it also points out that this incident happened to Isaac when he too was a child, like Marcus. The ninth vision reveals that the Messiah will first appear to the Hebrew people as a little 'sprout' who will eventually become great as he matures and grows.

So it was that, after presenting my arguments to Rory Boid, he eventually came up with a compromise position. With regards to the words 'the ninth vision' he made the case that both meanings – the reference to the ninth vision in the Book of Genesis (the *Akedah*) and the ninth vision in the Book of Zechariah were relevant. In each case the vision relates to a young boy. Moreover, Boid made the case that it has to be considered the words could have been there to explain why Isaac doesn't appear in the picture on the back of the throne. The words are meant to explain to the initiated witnesses that the little boy who once sat on the throne was both 'Isaac' and 'the sprout' of the respective texts.

We don't have to look far to see how easily the intention of the picture of the ram and the bush might be missed. The author of the Book of Revelations certainly got it wrong, as did every modern observer. Without the hidden words indicated by the bush, it would be very easy to mistake a ram for a lamb and a bush for a tree. The secret had to be whispered into people's ears. 'Count the number of fruits on each branch and convert the numbers to letters, and you will learn a great mystery.'

Apparently these words were meant to trigger the switching on of a light in the minds of those gazing at this object. The same codes used in the scriptures of the Bible and later in the gospels were also present in the throne. This realization makes sense of why Marcus Agrippa was greeted with Aramaic shouts of praise during his visit to Alexandria. His identity as Barabba (that is, Isaac, 'the son of Abraham') was confirmed on the very throne on which he was acclaimed as the Messiah. Anyone who could piece together these clues must have figured out that they revealed the truth that all Israel had awaited for centuries – here was the Messiah foretold by the sacred writings![100]

CHAPTER 21

THE AGRIPPA CODE

At this stage I seemed to have everything I would need to convince even the most diehard sceptic that the Throne of St Mark was much more than a randomly decorated reliquary, simply ornamented to suit the foibles and artistic prowess of whoever made it. The discovery of the number symbolism of the fruits or leaves on the backrest of the chair would surely prove to anyone that there was real 'intention' in the minds of those who planned this most extraordinary creation.

Could I reasonably expect anything more from this ornate piece of alabaster? It seemed unlikely. But by this stage I had come to realize just how clever the throne's makers had actually been. I knew the object was replete with symbolism created on many different levels. At the same time, some of my associates in this process, for example Rory Boid and Alan Butler, were advising caution, telling me that 'watertight' is not always enough, especially for people who consider themselves to be experts and to whom only the most rigorous explanation would do. As the days and weeks went by I continued to look carefully at the throne and its graphic representations, trying to reach into the minds of those to whom it had clearly been of the most tremendous importance to impart their secrets to the 'elect' by way of this 'throne of the Messiah'.

I could be certain that the image on the front of the backrest proved once and for all that the throne was not intended for Jesus. The words from the Book of Zechariah were very clear in this respect. Jesus was not the enthroned king. Nobody who accepted Jesus as the long-prophesied Messiah of the Jews would have hidden the ninth revelation of Zechariah in the throne's symbolism: the passage is explicit about two quite separate individuals being involved, one being the herald and sacrifice and the other being the prophesied messiah.

It is impossible to know *exactly* what those responsible for the throne and the new religion may have intended, but we might very reasonably speculate that, to them, Jesus, who died on the cross, was understood to be the 'high priest' in heaven, or perhaps even a corporeal counterpart of God. Yet the passage in question makes it unequivocal that the throne's makers understood Marcus Agrippa to be the messianic 'little sprout' mentioned in the ninth vision of Zechariah.

Bearing in mind the advice of my co-conspirators in this most remarkable adventure, I looked again at some of my evidence. I was certain that I had now proved beyond doubt that this little alabaster chair was intended to represent a solar throne. The four creatures depicted on the sides and back of the throne – the bull, the lion, the eagle and the man – all have a celestial representation, representing the zodiac path or ecliptic through which the Sun travels during the year. Each is connected with a different zodiac sign, and these four signs have been significant to observers for countless centuries.

The zodiac signs in question are Taurus, Leo, Scorpio and Aquarius. These zodiac signs can be seen as 'corners of the year', often called the 'cross-quarters'. Taurus marks the point at which the spring is at its fullest. Three months later comes Leo, with the heat of the summer. Another three months pass and the Sun is then in Scorpio, to mark the fall and then, after a further three months, the Sun appears in Aquarius, signifying the travails of winter. In this way these four zodiac signs, in the form of the four creatures, circle around the throne and, in a figurative sense, they appear to form an equidistant zodiacal cross. The throne, or rather that very special individual for whom it was made, represents the Sun itself, performing its annual dance through the zodiac signs.

Throughout the minutiae of a busy life the throne stayed in my mind and I often looked at the colour plates pinned to my study wall. Then quite suddenly this most fascinating of objects spoke to me again, and

I realized something that had been staring me in the face all along, but which I had previously failed to recognize.

I found myself focusing again on the palm trees on the right side and back of the throne (position indicated below).

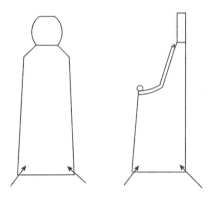

The palm trees appear in the bottom corners of the throne in each case, but there is something quite different about the way they are represented. In the case of the right hand side of the throne, where the human figure is to be seen, the trees are squatter and do not extend high into the image as they do on the back of the throne. It is as if whoever designed the throne wanted the viewer to recognize that there was a deliberate difference. One gets the impression that, in the case of the right hand side of the throne, the trees are younger – somehow less developed. The potential is there because the trees do have leaves and fruit, but when they appear close to the lion they are half as tall again and intended to be seen as fully mature plants. The lion even stands over another tree – this time a tamarisk – fully in bloom to emphasize this understanding. Bearing in mind everything else that had come to light it seemed certain to me that this state of affairs could not be accidental. What I needed was an explanation.

Was the way the trees were portrayed simply meant to represent ornamentation? If this was the case why did the trees reach above the diamond pattern in one case but not in the other? Had the artist intended us to view the cross-hatching as the Earth?

If this was the case, the small trees, in effect the 'shoots' or 'sprouts', might represent the *tsemah* concept we discussed in the last chapter, in which Marcus Agrippa, in his position as the Messiah, was described as a sprout – in other words a child.

Equally intriguing was the fact that the side of the throne containing the representation of the bull had no palm trees at all, and neither were there any palm trees associated with the fourth image, that of the eagle.

Of course it is easy to explain why there are no palm trees accompanying the eagle. It is depicted soaring above the lion. As such, here in the heavenly heights, it would be absurd to have palm trees present. Yet if we turn to the other panel on the outer left side of the throne – the one depicting the bull – the situation is quite different. One might reasonably expect palm trees to accompany this panel, and yet they do not.

Perhaps we are intended to look at the panels in a chronological order. If the trees are intended to represent the Messiah's growth and maturity we can be sure that the right side of the throne, with its tall trees, comes later in the story. That means the panels were probably meant to be viewed around the throne, starting at the left with the bull. From an astronomical point of view this would make great sense because the bull – Taurus – is a springtime zodiac sign, the earliest in the natural year of all the four zodiac signs represented.

I racked my brains for days until the solution came to me. The answer is connected to Hebrew Gematria, the traditional science of numerology and letter substitution.

The Hebrew word for palm tree is *tamar*. It has a value of 640 (t=400, m=40, r=200). As is well established in the Jewish mystical literature, the word for sun in Hebrew – *shemesh* – is a numerological equivalent for *tamar* (sh=300, m=40, sh=300). In other words, it's not just a plant that can be seen growing up from the underworld as our gaze passes around the throne from the human figure to the lion. It is a symbolic representation of the rising sun explicitly mentioned in the ninth vision of Zechariah.

As I demonstrated earlier, we have explicit proof that these earliest Alexandrian Christians did use Hebrew Gematria. We know for example that Marcus Agrippa's relative Philo was an expert in such matters. Moving a little forward in time, Clement of Alexandria, our earliest known Alexandrian Christian, employed Gematria to solve riddles in the Bible. He was aware, for example, that the reason the number 318 appears in the story of Abraham is because it is a numero-logical equivalent of his servant Eleazar. What is more, Irenaeus tells us in no uncertain terms, that *Marcus* and his followers used Gematria and other codes and ciphers on a regular basis.

Armed with this knowledge, we can now look even deeper into the encrypted Samaritan Aramaic Gnosis that lies at the heart of a full un-derstanding of St Mark's Throne. The palm trees have a fully intended double meaning. On the one hand they suggest that the Messiah will be a very young person but that as time goes on he will grow to full maturity. But the same trees also represent the Sun.

All that remains is for us to finally work out how the four tableaux might have been seen chronologically. The throne isn't unique in this regard, specifically in a Jewish context: archaeologists reporting on mosaic floors in ancient synagogues throughout Palestine and Jordan find much the same situation. In one particular study on such a syna-gogue mosaic from the ancient city of Sepphoris by Weiss and Netzer, a virtually identical state of affairs to that of the throne has come to light.

The synagogue mosaic has many of the same features as the throne – a Jewish sun god surrounded by images from the zodiac. There is also a pronounced emphasis laid on the *Akedah* story of the sacrificed ram mentioned in Genesis. The untrained observer might look at these mosaics and assume that they were all separate 'depictions' of various scenes from the Law of Moses. However Weiss and Netzer note that '… each of the scenes in the synagogue mosaic constitute a separate icono-graphic unit [while] at the same time, each one is thematically linked to those that border it.'

Weiss and Netzer identify the underlying theme of the images in Sepphoris as relating to a promise to, and a redemption of, the people of Israel. The *Akedah* – the story of Abraham, Isaac and the ram – represents the 'promise'. The redemption is brought about by the establishment of an organized priesthood for the Jewish religion. On the Throne of St Mark we have an identical starting point – the finding of the ram as a substitute for the slaughter of Isaac. However there can be no doubt that, in the case of the throne, the theme that follows is messianic in nature.

The image with the ram and the bush seen on the backrest of the throne is the *Gnostic* starting point. Anyone who receives proper instruction will understand that, hidden in the bush, is the reference to the ninth vision of Zechariah. With this knowledge it is possible to recognize that the story of the enthronement of Marcus Agrippa is meant to fulfil the promise brought about by Jesus' sacrifice. The panels that follow along the sides and back of the throne can be taken as applying directly to the life of Marcus Agrippa.

The people who designed the throne in 38 CE brought together four separate tableaux which, taken together, would explain how the ninth vision of Zechariah applied to Marcus Agrippa's enthronement.

We can now start at the beginning of the throne's story and work our way through.

First comes the necessary sacrifice, depicted on the backrest of the throne by the ram and the bush.

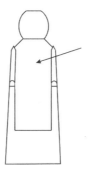

Next we must look to the left side of the throne to see the winged bull.

Like much of the iconography of the throne the bull is very Egyptian in context, which is hardly surprising considering the throne was made in Alexandria and that Marcus Agrippa was enthroned as the Messiah there.

The bull is, in one sense, Apis, the Egyptian bull god. The famous Apis bulls of Memphis were considered to be incarnations of the great god Osiris. They were perpetually kept indoors and buried with great ceremony when they died, but their chief place of residence was in the underworld. Those who designed the Throne of St Mark deliberately chose the bull for the left panel for two reasons. Firstly, it is an indication of the days immediately after the crucifixion of Jesus, at which time the Christ spirit was thought to have visited Hades, before being raised again in the form of Marcus Agrippa. At the same time the bull represents Taurus, indicating the starting point of Marcus Agrippa as the Messiah – not at birth, because that would be represented by Aries the Ram, but rather as a small child in the 'spring' of life, best represented by Taurus the Bull.

The lack of vegetation associated with this panel on the throne is easy to understand because of the panel's underworld connotations. Partly because the 'sprout' was not yet visible but also because the Sun God had not yet risen above the horizon in a figurative sense.

The next panel is that of the man – a hermit with bare feet. He is raised in all humility to his position as the Messiah, though with heralds and fanfares, to begin his task of redeeming humanity. The palm trees are still below the level of the Earth – the Sun is about to rise.

Following on from this we now refer to the back of the throne. The bottom picture is that of the lion. The Sun is at its zenith shining in all its glory, and the palm trees are mature. This is Marcus as a fully-grown man, having taken possession of his kingdom and seen perhaps as the

Lion of Judah, a familiar representation to anyone of Jewish origin. But the lion also represents the very hottest and most potent part of the year, as epitomized by the zodiac sign of Leo.

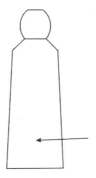

Finally we come to the top representation on the back of the throne, which is that of the eagle.

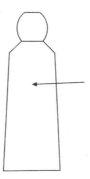

In this representation the eagle soars up to heaven. Above its topmost wings is what remains of a piece of carving that appears to have been partially destroyed when the top medallion of the throne was either replaced or added. In the original conception of the stone carver this was almost certainly meant to represent the Sun's disc. The wingtips of the eagle almost touch the edge of a Sun disc, and this is for a very important reason. We saw earlier how important the figure of Horus was in Egyptian religion; he was the son of Isis and Osiris, but he was also a reincarnation of Osiris. He was invariably depicted as a hawk and he too was often shown with his wings touching the solar disc.

The intention is clear: by portraying Marcus Agrippa in this way a comparison with Horus is being made and an appeal is being sent out to native Egyptian converts that they should come over to Agrippa's new religion. Upon doing so they could receive the new mysteries it imparts – though without losing the essence of their existing religious patterns.

None of this is as far-fetched as it might at first appear. For example, the idea of St Mark emerging as the light of the Sun from the inner darkness of the Earth is still present in the hymns and traditions of Coptic Alexandria, as in the example below ('Doxology of St Mark'). This tells graphically that Marcus Agrippa was present at the crucifixion of Jesus and that he went on to fulfil the expectations of the Messiah. True, there are modern Christian overtones, but the essence of the original meaning shines through as bright as the Sun itself.

> O Mark the Apostle, and the Evangelist,
> the witness to the passion of the Only-Begotten God.
> You have come and enlightened us through your gospel,
> and taught us the Father, and the Son, and the Holy Spirit.
> You brought us out of the darkness into the true light,
> and nourished us with the Bread of Life that came down from heaven.
> All the tribes of the earth were blessed through you,
> and your words have reached the ends of the world.
> Hail to you, O Martyr, Hail to the Evangelist,
> Hail to the Apostle, Mark, the Beholder of God.

As Christianity became changed and Roman ways began to predominate, Church leaders such as Irenaeus did their best to prevent this gnosis or knowledge from remaining at the heart of the faith. They deliberately established counter traditions regarding the symbolism of the throne in order to obscure its original meaning. If we want to make sense of this secret doctrine, we have to abandon our dependence on the familiar Christian story to be found in the surviving Gospel of Mark and its companion gospels. As I demonstrated earlier in the book, there was once a fuller text that undoubtedly related to the original conceptions of Christianity.

The Throne of St Mark is a tangible testimony to what happened after Jesus' self-sacrifice. It was created very early in the story of the emerging faith – a little over one year after the crucifixion – in order to celebrate the fulfilment of all that Jesus had predicted during his ministry. Now we can see why the throne must have taken such a central role in the faith of the Markan community. It was meant to confirm the veracity of the Passion spelled out in a 'picture book' form.

The Gospel of Nicodemus, a somewhat mysterious work that never found its way into the accepted Christian canon of gospels, has many features that lead back to the Throne of St Mark. It begins with Jesus' sacrifice and makes clear that Christ immediately went to the underworld to save those who had been waiting there for their salvation since the beginning of time. In the text the 'righteous' who lived in the world below say:

> When we were set together with all our fathers in the deep, in obscurity of darkness, on a sudden there came a golden heat of the sun and a purple and royal light shining upon us. And immediately the father of the whole race of men, together with all the patriarchs and prophets, rejoiced, saying: This light is the beginning of everlasting light which did promise to send unto us his co-eternal light. And Esaias cried out and said: This is the light of the Father, even the Son of God, according as I prophesied when I lived upon the earth ... and now hath it come and shone upon us that sit in death. (Gospel of Nicodemus, Part II, 2:1)

Little by little the throne reveals its secrets in a picture form that even the most illiterate devotee could come to understand. From the sacrifice the spirit passes to the underworld and from the underworld it returns to the world in the form of the novitiate Messiah. From there it is elevated to the rank of earthly king and then onto something much more – nothing less than the soaring eagle, God's direct emissary. Yet at the same time the whole story is emblematic of the life-giving Sun, which dies each day to be reborn at dawn, eventually rising to its full power and zenith. It is also the story of the Sun passing from the cold and hunger-laden months of winter to its ultimate triumph at midsummer. On one level the story fulfils the expectations of Jewish observers but at its heart it is also very, very Egyptian.

The eagle, the most elevated of the scenes on the body of the throne, completes the promise of the ninth vision that can be read in

Genesis 22. But of course there is also the ninth vision of Zechariah. The various Sun symbols on the throne prove that those who designed the throne certainly had this in mind. In other parts of the Old Testament we find passages such as that in Malachi 3:20, which says: 'The sun of righteousness will arise, with healing in his wings.'

And in Deuteronomy 32:11–12, we have: 'As an eagle awakens its nest, hovering over its fledglings, it spreads its wings, taking them and carrying them on its pinions. [So] the Lord guided [the Israelites] alone.'

It is also worth mentioning that the eagle is a bird that was of massive significance to the imperial Romans – in fact the eagle was Rome. Although with the passing of time it would be Rome that would obscure and subvert the original intentions of those who wrote their story into the Throne of St Mark, it cannot be doubted that at the start of the adventure a Roman emperor was primarily responsible for allowing it to take place. If Caligula had abandoned Marcus Agrippa there would have been no enthronement and no Messiah in 38 CE. The very first Christians owed a debt of gratitude to the empire. As we have seen, Marcus Agrippa threw in his lot absolutely with his friends, the successive Roman emperors.

There can surely be no doubt about the intentions of those who created the throne. They had the financial wherewithal, political influence and dogged determination to take the little king, who had so recently been favoured by a Roman emperor, and make him into a saviour. But right from the start Marcus Agrippa was meant to be a deliverer for both Jew and pagan alike. His presence and status reflected the very earliest human religious instincts, but it was also sophisticated and steeped in mystery. No wonder then that when Marcus Agrippa arrived in Alexandria in the year 38 the religious leaders of the pagans in Egypt complained that Marcus and his followers wanted to take over the entire world!

CHAPTER 22

KIDNAPPING A TRADITION

When we put all the pieces together, we can see nearly all of the thinking that went into the creation of a brand new religion that commenced in 38 CE in Alexandria. The Throne of St Mark is the previously unrecognized primary evidence in reconstructing something that is now almost totally lost to us in other ways. It is the smoking gun!

In the minds of Philo, Marcus Agrippa's family and high-ranking members of the Alexandrian Jewish community, everything was quite straightforward. Jesus appeared as a herald and a teacher; his primary role was to announce the coming of the Promised Messiah – though he went to great pains to point out that he was not himself the Messiah. The gospel offers us various names that Jesus applied to this individual. One of the most common is that of the *paraclete* or 'comforter'. Jesus said that after his own death God would give his followers 'another comforter' to be with them forever. This person would teach 'all things' to the community and would remind them of everything Jesus had said and done. Although Jesus never says so in as many words, we can take it more or less for granted that he knew the teachings would ultimately appear in the form of a written gospel – the new covenant.

The significance of this *paraclete* or 'comforter' is inherent in the Jewish word game we have looked at time and again. The Gematria, or word number substitution, was well known to all members of the rabbinic tradition. To learned individuals such as Philo the letters of the word *tsemah* – the messianic title from the ninth vision of *Zechariah* – add up to 138. This makes it a numerological equivalent of *menachem* or 'comforter'. Although such concepts are nonsense to us, they were taken extremely seriously at the time. Both *tsemah* and *menachem* are important names for the Messiah. The fact that Mark's original gospel identifies the Messiah to come as the *menachem* and that the hidden references on the throne point to the word *tsemah* is no coincidence. They respond to Gematria and are absolutely intentional.

The Copts preserve a story that seems to connect the two traditions together. By the middle of the third century the Markan community had already been torn apart. Two centres remained. One was in Alexandria and the other existed in the independent kingdom of Osorhone, which roughly corresponds to the Kurdish region of modern northern Iraq. The Copts of Egypt were well aware that followers of their tradition thrived in Osorhone and they still tell of an important day when a heretic named Mani visited Osorhone. Mani went on to found the dualistic Manichaean religion.

The Markan believers in Osorhone had been cut off from their Egyptian brothers for some time, nevertheless the bishop of Osorhone still sat in the 'Throne of St Mark' (perhaps even a copy of the original throne in Alexandria). The story tells how, at some unspecified date, Mani (or Manes) entered the church in Osorhone and seated himself on the Throne of St Mark. In Severus of Al'Ashmunein's *History of the Coptic Church* I, we are told:

> He went straight to [his] chair, and sat upon it in the midst of the house; and he thought that they would request him that they might receive instruction from him … [so] when [the bishop] saw Manes sitting on the chair, he was astonished at his want of shame. Then the bishop questioned him, and said to him: 'What is thy name?' Manes replied: 'My name is Paraclete.' Archelaus said to him: 'Art thou the Paraclete of whom the Lord Christ said that he would send him to us?' He said: 'Yes; I am he.' The bishop asked him: 'How many are the years of thy life?' He answered: 'Five and thirty years.' Archelaus, the bishop, said to him: 'The Saviour Christ said to his disciples: "Remain in Jerusalem, and do

not depart, nor preach the gospel, until you are clothed with the power from on high, which is the Paraclete, the Holy Ghost. And after ten days from his Ascension into Heaven," as he said, the Paraclete descended, on the day of Pentecost, which was the completion of fifty days after the Pasch. But according to thy words, the disciples are still awaiting thee at Jerusalem.'

There is much inferred in this story that isn't spelled out in words. The heretic Mani seemed to think that if he simply sat on the Throne of St Mark, it would prove that he was the awaited comforter. He wanted to make pronouncements and to bring new teachings to the Copts but the bishop of the Markan faith denied him this right.

Why was bishop Archelaus so sure that Mani was not the paraclete? The answer is quite obvious. The community in Osorhone was as certain as the Copts in Alexandria that the paraclete had already appeared. It was Marcus Agrippa, known to the Copts as St Mark. In Catholic tradition the paraclete was synonymous with the Holy Spirit, that appeared to the disciples during the Jewish celebration of Pentecost, fifty days after the crucifixion. The Copts believed, and still believe, that this event, described in the Acts of the Apostles, took place in St Mark's house in Jerusalem. It should by now be obvious that in reality it was little Marcus Agrippa who appeared to the disciples, 'dressed with the holy spirit' in order to show himself as the awaited Christ of the community.

That Christians go to their churches today to recognize Jesus as the Messiah is thanks to the perverted testimony of Church Fathers who had their own agenda, most likely with a burning political need to modify the developing religion. The creation of Christianity as we know it today is responsive to one specific individual – a man whose work I have examined closely throughout the pages of this book. It is quite clear to almost all scholars in this discipline that Roman Christianity is primarily the creation of Irenaeus of Lyons.

Irenaeus was deeply influential in terms of the surviving Christian tradition. His war against Mark and Mark's heretical followers was eventually joined by just about every other Church leader that followed him, and in almost every subsequent generation.

Irenaeus did most of his writing during the reign of Emperor Commodus, who sat upon the imperial throne between 180 and 192. Commodus was one of Rome's 'bad' emperors and, in his own way, he was clearly as mad as the Claudian emperors of Marcus Agrippa's time had been.

We cannot know the inner workings of Commodius' strange mind or why he may have preferred one form of Christianity to another, but it is clear that the beliefs of Irenaeus somehow better fitted the sensibilities of the Roman authorities than those surrounding a now long-dead Jewish king. For whatever reason, Irenaeus took it upon himself to restructure Christianity and to openly attack any believers who did not share his own peculiar home-grown dogmas. It is also entirely possible that Irenaeus' form of Christianity fitted better alongside other mystery religions, such as that of Mithras, which proliferated in the Roman Empire at the time.

As we have seen, amongst other things Irenaeus took it upon himself to replace the one original gospel of Christianity, that of St Mark, with four. There is no doubt that although the Gospel of St Mark is almost universally regarded by scholars as being the earliest canonical text, it is also recognized as being a battered and tattered version. To many, the narrative seems to have been completely gutted of its original content and scholars have often remarked about its patchwork appearance. Almost every scholar alive today acknowledges that the oldest texts of St Mark abruptly ended with Mary discovering the empty tomb. It is as if someone in the Catholic Church didn't want us to see what originally came next in the narrative.

Scholars also tell us that, very early in Catholic Christianity, someone tried to add a new ending to Mark. There is no actual proof of who may have been responsible, but it seems quite significant that Irenaeus cites the contents of this falsified ending as a way of disproving the original heresy associated with the Markan tradition.

Mary's discovery of the empty tomb was almost certainly followed in the original version of St Mark's Gospel by the acclamation of little Marcus Agrippa by the disciples. The heretic Mani, whom we met a moment ago, certainly thought so. Scholars have unearthed fragments of a gospel from Mani's time that indicate this to have been the case.

That is why Mani believed he had the right to occupy St Mark's Throne. He saw himself as representing Mark's 'second coming'.

Irenaeus took it upon himself to regularize a faith that was developing differently in different places but, in order to do so, he had to take the symbolism that was important to those he referred to as heretics and use it to his own ends. I think it is possible to prove that this also included the Throne of St Mark.

With a thorough examination of one particular section of his great work, *Refutation and Overthrow of Knowledge Falsely So-Called*, book three, chapter eleven, it is possible to show that he used his intimate knowledge of the beliefs and practices associated with the throne against the very community that held the relic in such reverence.

As far as Irenaeus himself is concerned, there is much we don't know. We cannot be certain whether or not he ever visited Alexandria, though he was certainly familiar with the Throne of St Mark, so it seems almost certain that he had either seen it or a very good copy at some time.

For the moment let us go back to the current situation with regard to the Gospel of Mark as it stands in the present Christian canon. Most commentators have pointed out that it ends rather suddenly, as if an original ending was deliberately cut off. At the same time Irenaeus can be associated with a late second century effort not only to establish four gospels but in particular to tack on a new ending to Mark. Irenaeus put forward an alternative ending for the gospel that concluded with Jesus being enthroned. He emphasizes that:

> Towards the conclusion of his Gospel, Mark says: 'So then, after the Lord Jesus had spoken to them, He was received up into heaven, and sitteth on the right hand of God' confirming what had been spoken by the prophet: 'The LORD said to my Lord, Sit thou on My right hand, until I make thy foes Thy footstool.' (Irenaeus AH 3:10:5)

What most Christians today don't understand is that nobody prior to Irenaeus ever saw or bore witness to this alternative ending. What seems to be happening here is that, as part of his onslaught against Markan Christianity, Irenaeus is insisting that heretics should give up their notion of some other Christ being enthroned at the end of the gospel.

They should accept, as he does, that the Messiah was Jesus. If the Gospel of St Mark, complete with Irenaeus' new ending, is accepted by the majority of Christians, the heretics can then be accused of spreading falsehoods!

Irenaeus was not a scholar in the strictest sense of the term. He was first and foremost a spokesman for a particular set of ideas he was trying to promote. He vehemently argued on behalf of his own understanding of what the new canon of the Catholic Church should look like. His influence cannot be doubted because, within only a few years, his innovations were being echoed in the writings of leading churchmen – even in Alexandria. But whether the Alexandrians really *believed* what he was saying is a different matter altogether.

But no matter how well Irenaeus might have got on with the Roman emperor of his period, and despite his great capacity for arguing that black was white, it would have been impossible for Irenaeus to coerce Christians all over the known world to accept something that he had apparently drawn from thin air. Even his concept of a fourfold gospel is actually based on *something*, and that something turns out to be the Throne of St Mark. In the end, and almost paradoxically, Irenaeus uses the throne's symbolism to support his claims of orthodoxy.

Almost immediately after his mention of the corrected Gospel of St Mark, with its strange and obviously artificial ending, Irenaeus sets out to prove the validity of the fourfold gospel with the statement:
Of course this comes at the end of a section in which Irenaeus had imposed an ending on the Gospel of Mark in which Jesus Christ is specifically referred to as being seated on a throne.

> It is not possible that the Gospels can be either more or fewer in number than they are … it is evident that [Jesus] the Logos, the Artificer of all, He that sitteth upon the cherubim and contains all things, He who was manifested to men, has given us the Gospel under four aspects, but bound together by one Spirit. As also David says, when entreating His manifestation, 'Thou that sittest between the cherubim, shine forth.' For the cherubim were four-faced, and their faces were images of the dispensation of the Son of God. (Ibid 3:11:8)

It is towards the Throne of St Mark that Irenaeus looks for his ultimate proof of the fourfold gospel, because he takes the four creatures (or seraphim) and makes each one of them into a gospel writer. Of course he doesn't specifically mention the throne and talks instead about the vision in the Book of Revelation, but nevertheless he gives his position away time and again. This is because he cannot help embellishing his description at every opportunity. By so doing he proves that he is aware of facts and descriptions that do not appear in any written context – either in the Book of Revelation or anywhere in the Old Testament.

Irenaeus also explains the creatures around the throne in terms of the Christ. He tells us:

> 'The first living creature was like a lion,' symbolizing His effectual working, His leadership, and royal power; the second was 'like a calf', signifying [His] sacrificial and sacerdotal order; but 'the third had, as it were, the face as of a man' – an evident description of His advent as a human being; 'the fourth was like a flying eagle', pointing out the gift of the Spirit hovering with His wings over the Church. (Ibid 3:11:8)

Eventually Irenaeus also connects the creatures to the familiar figures of the gospel writers Matthew, Mark, Luke and John. But Irenaeus has already demonstrated that his source, whoever wrote the Book of Revelations – must have seen the throne. Irenaeus' development of these themes appears to demonstrate that he too had seen the Throne of St Mark and that he adapted its symbolism to suit his new innovations.

A careful review of Irenaeus' statements about the relationship between the four living creatures and the gospel proves that he not only saw the Throne of St Mark first hand, but that he knew that the story we just deciphered follows from right to left along the surface of the throne (exactly as one would expect if the throne originated among Hebrews). It is important to note that Irenaeus emphasizes that there is a correct order to the living creatures. In his conception it is lion, calf, man and then eagle. Yet it is worth noting that he uses the term 'cherubim', which comes from Ezekiel, chapter 1, where the order is man, lion, ox and eagle.

The ultimate question now is what made the Book of Revelation and Irenaeus contradict scripture? After all, Irenaeus instructs us to go no further than what is literally laid down in the written word of the prophets. Clearly there was something tangible that compelled both him and the author of Revelations to deviate from the words of the Old Testament. The only possible explanation is that both Irenaeus and the writer of the Book of Revelation got their notion from the Throne of St Mark. If we start from the back of the throne and then move counter-clockwise you would get lion, calf, man and then the eagle, which is, as it were, on the second level.

Irenaeus links the rightful existence of four gospels to the four creatures and there can be no doubt that the creatures around the Throne of God already had a central place in Christianity. Irenaeus tries to convince his readers that the correct number of gospels is four because Christianity already venerates the cherubim. But why should the number of gospels have anything at all to do with the Throne of God or the number of creatures surrounding it? There is no tradition whatsoever for this departure, which is clearly a figment of Irenaeus' imagination.

What was so right about the number four? Surely Irenaeus could have argued for the holiness of the number three, because of the Father, Son and Holy Spirit, or the three angels, who visited Abraham? In other words, there had to have been some pre-existent understanding in Christianity that helped guide him to the rightness of the fourfold canon. The most likely explanation is that Irenaeus was reshaping an existing secret tradition associated with the Throne of St Mark and its esoteric interpretation of the four cherubim.

Irenaeus' point of view is identical with the author of the Book of Revelation: the throne should be taken as the rightful seat of Jesus rather than of Mark. To Irenaeus, Jesus is the Creator who sits surrounded by the images of the four creatures, which are also representative of the four Evangelists. Irenaeus emphasizes the point by suggesting: 'Therefore the Gospels are in accord with these things [the living creatures], among which Christ Jesus is seated.'

However, what follows proves beyond a shadow of a doubt that Irenaeus had indeed seen the Throne of St Mark. This is because he goes on to interpret each creature around the Throne of God as if the very pictures we see carved into the throne were right in front of him as he penned the words.

He begins by saying that the lion symbolized Jesus' 'royal power', the calf is connected with sacrifice (where somebody or something dies and goes to the underworld), the man signifies the advent of Christ as a human being, and the eagle hovers 'with His wings over the Church'.

Everything that is said here matches perfectly with the basic outline I developed for the Alexandrian mystery religion in the last chapter. There I suggested that the bull was connected with Mark in the underworld, the man represented Mark's messianic enthronement, the lion represented his royal authority and the eagle was a symbol of protection. However, Irenaeus actually goes one step further and proceeds to develop these four characteristics into four separate evangelists.

Irenaeus goes on to explain to his readership that the characteristics of the lion, the calf, the human and the eagle are descriptive of his fictitious gospel writers:

> That [Gospel] According to John … is that gospel full of all confidence [like a lion], for such is His person. But that [Gospel] According to Luke, taking up [His] priestly character, commenced with Zechariah the priest offering sacrifice to God. For now was made ready the fatted calf, about to be immolated for the finding again of the younger son. Matthew, again … is the gospel of His humanity; for which reason it is, too, that [the character of] a humble and meek man is kept up through the whole gospel. Mark, on the other hand, commences with [a reference to] the prophetical spirit coming down from on high to men … pointing to the winged aspect of the gospel; and on this account he made a compendious and cursory narrative, for such is the prophetical character. (Ibid)

In this description Irenaeus has gone beyond anything that appears in the Book of Revelation, Ezekiel or even Isaiah. However, we can say with certainty that Irenaeus did not simply draw his information from thin air. He is referring specifically to the carvings on the Throne of St Mark.

Let us start with the Lion.

This is surely a 'confident' lion as Irenaeus describes. In fact its pose captures the description perfectly. The lion stands on its hind legs in an attitude that would eventually become known as a 'lion rampant'. In heraldry the lion is seen as being brave, royal and strong, attributes that are emphasized all the more when it stands on its hind legs or 'rampant'. As such anyone would see the animal as being 'confident'.

Now for the animal that Irenaeus describes as a calf, though it is more likely to represent a bull.

According to my interpretation the bull comes first after the central theme of the ram and bush on the backrest of the throne. Irenaeus connects this animal to the Book of Zechariah in which a calf is sacrificed or 'immolated for the finding again of the younger son'. Again there is a connection with the sacrificial nature of the bull's residence in the underworld.

Next comes the human creature.

In this instance there can surely be no doubt whatsoever that Irenaeus got his idea from the throne. We hear him speak of 'a humble and meek man'. The question that scholars might rightfully have asked a long time ago is, where did Irenaeus get this idea? True, we are familiar these days with 'gentle Jesus meek and mild', but such a reference, or even an inference, is completely absent in the prophetic writings. The Book of Revelations speaks instead of a 'beast that has a face of a man'. We surely wouldn't normally expect a beast either to be meek or mild. So where is Irenaeus getting his information? It isn't from the Old Testament, neither from the Book of Revelation. Arguably, it could only have come from one place – the Throne of St Mark.

Irenaeus wasn't simply quoting scripture as he described any of the creatures. In the case of the eagle we see even clearer evidence that Irenaeus' source material must have been the Throne of St Mark. In each of the four references Irenaeus makes to the eagle, which he associates with St Mark, he waxes lyrical about its form. He tells us:

- 'The fourth was like a flying eagle,' pointing out the gift of the Spirit hovering with His wings over the Church;

- Mark, on the other hand, commences with the prophetical Spirit coming down from on high to men ... pointing to the winged aspect of the gospel;

- he sent the gift of the celestial Spirit over all the Earth, protecting us with His wings;

- the fourth, that which renews man and sums up all things in itself by means of the gospel, raising and bearing men upon its wings into the heavenly kingdom.

Notice the continual mention of 'hovering', 'spread out wings' and 'height', all of which would make no sense at all from anything written in Ezekiel, Isaiah or the Book of Revelations. Irenaeus not only saw the throne, but he must have been at least partly familiar with the secret narrative associated with the pictures.

In the first reference, the eagle is 'hovering over' something – this is definitely not present in Revelations. In the second the eagle is seen 'coming down from on high', which is once again something outside of that text. In the third reference the eagle's wings are 'spread out' in order to 'protect us', exactly like the eagle on the throne, which has an attitude borrowed from the Egyptian hawk Horus. Finally, in the last reference, the eagle is directly connected to the gospel, something implicit in the other references, but unmistakably drawn from the Alexandrian image. Notice also that it is now specifically conceived as flying upwards toward the heavenly kingdom of light. This is the grand finale of the throne's secret message.

When taken entirely from scripture, there was no reason for Irenaeus to emphasize the eagle to such a degree – unless of course he had already seen the Throne of St Mark, on which the eagle is placed above all the other creatures. Why should Irenaeus assume that the eagle could fly better than the other creatures – given the fact that the scriptural references identify all the creatures as being 'winged'? One would assume that all of these supernatural creatures could fly as well as each other. The only reason that the author of the Book of Revelations and Irenaeus think otherwise is because of the carvings on the throne.

Nevertheless I am certain that there will be some readers who ask whether or not the throne was manufactured *after* Irenaeus' description and whether, as a result, the similarities are actually the other way around. In other words, there might be a suggestion that those creating the throne were copying from Irenaeus. This notion holds no water, not least because the throne is remembered as the Throne of St Mark.

The bottom line is that Irenaeus could have described the creatures surrounding the throne in any way he wished. But in the midst of a fractured Church where heresies and alternatives were everywhere, Irenaeus wished his descriptions and explanations to be accepted without question. For this to be the case, he had to tie his descriptions and explanations to imagery that was already known and accepted. But as an example, we might ask why Irenaeus had to describe the eagle as taking its gospel up to heaven? Why would there be any need to do this if the eagle is one of the evangelists? In fact, when looked at closely, this statement makes no sense whatsoever.

The only plausible explanation is that Irenaeus knew that the eagle on the throne was indeed carrying a book in its bill and, as a result, he was obliged to invent an explanation that sounded vaguely pious – in the sure knowledge that the piously vague would accept it. The same is broadly true regarding all his other associations between the various seraphim and the evangelists. The images had to come first and Irenaeus' explanation later. Since the images he describes don't appear in scripture, it stands to reason that he must have seen this throne, or maybe a faithful copy.

Irenaeus found himself living, as the Chinese would have it, 'in interesting times'. Nothing was certain. Even life and liberty depended on the caprices of mad emperors and their sycophantic followers. We have to maintain at least a little sympathy for him and his contemporaries. True, they were attempting to forge a new religion, but they were also trying to stay alive. The Church Fathers in and around Rome had to come up with something that suited the times in which they were living and Christianity was open to competition from numerous other religious options. Its only chance of survival lay in everyone singing the same song, and that is what Irenaeus wanted. But there is another factor involved that cannot be ignored.

By the time of Irenaeus, Marcus Agrippa had been dead for some time. His land was in ruins and his people, the Jews, were dispersed all over the known world. Even as Irenaeus wrote his words, Judea continued to be in a state of turmoil and remained a continual thorn in the side of the Roman empire. The only way forward for Christianity under such circumstances was for it to adapt to suit the needs of the time. There was no room for rebels; conformity was king, as far as successive emperors were concerned.

Marcus Agrippa had been a loyal friend to Rome, or at least that is how it had seemed to successive emperors, but was this really the case? Was it not more the case that Marcus Agrippa had *used* circumstances and rulers to achieve his own objectives? And, in any case, from the perspective of those ruling the empire, Marcus Agrippa seemed to have achieved very little. It is freely admitted by historical experts that, with the rule of Emperor Commodius, the gradual disintegration of the Roman Empire began. What was needed in all parts of the ailing empire was cement – not hammers.

Jesus may have been a Jew like Marcus Agrippa, but his biography was vague. In many respects he could be made to look like Mithras, Dionysus, Horus or any one of a dozen or more similar religious figures that proliferated across the empire. Probably most important of all was the realization that Marcus Agrippa had meant his new world to be in the 'here and now'. The New Jerusalem he had in mind was for the temporal world, and it was intended to be bigger and better than anything that had gone before – including the Roman Empire.

This idea simply could not be countenanced in Rome itself, and if the Christians there wished to survive they had to think up something quite different. Nobody wants to get off the gravy train at the next station, let alone end up being crucified on the Appian Way. So, all things considered, Jesus was a better option than Marcus Agrippa. He was meek and mild, easy to manipulate and, most important of all, it could be made to appear that he had always intended his Kingdom not to be of this world but of another.

It was a case of 'liberation suspended' and it worked excellently across almost 2,000 years, in terms of keeping people in their place. Christianity became a *tool*, often a tool of oppression and always one of manipulation. That was a state of affairs that admirably suited the ailing Roman Empire – so much so that a couple of centuries after Irenaeus, Christianity, by this time totally sanitized and systemized, became the official religion of the empire.

Irenaeus was not the only man to make this possible, but he was quite likely the first. He was the slick car salesman of his time and he knew how to twist anything to suit his ends. Anyone who held to old beliefs immediately became a heretic – a word that would strike fear into humanity for centuries to come. Irenaeus made his position clear, especially with regard to the abandonment of the one true original gospel and the acceptance of the new fourfold gospel of his own manufacture. He wrote:

> These things being so, all who destroy the form of the Gospel are vain, unlearned and also audacious – those who represent the aspects of the Gospel as being either more in number than as aforesaid or, on the other hand, fewer. The former class [do so], that they may seem to have discovered more than is of the truth; the latter, that they may set the dispensations of God aside. For [those of] 'little Mark', rejecting the entire [fourfold] Gospel, yea rather, cutting [themselves] off from the [fourfold] Gospel, boast that he has a part in the Gospel. (Ibid 3:11:9)

Now, in a new age of enlightenment, when men and women will not be burned or strung up for examining even the most revered conventions in the light of reason, it is possible to look again at what people such as Irenaeus were really all about. For some he stands as the voice of reason, so close to the start of Christianity that he seems to be looking directly at the events he describes.

But we must never forget that Irenaeus was a propagandist and not a historian. When we see how he took the images from a throne that was already deeply sacred before he was born, twisting them into something that was so much at odds with the mixture of religion and philosophy that had started the adventure, there is only one question worth asking: would you buy a second-hand car from this man?

CONCLUDING THOUGHTS

Every day tourists from all over the world avail themselves of the pleasures and delights of the city of Venice. A fair proportion of these find their way into the treasury of the Basilica of St Mark and many find themselves confronted by the strange little alabaster throne. Until now none of them, not even the experts, had any real idea of how old the throne actually was, or of the numerous messages it imparts. For my part it has afforded me the necessary information to set the seal on discoveries that have filled my life for the last two decades.

Some of the most recognized experts in historical Bible studies, ancient Judaism and Samaritanism have joined me on my quest across the years and it has been possible to obtain their opinions regarding the throne of St Mark. There can be no doubt that the patterns, codes and ciphers contained within its carvings were intentionally placed there to serve as a 'language to the initiated'. They once formed part of the new mystery religion that had been founded in Alexandria and in Judea by Marcus Julius Agrippa, the last King of the Jews. Doubtless would-be aspirants were gradually instructed as to the meaning of the throne's carvings and learned, probably across many years, what has now, at last, revealed itself to an unsuspecting world.

It is especially odd that these findings should become known at this particular point in time. The world has recently been captivated by another series of codes, this one cobbled together by a writer of fiction in order to provide an exciting adventure that has spawned a number of imitators. *The Da Vinci Code* has sold millions of copies worldwide and eventually became a blockbuster movie that has captivated tens of millions more. How strange then that the Throne of St Mark should reveal its secrets at this specific time, because the result has all the excitement of Dan Brown's novel. Though, as the saying goes, 'truth is stranger than fiction'.

My previous research had shown that the origins of Christianity were far more surprising than most people have previously suspected. They demonstrate that, almost at the start of this adventure in Christian belief, the original story was changed to suit the times and political circumstances. There is nothing so odd about this. If we were to delve into the recesses of all world beliefs we would almost certainly discover that the kernel of truth at their heart was very different from the fruit that is apparent today. But in the case of Christianity, these revelations will be particularly difficult to digest for diehard believers.

I make no apology for throwing a number of preconceptions into a state of potential turmoil. Truth takes us where it will and, as historians, it is our duty to follow the evidence and reach the inevitable conclusions that might lead from it. The truth is that one very inspirational king, fabulously wealthy and with endless time on his hands, decided that the time was right to end the fractured nature of belief. It was his clear intention to create a faith that could be open to anyone. Doubtless he hoped that his new departure would weld communities together, and his attempt was a forerunner of what the Roman Empire tried again to do some three centuries or more after his birth. The result of the efforts of Emperor Constantine is the massive edifice of Christianity as we see it today across the world, but it is a religion that is quite different in many ways from the conception of Marcus Agrippa.

Marcus was looking for something that would change the world in the 'here and now', and this may ultimately be the reason why it did not perpetuate. In all strata of society there have always been and always will be those who consider themselves born to rule, and history shows that such people will use any means at their disposal to rise to the top of the pyramid. Meanwhile, the vast majority of people have been content to follow in the wake of these movers and shakers. The rule of a king or even a dynasty is restricted, but that of a religion can last for millennia.

So it was that, generation by generation, slowly but surely, Christianity gradually modified itself in order to keep a few people firmly in charge of millions. True, it promised everlasting life to its followers and there are still very many people in the world who firmly believe the promises handed down by the Church hierarchy. Some will doubtless remain convinced that Christianity has been a force for good, but many others who look back across the indoctrination, torture, murder and wars engendered by religions of any sort will have their doubts.

I hope I have explained satisfactorily why the efforts of Marcus Agrippa ultimately failed, but doubtless readers will form their own conclusions. What matters is that we now have a clearer window onto the ancient past. What is truly remarkable is that, against all odds, one specific piece of evidence has survived the ravages of time in order to stand as a witness for something quite remarkable. It appears that Marcus Agrippa was quite willing to countenance the death of many thousands of people in order to change the world, but of course he lived in a very different age and, in any case, like many who have come and gone since, he most certainly believed he was doing 'God's work'.

In his own conception, bolstered by a series of phenomenal coincidences, Marcus Agrippa almost certainly thought he was the Promised Messiah, not just of the Jews but of all humanity. His efforts have been obscured and even deliberately buried by successive generations, but it has never occurred to anyone since then to destroy the most vital piece of evidence – the Throne of St Mark. Why should they have done so? Either they did not understand the various messages the throne had been created to impart, or else they perverted the symbolism in order to make the Throne of St Mark tell a story its creators had never intended.

Someone had doubts, because the very top of the throne was significantly altered. It now shows the four evangelists, the gospel writers Matthew, Mark, Luke and John, but the evidence supplied by experts demonstrates that this was not how it once looked. What once stood atop the throne, if anything at all, we will never know but, whatever it was, it clearly wasn't 'Christian' enough to survive.

For those who want to go into this story further, and for whom the evidence contained in this book is not enough, I have created a website that sets everything out in a much more detailed way: www.therealmessiahbook.com and www.therealmessiahbook.blogspot.com There scholars, or simply interested laypeople, can find the notes from twenty painstaking years of research which, when taken in total, will I hope make my case even more certain.

Just when it seemed my work was over for the moment, I realized that every Scorpion has a last and sometimes very potent sting in its tail. I was left with one final puzzle – a question I just could not answer. It wasn't anything too important, apparently, but it was a broken sentence, a loose twig on the bush of life that somewhat spoiled the geometry of the whole. Even allowing for the fact that journeys took time to arrange and complete in this remote period it was difficult to work out why a full year had elapsed between Marcus' raising by the Emperor Caligula until the time he went to Alexandria to be enthroned as the Messiah. Had Caligula sent him there at that time? There wasn't any evidence to suggest this was the case. Though many historians have since suggested that part of the reason Marcus went to Alexandria was to try and quell the pogrom taking place in the city, it now seems that this is actually the opposite of what happened.

We have seen that Philo's protestations regarding the uprising tend to suggest that the trouble came from nowhere. He seems to assert that the Greeks attacked their Jewish neighbours for no tangible reason and that the Roman governor, Flaccus, had either ignored what was going on, or had actually added fuel to the flames. If this was the case, it was entirely out of character for a man who had always previously managed to keep the lid tightly on the powder keg.

As I have suggested, it seems much more likely that the Greek citizens of Alexandria were spurred into attacking the Jews for some tangible reason which, it seems, could only have been Marcus' presence in their midst and his enthronement there. They accused Marcus and his followers of wanting to take over the world and, in a sense, they were correct.

But there was one last piece of evidence from the throne that explained this final puzzle – or rather two pieces of evidence that fitted together like a hand in a glove.

Firstly, there were the dimensions of the throne. The Italian art expert Wladimiro Dorigo had measured the throne very carefully. As I pointed out in Chapter 19, he came to the conclusion, though he did not attempt to prove it, that there was something very special and almost certainly deliberately informative about the throne's dimensions, particularly when measured in the ancient inch and foot he considered to have been used in its creation. At the time I discovered Dorigo's work, whatever message the measurements of the throne might impart were not immediately apparent, but in another of those flashes of inspiration that often occur when one least expects them, something interesting did come into my mind.

Dorigo suggested that in a series of measurements the ancient inch, known to have been used extensively in the region, occurred in whole numbers, all of which were divisible by 2. He quotes the list as being 12, 52, 40, 12, 20, 18, 20 and 18. Two of these numbers, the width and the depth of the throne, represent 18 inches and 20 inches. When multiplied together, the result is 360, a nice round number it's true, but probably just a coincidence. However, it was worth a second look because it is known that, to the Egyptian culture (and of course the throne was made in Egypt), 360 was the number of days in a year.

Of course we all know, just as the Egyptians knew, that there are actually 365.25 days in a year. Unfortunately 365 is a particularly difficult number to split into months with an even number of days. So the Egyptians, like many other cultures, celebrated 12 months of 30 days, equalling 360 days. The odd five days were kept out of the calendar. Some cultures simply added them onto the end of the year as 'extra days', or waited until they accumulated to 30 days, when an extra month was added to the year.

The Egyptians did the former and added five days (the *epagomenes*) onto the end of the year. Many cultures started their calendar in a seasonal way by, for example, making the first day of the year conform to the time of the spring equinox, around 21st March. This is understandable to cultures whose farming relied on the seasonal changes of the year but, to the Egyptians, the situation was quite different. It rarely rains in Egypt and the culture was entirely reliant on the River Nile, which passes through the whole length of Egypt. However, it does rain heavily in the mountainous regions southward (in today's Sudan and Uganda) where the Nile rises at a particular time of year. This leads to the flooding of the Nile on a yearly basis, which ultimately allowed the ancient Egyptian farmers to harvest the water their crops needed and thus make the desert bloom.

The flooding or inundation of the Nile was of critical importance and, without it, the whole civilization would have starved. It was crucial from the very earliest times of farming in the area to know when the inundation would take place and the Egyptians invented a neat, foolproof little trick. The most important star to the Egyptians was Sirius, which can be seen in the northern hemisphere throughout the winter months and into the spring, but which is much more prominent at the latitude of Egypt. In Egypt there are only seventy days each year when Sirius cannot be seen. Being the brightest star in our night skies, to the Egyptians it was deeply sacred. It represented Isis, the goddess about whom I have spoken extensively in this book.

The Egyptians realized very early in their history that, after Sirius had disappeared from visibility (blocked out by the brightness of the Sun), it would not appear again for over two months. When it did first appear just before dawn and ahead of the Sun (known as the *heliacal* rising), the flooding of the Nile would follow in only a few days. The heliacal rising of Sirius was therefore of the most critical importance. This may explain why the star became so absolutely important to the Egyptians in a religious as well as a practical way. The seventy days on which Sirius was invisible in Egypt was considered to be the period during which Isis, together with her husband Osiris, travelled through the 'Duat', the Egyptian underworld. On the day Sirius reappeared there was great rejoicing because it meant the royal pair had returned and could be crowned again as the most important of the Egyptian deities.

Sirius was associated with Isis under one of her alternative names, this one being *Sopdet*. The festival held when Sopdet appeared marked the start of the new year, attended with great reverence and also merrymaking. Sopdet was also associated with protecting pharaohs after they had died, and the period it took to prepare a royal mummy was seventy days, the same as the period during which Sirius was invisible in the night sky of Egypt.

Little Marcus Agrippa had gone to Alexandria in July or August of the year 38 and there, doubtless with great ceremony, he had been enthroned as the Messiah. What I did not know was whether there was a direct connection between his enthronement, the ritual 360-day year, and Sirius and its heliacal rising. So I once again got in touch with Alan Butler, who checked his historical astronomical computer programmes for the year in question. He soon got back to me and confirmed that, in 38, the heliacal rising of Sirius took place around July 15th, which was precisely the period I knew Marcus Agrippa travelled to Alexandria.

This could easily be the explanation I had been looking for, as to why Marcus Agrippa's family waited well over a year after his elevation by Caligula before taking him to Alexandria. In the previous year, 37, Marcus did not receive his good news from Caligula until sometime early in April. That left only four months or so before the heliacal rising of Sirius, which would not have been sufficient time either to plan the journey or for preparations to be made in Alexandria. It was therefore natural to leave the ceremony until the following year, by which time the throne could be made and all necessary arrangements sorted out.

What other messages do the measurements of the Throne of St Mark carry? No doubt I and other interested parties will sift through them in order to understand what else they might be trying to tell us, but there is now absolutely no doubt that the little alabaster throne was extremely carefully planned and created. The throne is a veritable treasure house of codes and, although I have tried extremely hard to understand them all, I don't doubt that there are other messages here for anyone clever and knowledgeable enough to tease them out.

All of this taken together gives us the best glimpse imaginable into the minds of people who lived 2,000 years ago. It shows us that the religion they had planned had much in common with Judaism but that it was also closely allied to pagan religions and of course to cosmology. It is quite likely that only those elected to be Marcus Agrippa's direct followers as the head of his new religion would have possessed *all* the information the throne could impart. Over a period of time Christianity changed its appearance to such an extent that in probably only a couple of centuries the true symbolism encapsulated into the throne was lost – until now.

The alabaster throne, the name of which can now be rightfully altered from the Throne of St Mark to the Throne of Marcus Agrippa, is undoubtedly of the greatest importance. It is a rare survivor and it literally speaks to us of the origins of a religion many of us have known and followed since childhood. We may be shocked by what it has to tell us, and it might even destroy the very principles many of us have held to for most of our lives.

The problem for the Church is now going to be what henceforth it does with the throne. Of course the established Church will simply shrug its shoulders and shout 'foul', as it has always done to those it calls heretics. It will say that Christianity has a proven track record and that true believers will not be diverted from the path of their faith. Fortunately we live in a very different world these days. The majority of people are more likely to accept evidence rather than blind faith. If my findings serve to swell the ranks of those who visit Venice to see the throne for themselves, the Church will even gain in terms of the revenue it accrues.

Questions that now deserve to be asked include the following. For how long after the time of Marcus Agrippa did people continue to know the truth about his existence and his role as the Messiah? Is it possible that some heresies, even in the Middle Ages, were founded by Markan doctrines? How hard has the Church struggled to keep quiet what it knew of the true origins of Christianity for all the intervening centuries?

These are queries for another day. But the answers, when we do discover them, are likely to be as intriguing as the throne itself, perhaps one of the most important historical artefacts in the world today. If we still can't bear to rename it the Throne of Marcus Agrippa, maybe we can tolerate its ultimate title: the Throne of the Messiah.

APPENDIX A

THE RESURRECTION OCCURRED
ON MARCH 25TH

At its most basic, the gospel makes clear two basic facts – the mention of a Wednesday Passover when Jesus and the disciples ate the 'Last Supper' and his resurrection on the subsequent Sunday. Notice that it is said here that Wednesday and not Thursday is the proper date of the meal. The list of events in the narrative demands a starting point on Wednesday night. As Epiphanius (367–403 CE), the bishop at Salamis, wrote, 'Wednesday and Friday are days of fasting up to the ninth hour because, *as Wednesday began* the Lord was arrested and on Friday he was crucified.'

The list of dates for the sunset starting on the 15th of the first month of Nisan, from Jack Finegan's *Handbook of Biblical Chronology*, reveal that only two dates from the period support this Wednesday date for the Passover and a corresponding Easter Sunday:

30 CE **Wednesday April 5th (Easter Sunday April 9th)**

31 CE Monday March 26th

32 CE Monday April 15th

33 CE Friday April 3rd

34 CE Monday March 23rd

35 CE Monday April 11th

36 CE Friday March 30th

37 CE **Wednesday March 21st (Easter Sunday March 25th)**

38 CE Monday April 7th

39 CE Friday March 28th

40 CE Friday April 16th

Jewish days begin at sunset and continue through to the next sunset. A day that begins at sunset on Wednesday carries through to Thursday in a Roman calendar. So it is that the gospel narrative really began on Wednesday. Thus we are left with only two real possibilities to choose between for the correct dating of the Passion. It is either Wednesday April 6th, 30 CE, or Wednesday March 22nd, 37 CE.

As we said earlier, only one minor sect in second-century Christianity picks the former date, 30. Irenaeus' gospels can be used only to superficially confirm this date as the beginning of Jesus' ministry. Nevertheless Irenaeus goes out of his way to emphasize many years of preaching for Jesus. In later times a two or three year ministry is developed, but Irenaeus emphasizes one which lasted 19 years. Why 19? It should be obvious: by then the same cycle of days from year 30 repeat themselves in year 49. The whole idea is undoubtedly rooted in a tradition that Jesus was also crucified in a 49th year. We will develop this further in the next section.

While all modern scholars and ancient Church Fathers naively use Irenaeus' texts to arrive at a date *around* 30–31, 32 or 33, most typically, all these efforts prove ultimately misguided. None of these dates allow for a Wednesday start to Passover. None of these dates allow for an Easter Sunday Resurrection. Indeed, not a single ancient Church tradition argues for a 30 date.

So we have to abandon 30 and look again at the Alexandrian tradition's choice of 37. We have to begin with the clear understanding that the earliest Alexandrian witnesses, based on their preference for the Gospel of Mark, emphasize only a one year ministry for Jesus. We have already seen that one of its most famous representatives from the fifth century emphasizes Sunday March 25th. It all comes together when we realize that the Passover in 37 begins on Wednesday March 21st. Easter Sunday would correspond to March 25th in that same year.

The point now becomes clear that, when we look at all the surviving reports from the Church Fathers, the traditional Alexandrian emphasis on the dating of the Passion in 37 was widely influential. Even if most of these authorities got the year wrong, or the specific identification of March 25th as the date of the Resurrection, something of the original Alexandrian understanding has made its way past Irenaeus' deliberately falsified gospels, often in an admittedly garbled form.

It is absolutely significant that almost every single surviving remembrance of the month and day of the Passion never goes any later than March 25th. This will finally help solidify our 37 dating in the Alexandrian tradition. The one tradition which dissents – that associated with a late-second-century prophetic Church from the province of Phrygia in Asia Minor – is intimately connected with the tradition behind Irenaeus. It attempts to argue for that earlier date in 30. This tradition is wholly unreliable and has at its core a belief in the new truths coming from 'new spiritual revelations', which accounts for its going against the grain of virtually every other ancient witness out there.

On the website connected with this book www.therealmessiahbook. com, we shall examine why it is that at least a handful of Christians got confused about the dating of Easter, by systematically categorizing all references to the dating of the month and date of the Passion.

The Conclusion

There is a unanimous tradition that the Passover in question fell on the earliest date possible, just after the equinox. This makes it all the more remarkable that the tradition concerning the year has almost been lost. With the partial exception of Lactantius, the sources have a year that could be guessed at, either 32 or 33. But the very fact that both 32 and 33 are put forward shows that there is no tradition, and that both years are academic reconstructions. They are not very good even as reconstructions, since the Passover in both years was nowhere near these dates. There was an appropriate correspondence of dates in 34, but the day of the week does not fit. We shall therefore dismiss the years 32 and

33 as superficially plausible, but actually impossible new guesses predicated on the assumption of a birthdate for Jesus at the end of 1 BCE and a ministry of three years. We treat the date given in the Acts of Pilate as a fusion of March 24th and 25th, both only reconstructions and neither falling on a Friday near the Passover.

Suppose we accept Lactantius' date of March 23rd. Although he does not specify the year, he does say it is towards the end of the reign of Tiberius, so he is definitely not thinking of 32 or 33. In the text of Malalas the context shows the date of 3rd Nisan to be a mistake for 13th. Jesus' appearance before Caiaphas is then on Wednesday night, 13th Nisan, the fifth day of the week. Both agree with the canonical John in not making the Last Supper a Passover. Of the two, only Malalas gives a year, 32, but this can be disregarded as his own reconstruction, since March 23rd that year was not near the Passover. The absence of a year in one source, and the wrong correspondence in the other, indicate the omission or deletion of a year thought impossible because too late. Malalas certainly, and probably Lactantius, would have known that the only year when the afternoon of 14th Nisan fell on Friday March 23rd was 37.

The date of Friday March 23rd in Malalas and Lactantius is the correct date by the Roman calendar, and these two are definitely the only bearers of a tradition of the date. However, they are both mistaken in saying the date was 14th Nisan. It was 16th Nisan. They have unthinkingly taken over the dating in John, and their evidence can be discounted in respect of the Jewish date. The only way their evidence can be accepted is if their tradition correctly says it really *was* 14th Nisan or Sunday March 25th, 37. Given the widespread echoes of this date of March 25th as a seminal date in the Passion narrative (and no reference to anything related to early dates in April) the year of 37 has to be considered to be the correct one.

APPENDIX B

ALEXANDRIAN CHRISTIANITY AND THE PASSION OF 37 CE

There is now no doubt that Sunday, March 25th, was remembered as the date for the Resurrection. Alexandria was the ultimate epicentre of that tradition. One would think that this date alone should convince the world that the accompanying year was 37 CE; this is after all the only year in which a Sunday, March 25th could have been the date of the Resurrection. Nevertheless, as is well known, science alone doesn't convince Christian religious minds and 37 was a problem for the Church. Indeed, the Catholic New Testament canon was deliberately established to obscure the true date of the Passion.

It is not without purpose that Irenaeus puts forward the seemingly laughable claim that Jesus was in his 49th year when crucified. This is a deliberate obscuring of the original understanding that the Passion occurred 'in a 49th year' – the year before a Jubilee. If we look carefully, the 49th year plays a central role in Alexandrian reflection on the dating of the death of Jesus. Yet in order to get there we have to pay careful attention to Irenaeus' disinformation campaign against the tradition.

In a famous section from his *Against Heresies*, he accuses the heretics of falsely putting forward that Jesus preached only for one year. The Gospel of John he introduces proves that Jesus was 'almost 50'. We can be sure that Jesus' 49th year was a deliberate spin on the Alexandrian community's insistence that Jesus was crucified in a 49th year. For if we look closely, Irenaeus attacks their Markan tradition on the Jubilee in the same breath as he invents a 49-year-old Jesus.

The heretical belief that Jesus only took part in the 49th year while the Jubilee was reserved for 'Christ' seemed to Irenaeus to subordinate the man from Nazareth. As a result, the Roman Church Father went out of his way to re-engineer the gospel. Not only do we see the whole concept of 49th years and Jubilees wiped clean from the Catholic tradition, so too is a one-year ministry of Jesus (through the development of the Gospel of John).

Of course, once Irenaeus started fiddling around with gospel dates, it is not at all surprising that the subsequent Catholic tradition loses touch with the actual year of Jesus' ministry. The problem of course becomes quite simple: you can't have a Resurrection on Sunday, March 25th in any year around the time of Jesus' 30th birthday except 37. Nevertheless the gospels now speak of a beginning of Jesus' ministry around 30. So none of the dates usually bandied about to explain when the Passion of Christ occurred make any sense, and most scholars avoid the whole science of lunar months, instead giving any number of years which can't possibly work.

Indeed most academics typically dismiss the year 37 as a potential candidate because, they say, the Jewish historian Josephus 'makes it clear' that Pilate had already been dismissed from his post in 36. Yet these readings of Josephus are utterly superficial. Daniel Schwartz, the author of the only other book ever published on the subject of Agrippa, agrees with us here. He emphatically argues that a careful reading of Josephus makes clear that in fact Pilate was sent back to Rome to answer for his mistreatment of Samaritan messianists in 37. Any other reading is simply ridiculous.

Once we acknowledge that Pilate was procurator of Judea right up until the Samaritan Passover of 37, and relieved of his post by Vitellius while the eight-day Jewish festival was still going on, we can now examine the hitherto unexplored question as to whether the Passion might have occurred in that same year. Immediately an intriguing possibility suddenly becomes manifest: could Pilate's brutal assault against the Samaritan messianic gathering, which Josephus tells us occurred in that same year, have been one and the same with the gospel narrative's description of the arrest of Jesus? At least one ancient Samaritan Christian seems to think so.

Some ancient Christian traditions believed that it was his mistreatment of Christ and the disciples which led to Pilate's recall to Rome. Texts like the Acts of Pilate come from a tradition which connects the events described in Josephus with the Passion. We can only imagine what was in the original text or what was claimed to be Pilate's original explanation of his actions, which the anti-Christian emperor Maximin used to disprove the gospels.

All of these points will likely never be settled to anyone's satisfaction, yet they necessarily lead us back to the year 37 as the only possible date available for the Passion. Of course, that it has never even been considered by theologians is not as problematic as it seems at first. For them the world doesn't have to make sense. Indeed the more it seems to contradict logic, science and reason, the happier they inevitably are.

Placing Christ's resurrection in 37 would only serve to prove the greatness of their God. This, given the fact that an immediate recall of Pilate would only have proven to contemporaries that God indeed did punish those who harmed his beloved Christ. Having the wicked emperor Tiberius also meet his end in the lead-up to this event didn't hurt either.

So what did Irenaeus have against 37? The question could easily be turned around and posed in a different way: why did the Alexandrians continue to venerate the date? The answer in either case is that it is clearly the year that Marcus Agrippa claimed to be resurrected in Jerusalem.

The underlying knowledge shared by both Irenaeus and his enemies in Alexandria was the same. This is why the information is now only preserved in a fragmentary form, scattered around the pages of the Church Fathers. Sunday + March 25th + 49th year + 37 CE = 'another Christ' + coronated + Jubilee + Alexandria = Marcus Agrippa. It really is that simple.

The final proof for this assertion is to be found preserved in the writings of an eighth-century Byzantine scholar named George Syncellus, who thankfully preserved the writings of two ancient Alexandrian monks. Many scholars who have heard a little about the text will likely shake their heads about now. 'George Syncellus' Chronology doesn't put Jesus' crucifixion in 37 CE!' they will say. 'In fact it is strangely placed in 42, the second year of the Emperor Claudius.'

All of this may be true, but as we remove the various layers of this text we will be able to see what has happened. Nevertheless, let us ask, even with all of this incorrect information coming from Alexandria, when does this same ancient Church understand that its St Mark first appeared in the city? The current pope makes clear in his *Evangelist Mark* (p42) that, while '… It is difficult to determine the exact dates for the journeys of the apostles [they are] usually calculated in relation to [other] events, and the time of the arrival of St Mark was no exception … St Mark came to Alexandria in 43 CE.' In other words, as silly as it might seem to have Jesus' crucifixion end up being in 42, it is uncanny the way the follow-up appearance of Mark nevertheless immediately comes right after it.

So how did the official tradition get the dates so wrong? Let us go back to the beginning again. As Adler notes, 'Since Clement, Christian chronographers in Alexandria had experimented with [dating the Crucifixion from] the era from Creation.' Yet over 200 years lay between Annanius of Alexandria, George Syncellus' main source for his 42 CE, and Clement. In that time the Catholic innovations of Irenaeus had forced changes in the outer appearance of Alexandrian orthodoxy.

Nowhere is this clearer than in Clement's repeated insistence that Jesus was 30 at the time of the crucifixion. This clearly explains where all these extra years develop by the time of Annanius, who is repeatedly congratulated by the Byzantine George Syncellus for abandoning much of the heresy native to the city.

Annanius still dates Jesus' birth to 7 CE. With the original Alexandrian claims for Jesus only reaching his 30th year, the date for the Passion remains at 37 CE (7+30 = 37). However, it is apparent that Annanius finally came around to accepting the claims of the Gospel of John with regard to multiple years for Jesus' ministry. As such, almost all scholarly readings of the gospels note that there are five Passovers demonstrated to have occurred during Jesus' ministry. Annanius' new date of 42 CE would seem to follow from the Catholic augmentation.

So it is now apparent we need to get out from under Annanius' influence if we wish to get at the original Alexandrian understanding. Scholars like Adler assist us in this regard by constantly emphasizing that Annanius was only a later redactor of an original work by another Alexandrian monk named Panodorus, whose conclusions Syncellus vehemently opposed. Panodorus likely lived slightly before Annanius. He certainly acknowledged March 25th as the date of the Crucifixion. However he maintained the original Alexandrian interest in the first of Thouth (the date I suggest Agrippa was enthroned during the Jubilee).

Annanius undoubtedly retained most of his predecessor's original work but sought to 'correct' its indebtedness to pagan and heretical teachings. The thing which bothered Syncellus most about Panodorus' original calculations was that it 'contained not only interest in astronomy but tables of lunar and solar motion'. As we shall demonstrate shortly, this deliberate emphasis on the 19-year metonic cycle helps solidify the 37 date once and for all.

What Annanius should be credited with is perfectly reconciling the 254-day lunar calendar of the Hebrews with the traditional 360-day solar calendar of Egypt. As George Syncellus (the Byzantine scholar who preserved most of the information about these figures) notes,

> 'It should be recognized that the exposition of Annanius is more concise and more accurate and in line with the apostolic and patristic tradition; in it he assigns the divine incarnation to the end of the year 5500 and the beginning of the year 5501, and the holy luminescent day of the Resurrection in the 25th of the Roman month [of] March, the 29th of the Egyptian month of Phamenoth, which in the 532-year Paschal tables compiled by him, he also shows with the aid of learned investigations was the first formed day.' (*Sync* 35:20–7)

This new system devised by Annanius was an innovation. All that Panodorus originally established was the standard 19-year metonic cycle dating back from 284 CE – the so-called Era of Martyrs – which has become the standard Alexandrian chronological reference point. Panodorus seemed to have fixed that date in relation to a March 25th Resurrection and, furthermore, Creation on 1 Thouth. Annanius developed the system one step further and brought March 25th into harmony with all-important Christian dates (Creation, Incarnation and Resurrection) in relation to his cycle of 532 years.

Yet let's step back from Annanius' innovation. The earliest Alexandrians knew only the 19-year cycle used by Panodorus. This system was known also to Jews and Samaritans living in the city from before the time of Christ. Together they knew that every 19 years the dating of Passover necessarily repeats almost down to the day. The most holy year in the Christian calendar was the year in which the Passion fell. The next most significant was the Era of Martyrs.

It cannot be a coincidence when we discover that the year 37 falls within the 19-year cycle established by the Coptic 'anchor' of 284: 37+(19×13) = 284.

It has to be seen as the germ from which Annanius' grandiose claims about the Creation being established on March 25th grew. Thirty-seven is the only year anywhere near the traditional dates of Jesus' ministry that falls within the metonic cycle calculated from 284 CE. As such, we must assume that the tradition from which Panodorus drew his information necessarily acknowledged not only March 25th as the date of the Passion, but also 37 as its proper year.

This is how Panodorus must have reconciled his system. Diocletian ascended to the throne around August 29th, 284. This date must have been very close, if not falling exactly upon, 1 Thouth, the traditional first day of the Egyptian calendar (and still the first day of Creation, according to Panodorus). Just a few months earlier in the same year, the Church celebrated its 13th repetition of the original March 25th, 37 CE date of Easter. Thirteen has always been an unlucky number in Christianity. The persecutions which followed Diocletian's ascension must only have seemed like heavenly confirmation of that belief.

APPENDIX C

AGRIPPA AS THE MESSIAH
OF DANIEL 9:26

The word *mashiach* (Hebrew, 'anointed one' or 'messiah') appears in numerous places in the Jewish Scriptures. Nevertheless Daniel 9:26 is almost the only explicit reference to a future messiah in all the books of the prophets. Of course the rabbinic tradition no longer counts Daniel among the prophetic writings. This certainly was not always the Jewish position, as Josephus clearly testifies. The universal acceptance of Agrippa as the *mashiach* of Daniel must be reason for the change of heart. By denying Daniel a place among the prophetic writings one effectively denies Agrippa's original claim to be 'the messiah of the prophets'.

It is enough to paraphrase Daniel's oracle in the following terms. At the end of a period of 70×7 years (a concept intimately connected with the Jubilee) the Temple would be destroyed. However Daniel seems to indicate that, just before this catastrophe, the Messiah would reveal himself and then just as suddenly 'disappear'. He is specifically identified as an anointed leader, נגיד משיח. This is the title that our canonical gospels make Jesus explicitly reject (Mark 12:35–7 and the parallels). What Jesus implicitly claims for himself is something quite different. It is for this reason that we see the early Christian commentators were right in saying the figure in Daniel can't be Jesus, not only from the chronology of the 70×7 year period, but also from the use of this term *nagid* (leader).

Agrippa by contrast was almost universally acknowledged to be this figure by the rabbinic tradition. A partial list of sources would have to include the *Seder 'Olam Rabba* (mid-second century), which has official standing as the authoritative chronology, the *Yosippon* (second century, but the editing is probably late Amoraic), Samuel b. Nahmani (fourth century), pseudo-Saadiah Gaon (eleventh century), Rashi (eleventh century), Ibn Ezra (twelfth century), Ibn Daud (twelfth century), Joseph Kimchi (twelfth century), Maimonides (hostile, twelfth century), Nachmanides (thirteenth century) who also imputes this information to the Sages, [but,] as the editor of [his work] notes, his sources are unknown', Moses ha Cohen of Tordesillas (fifteenth century), Abarbanel (fifteenth century), John Calvin (hostile), Martin Luther (hostile), the author of the Metsudat David (seventeenth century), Ishac Orobio de Castro (seventeenth century), David Levi (eighteenth century).

The early Christian tradition shows remarkable agreement with the rabbinic interpretation, especially among second- and third-century Alexandrian commentators. Clement and Origen accept this understanding and Origen goes one step further. As Adler emphasizes, Origen's reliance on this 'Jewish history' is referenced elsewhere in the same work.

We should note that the wildly influential *Yosippon* text – a Hebrew version of Josephus – represents only a particular enhancement of the existing tendencies of the rabbinic tradition. In keeping with its development of themes from Daniel, Agrippa is not merely 'cut off' but 'killed'; a traditional rabbinic interpretation of *yikareth*. Instead of merely giving the speech found in Book Three of *Jewish War* and disappearing, Agrippa gives the speech and dies. The speech and Agrippa's subsequent death become a major focus of the *Yosippon*. We hear a number of Jewish characters come forward to remind their fellows about Agrippa's warning about the impending fulfillment of Daniel if he is rejected by his people. The text ends with Titus acknowledging Agrippa as the *mashiach* of Daniel.

The author's central claim is that, because of what the Jews did to Agrippa, the daily offerings in the Temple ceased. Agrippa is 'cut off', both in the sense of being killed and in the sense of having no heirs. His end is the prelude to the permanent end of the Temple service, brought about by its symbolic desecration. It was his death, along with Titus' erection of 'the Abomination' mentioned in Daniel's prophesy, that marked the absolute end of Judaism in the period. The details of the timing of the demolition don't matter very much after this. Indeed, according to the *Yosippon*, Agrippa's 'cutting off' is taken to be the real defining moment for Israel.

The *Yosippon* makes clear that Agrippa offered the nation an alternative to the suffering which beset it for the next thousand or so years. It is written with later events very much in mind. In the material that follows in the *Yosippon* about the execution of Agrippa it says, not in words, but by its allusions to words in Daniel 9 and 12, that this collective slander brought about the absolute end of the anointed line, which immediately brought about the end of the Tamid offering and then eventually the erection of the Abomination of Desolation and the destruction of the Temple for ever.

This is a most remarkable development, for the *Yosippon* places Agrippa on a timeline that reaches back to Moses and the founding of Israel. It is inferred that there was something unique about Agrippa in the history of this people whereby his being 'cut off' leads directly to abandonment of Jerusalem sanctuary. While it is never said explicitly, it has to come down to the fact that he was the awaited Messiah, and that the actions of the wicked caused his downfall, since the offerings could no longer continue.

FURTHER EVIDENCE OF THE 'REAL' INTENTION OF JESUS' MINISTRY

The Gnostic interpretation of the gospel assumed the existence of a 'messianic secret' in the narrative. This idea is reinforced in the reports of the ancient Church Fathers since the time of Irenaeus of Rome. The evidence from these and various other sources is that this 'secret doctrine' was one in which Jesus came to announce someone else as the messiah. This remains the cornerstone of early Islamic theology (which is now the near-universal faith of people from Jesus' 'part of the world'). What is more, second- and third-century witnesses within the Church preserve an identical understanding. Origen of Alexandria, one of the most influential Church Fathers of all, went so far as to argue that the understanding that 'Jesus was the Christ' was not only unknown to Jesus' disciples but was actively discouraged by Jesus himself (Origen Commentary on Matt 12:15–17).

I have assembled a sampling of some passages that have traditionally been used to support this point of view. Where possible I have given textual variants found in early Christian sources.

A. Those sayings where Jesus was understood to deny that he is the messiah:

- 'But what about you?" Jesus asked. 'Who do you say I am?' Simon Peter answered, 'You are the Christ.' *And he rebuked Peter and enjoined His disciples that they should tell no man that He was the Christ.'* [cf Matt 16:20; Lk 9:19–21; Orig. Comm. Matt 12; Tert AM 4:26]

- Those who were healed shouted out 'Thou art the Messiah, the Son of God' *and Jesus rebuked them much.* [Diat. 6:52–4; Mk 3:11–12, Lk 6:18f]

- And those that had plagues and unclean spirits, as soon as they beheld him, would fall, and cry out, and say, 'Thou art the Son of God'. *And he rebuked them and ordered them to be silent.* [Lk 4:41 from Tert. AM 4:8]

- And the demoniac cried with a loud voice and said, 'What have we to do with thee, Jesus, Son of the most high God?' … and Jesus commanded the unclean spirit to come out of the man [Mk 5:1–20; Lk 8:26–36; cf Tert AM 4:20]

- A blind man was sitting by the roadside begging. When he heard that Jesus was coming he began to shout, 'Jesus thou Son of David, have mercy on me!' … Jesus stopped and said to him, 'What do you want me to do for you?' The blind man said, 'Rabbi, I want to see.' 'Go,' said Jesus, 'your [new] faith has just healed you.' [Mk 10:46–50; Lk 18:35–40; Tert AM 4:37]

- Jesus said 'Many will come claiming that I am the Christ and will deceive many. *Do not follow them.'* [Matt 24:5 from Tert AM 4:39 cf. Lk 21:8; Mk 13:6]

- And the chief priest and teachers of the law said 'If you are the Christ, tell us.' Jesus answered, 'If I tell you, you will not believe me.' [Lk 22:67]

- Pilate asked Jesus, 'Are you the Christ?' Jesus replied 'That is what you say.' [Lk 23:3 from Tert AM 4:42 cf Matt 26:62,63]

B. Those sayings where Jesus was understood to announce someone else as the messiah:

- Jesus said '*I have come and ye have not received me: when another shall come him ye will receive.*' [Iren Haer 5:25:4 cf Jn 5:43]

- Jesus said '*The Father will give you another Paraclete to be with you forever ... The world cannot accept him, because it neither sees him nor knows him. But you know him, for he lives among you ...*' [Jn 14:16f]

- Jesus said '*I will not leave you bereaved; I will come to you in another little one.*' [Jn 14:18 Peshitta]

- Jesus said '*When I will go I will send you the Paraclete.*' [Jn 16:7 from Coptic Manichaean Kephalaia 19:7]

- Jesus said '*I will go to my Father and will send the Paraclete straightaway to you.*' [Jn 16:10 from Act Arch. 31]

- Jesus said '*If I go not away, that Paraclete shall not come to you; but if I go away, I will send Him to you.*' [Jn 16:7]

- Jesus said '*I have yet many things to say unto you, but ye cannot bear them now; but when the Paraclete is come, He will teach you all things, and will bring all things to your remembrance, whatsoever I have said unto you.*' [Jn 16:12 from Act Arch. 28]

- Jesus said '*Whosoever shall deny me and my sayings in this sinful and adulterous generation, the Son of Man also will deny him when he comes. For the Son of Man is about to come and reward each man according to his works.*' [cf Diat 23:49,50; Mk 8:38]

- Jesus said '*The Son of Man will come at an hour when you do not expect him.*' [Lk 12:40]

- Jesus said '*When the Son of Man comes, will he find faith on the earth?*' [Lk 28:8]

- Jesus said '*Whoever acknowledges me before men, the Son of Man will also acknowledge him before the angels of God.*' [Lk 12:8]

- Jesus said to his disciples '*I tell you the truth, you will not finish going through the cities of Israel before the Son of Man comes.*' [Matt 10:23]

- And Jesus said unto them, '*Verily I say unto you, There be here now some standing that shall not taste death, until they see the kingdom of God come with strength, and the Son of man who cometh in his kingdom.*' [Diat 24:1–3; Mk 9:1, Matt 16:28b]

- Jesus said '... *the Son of Man shall sit on his throne.*' [cf Mt 25:31]

- Jesus said '*Watch at all times, and pray, that ye may be worthy to escape from all the things that are to be [in Jerusalem] and that ye may stand before the Son of Man.*' [Lk 21:36]

- The high priest said to him, 'I adjure you by the living God to tell us if you are the Christ, the Son of God.' Jesus said to him '*You say that. But I say to you that after me you will see the Son of Man sitting at the right hand of power.*' [Matt 26:63, 64 Peshitta]

ENDNOTES

1 Adamantius, 'Dialogues Against the Marcionites', II, 15a. The speaker, a Catholic named Adamantius, bristles at the same suggestion associated with a heretic named Marcus of the Marcionite sect. Adamantius can be roughly paraphrased as asking 'What right has he to assert that the Messiah wrote the gospel? The gospel writer did not refer to himself as the Christ but to Jesus who he is proclaiming.'

2 In the first century there were as many as half a million Samaritans in central Palestine and about three times that many in other areas of the Roman Empire and in areas mentioned above (Crown, Alan, *The Samaritans*, Tübingen: J C B Mohr, 1989, p201). Avi-Yonah, in 'The Samaritan Revolts against the Byzantine Empire'(*EI* 4 (1956), 128) calculates that there were upwards from 300,000 Samaritans in Palestine in the fifth century after their numbers had already dwindled quite substantially. This doesn't take into account the large Samaritan diaspora outside of Palestine proper. On the influence of the Samaritans in Alexandria, their largest community outside of Palestine, see Alan Crown, *The Samaritans*, p211f.

3 *cf.* Fossum, Jarl E, *Name of God and the Angel of the Lord: Samaritan and Jewish Concepts of the Origin of Gnosticism*, Coronet Books, 1985.

4 Samaritans are typically slandered as '*Kutim*', that is, descendants of Babylonian settlers and not even blood relatives of the original patriarchs – *cf.* Lawrence Schiffman, 'Samaritans in Rabbinic Literature' in Crown *et al* (eds), *Companion*, pp198–9.

5 Justin of Neapolis, *Apology*, Chapter 26.

6 The later Catholic Gospels cast into the mouth of Jesus words like 'Do not enter any town of the Samaritans,' *Matt* 10:5.

7 See IRM Boid's forthcoming article, 'Recovering the Absolute Chronology in Abu'l-Fath'.

8 Dio Cassius tells us: 'Thus Tiberius, who possessed a great many virtues and a great many vices, and followed each set in turn as if the other did not exist, passed away in this fashion on the 26th day of March. He had lived 77 years, 4 months and 9 days, of which time he had been emperor 22 years, 7 months and 7 days. A public funeral was accorded him and a eulogy, delivered by Gaius.' Suetonius seems to disagree, saying that Tiberius: '... detained, however, by bad weather and the increasing violence of his illness, (he) died a little later in the villa of Lucullus, in the 78th year of his age and the 23rd of his reign, on the 17th day before the Kalends of April, in the consulship of Gnaeus Acerronius Proculus and Gaius Pontius Nigrinus. Some think that Gaius gave him a slow and wasting poison; others that during convalescence from an attack of fever, food was refused him when he asked for it. Some say that a pillow was thrown upon his face, when he came to and asked for a ring which had been taken from him during a fainting fit.'

9 (Josephus *Ant.* xiv 9, 2).

10 (Slavonic Josephus, Book II ix 6).

11 (Dio Cassius, Book iix 8).

12 Schwartz, Daniel R, *Agrippa I: The Last King of Judaea*, Zalman Shazar Center, 1987, with same title published as *Texte und Studien zum Antiken Judentum 23*, Tübingen: J C B Mohr (Paul Siebeck), 1990.

13 *cf.* Josephus' *Antiquities* 18:5:4, 'Salome was married to Philip, the son of Herod, and tetrarch of Trachonitis; and as he died childless, Aristobulus, the son of Herod ... married her; they had ... Agrippa.' *The Acts of the Pagan Martyrs* has a certain Isidorus identify Agrippa as having a 'Jewess named Salome' as his mother (unless scholars want to imagine that it was the Emperor Claudius so referred). The Coptic tradition similarly identifies the parents of St Mark as Aristobulus and Mary (Salome). Coins have been uncovered which identify Aristobulus and Salome as rulers of Chalcis.

14 This is a well established Jewish custom especially among Ashkenazi: a father never names his son after himself. Indeed children are never named after living relatives. The practice is very rare among Sephardic Jews where naming after paternal and maternal grandparents is preferred; *cf.* Kolach, Alfred J, *Inside Judaism*, Jonathan David Co, 2006, p362.

15 While the existing texts of Josephus stress that Herod ultimately killed both of his sons, Alexander and Aristobulos, born to the Hasmonaean princess Mariamne, there are also texts that insist they managed to escape execution and live on into a later age (cf. Antiquities 17:12). The Coptic tradition identifies St Mark as having Alexander as a wealthy Alexandrian uncle. The surviving text also preserves an Agrippa born of these two parents: 'Salome ... was married to Philip, the son of Herod, and tetrarch of Trachonitis; and as he died childless, Aristobulus, the son of

Herod, the brother of Agrippa, married her; they had … Agrippa' (Antiquities 18:5:4). Not only does the Jewish tradition necessarily assume this Agrippa to be our Marcus but the Coptic tradition also notes that St Mark was born of Aristobulos and Mary Salome. It is also noteworthy to further identify the pedigree of both Mark's Christian parents. However there also happens to be a legend repeated in many sources (Lionel Lewis, *St Joseph of Arimathea* p 120) that 'Aristobulus was the same with Zebedee, the father of St John'. This historian notes (ibid) that the legend says moreover that 'Aristobulus was Zebedee, the father of St James and St John and the husband of Mary Salome'. Indeed Lionel Lewis in his study of legends related to Aristobulus almost recognizes the significance of these ancient legends when he asks, 'may not Mary Salome be muddled with another Salome? Was Aristobulus one of the family of Herods? Aristobulus was a common name in that family. An Aristobulus (a Herod) was uncle of the saintly St Sabrina. He was the son of another Aristobulus who married Salome, daughter of Philip and Herodias of dancing fame.' The reason Lewis is drawn to the Herodian hypothesis is that many of the legends actually make reference to the connection. His arguments can be supported with various statements from the Church Fathers.

16 Lewis, *St Joseph of Arimathea* p 121.

17 Daniel Schwartz, *Agrippa*, p12.

18 This recognition that Agrippa owed his success ultimately to good fortune might explain why many of his coins feature the symbol of Tyche, the god of fortune.

19 Philo, *On the Embassy to Gaius*, 288.

20 As is suggested by the existing texts of Josephus. See my *Getting a Grip on Agrippa*, ch 3, for a detailed examination of the implausibility of the existing account. Daniel Schwartz sees the whole account as deriving from the story of the Patriarch Joseph; cf. Schwartz, *Agrippa*, pp53–5.

21 The surviving texts of Josephus get around this difficulty by having Antonia the grandmother intervene to make his imprisonment more bearable; *ibid*, p10.

22 49th years shared many of the characteristics of Jubilees; however in this case the Jubilee certainly followed the year 37 CE.

23 On the subject of the Jubilee, cf. 'Once Again, the Jubilee, Every 49 or 50 Years?', Bergsma, John S, *Vetus Testamentum*, Volume 55, Number 1, 2005, pp121–5 (5).

24 *cf.* Qumran text, I I Q, Melchizedek.

25 Knight, Christopher and Lomas, Robert, *The Hiram Machine*, Century Books, 1999.

26 A sign of how important astronomic observation in contemporary Judaism was can be found in repeated reports that the Jewish War of 66 CE was 'caused' by a streaking comet.

27 The name Markion might be a back-formation from Aramaic *Marqiyônê* (singular *Marqiyona*) meaning the followers of Mark. So there might never have been a Markion, only a Mark.

28 The very position of the billion or so Muslims whose faith inherited the part of the world Jesus came from. The idea is also present in the followers of 'little Mark', that is, Markan. See the Marcionite interpretation of Matt 11.11 / Luke 7.28 in Tertullian, where Jesus is understood to answer the question posed to him, 'Are you the one we are looking for or do we look for another?', with the answer that he was only the messenger; someone else, a 'little one', was the one they should look to (Tertullian, *Against Marcion* 4:18).

29 At its most basic level the arguments for how Jesus was 'like Moses' are the most implausible – a point emphasized in many anti-Christian polemics circulating among Jewish and Muslim writers.

30 Hegesippus, Book 5.

31 The idea is reinforced in several Gospel passages, but most notably his reading from Isaiah 60 in the Galilean synagogue (Luke 4:19).

32 *cf. Irenaeus*, Haer, Book 2:20:1. This is certainly the original Markan tradition because it is reinforced by Clement of Alexandria (*Stromata* I 21:146) and various others.

33 Mark 14:32.

34 'Gethsemane' is a meaningless Aramaic term which, even if it meant 'the oil press', could have been located just about anywhere.

35 See my *Marcus Agrippa: From Messiah to Pariah*, St Mark's Press, 2006, p56.

36 Diatessaron 50:22; Matt 27:17.

37 Even the term 'the other' is identified by Irenaeus as being a moniker to identify the 'other Christ'. Irenaeus, Haer, Book 5:25:4. He goes so far as to claim there that Jesus warned against this heretical doctrine: 'The Lord also spoke as follows to those who did not believe in Him: "I have come in my Father's name, and ye have not received Me: when another shall come in his own name, him ye will receive", calling Antichrist "the other", because he is alienated from the Lord.'

38 It is the Jews who have this custom as part of some festival. Pilate notes, 'You have a custom, that I should release unto you a prisoner.' Diatessaron 50:23; John 18:39.

39 Instead the texts have Pilate declare to the Jews that 'You have an *eida*, that I should release unto you a prisoner at the Passover: will ye that I release unto you the King of the Jews?' Eida means 'custom', yet the only custom where prisoners are released in this manner is associated with the sabbatical year.

40 Diatessaron, 50:23.

41 Philo, *An Embassy to Gaius*, 41:325.

42 Ant, XVIII, iv, 1, 2.

43 Ant, 18.85-87. See my *Messiah to Pariah*, ch. 5, for more details on this.

44 Cassius Dio and others claim that Agrippa was to receive all the lands of his grand-father. Perhaps this came later in Caligula's reign and he was confused. Daniel Schwartz makes the argument that Josephus' account that the bestowal of these lands happened in Claudius' reign doesn't make sense and the claim is undoubtedly incorrect. As such the transfer must have happened during the reign of Caligula. Schwartz, *Agrippa*, pp13–15.

45 There is an established history among the Jews for 'boy kings'. Solomon was said to have been twelve when ascending to the throne, Herod fifteen and Josiah eight.

46 For a detailed study of this text see *Philo's Flaccus, The First Pogrom: Introduction, Translation and Commentary*, by Pieter W van der Horst, Leiden: Brill, 2003.

47 As van der Horst admits, Philo '… was a witness of the events. That would seem to inspire confidence, but closer analysis of his book raises doubts.'

48 Erich Gruen (*Diaspora: Jews among the Greeks and Romans*, p. 57) notes, 'Can fault be fastened to Flaccus? It is not easy to see why the prefect already in a precarious position [with Caligula] should make matters worse for himself' by insulting his friend Agrippa.

49 Indeed van der Horst takes matters one step further when he writes, 'No one else makes mention of these dramatic events apart from Philo's somewhat later contemporary Flavius Josephus … Josephus does confirm the historicity of the event. But his relative neglect of it – eleven words in Josephus compared to over eleven thousand in Philo – makes us wonder whether the large scale of the pogrom as suggested by Philo was somewhat exaggerated.'

50 Philo, *Against Flaccus* 43.

51 *The Evangelist Mark*, HH Pope Shenouda, p9.

52 This pattern is demonstrated in the *Acts of the Pagan Martyrs* under Claudius.

53 Flaccus, 28.

54 This is echoed in later anti-Agrippan statements in the *Acts of the Pagan Martyrs*.

55 (*Phil Leg* 190). We know that they saw Caligula on two separate occasions.

56 Flaccus, 28.

57 *cf.* Gruen, *Diaspora*, p63, 'When Agrippa appeared in the city, says Philo, his arrival set off fierce emotions among those, bursting with envy.'

58 *Acts of the Pagan Martyrs*, 'My lord Caesar, what do you care for a twopenny-halfpenny Jew like Agrippa? I accuse them of wishing to stir up the entire world … They are not of the same nature as the Alexandrians, but live rather after the fashion of the Egyptian … I am neither a slave nor a girl-musician's son but gymnasiarch of the glorious city of Alexandria, but you [Agrippa] are the cast-off son of the Jewess Salome!'

59 *cf.* van der Horst, p130f.

60 *ibid*, citing Dalman, 1905.

61 Flaccus, 36f.

62 Flaccus, 116.

63 The *Succot* was also well known to be the time when the Messiah would appear for all nations, *cf*, Zechariah 14:16–21.

64 This specific Hebrew term resurfaces time and again in Judaism and Christianity as a deeply significant religious concept. As we shall see, it will ultimately solve for us the mystery of why Agrippa was hailed as 'Barabbas'.

65 'Mark and His Readers: The Son of God among Jews', *Harvard Theological Review*, 92.4 (1999): 393–408.

66 She cites Abraham's Studies in *Pharisaism* 2:202 and *Tertullian Against Marcion* 4:34, 11-14.

67 It has also been demonstrated by various New Testament scholars including Quispel that 'Mark', the author of the original gospel, developed his gospel as a kind of contemporary *Akedah* narrative.

68 Ant, 15:267.

69 *Galilee: History, Politics, People*, p72.

70 The fact that Berenice was Marcus Agrippa's sister is borne out by a number of sources. The authoritative *Greek English Lexicon of the New Testament and Other Early Christian Literature* by Walter Bauer, among others, is a good example. There it is stated as fact, not conjecture, that Berenice was married to Marcus Agrippa, her brother, and to 'others'.

71 Gospel of St Luke, 8:43–48.

72 'De imaginibus Oratio 3' (Migne, PG 94, 1369–74); Ailes 1898, pp125–6 in John Francis Wilson's *Caesarea Philippi: Banias the Lost City of Pan*.

73 This is clear from Scripture as well as rabbinical exegesis. It is specifically spelled out in the Book of Isaiah. In Chapter 2, Verses 2 and 3 we learn: '… and He shall be hallowed by all the nations. And a multitude of nations shall go forth and declare,

"Let us climb the mountain of the Lord, to the house of Jacob's God; we shall learn His ways and walk in His paths".' To confirm this, in Isaiah 11:10: 'And on that day, the Root of Eashai that rises shall be a sign to the nations, and to him the nations shall hold fast, and his fine garments shall be their honour.' In other words people who are not Jews and never were will finally come to accept the God of Israel as their own.

74 The great Jewish scholar Abraham Heschel points out that we already know what Agrippa's theological leanings were. He was a *min*, a term used in rabbinic literature to describe a type of sectarian which later would be associated with Christianity. The definition that often comes up here is that of 'Jewish Christianity' but even that is something of misnomer.

75 Here as well as elsewhere the reader should take any reference to 'little Marcus' as referring to the heretical figure ' markan' (Greek or Aramaic = 'little Mark') mentioned by the Church Fathers.

76 Cassio Deo, *Roman History* LXVI 19.

77 Morton Smith, *Clement of Alexandria and a Secret Gospel of Mark*, Harvard Univ Press, 1973.

78 Adamantius, Dialogue Book 2 15b, p93.

79 The gospel was written by Mark long after Jesus had been crucified. Most scholars put the date of its appearance at around the time of the destruction of the Jewish Temple. The author of the text has Jesus repeatedly emphasize that it will take some time for his words to crystallize into something approaching the literary work with which we are now familiar. He speaks of the eventual coming of a 'Paraclete' (a Jewish title of the Messiah) who would 'remind them of his words' in some future age. In other words 'the Gospel' strictly speaking was not established with Jesus; it would only come some time after Christ's resurrection.

80 *cf. The Coptic Doxology of St Mark.*

81 Marqe's writings are filled with kabbalistic explanations like this. While such an approach is typically viewed as utterly nonsensical among traditional Western scholars, they were the backbone of the Markan tradition in Samaria, Alexandria and throughout the world, as Irenaeus and Clement acknowledge.

82 Neubauer, A, 'Chronicle Samaritaine etc.' *Journal Asiatique* 14 (1869) p404.

83 See Boid's article on a first- or second-century dating for Marqe.

84 David Magie, *Augustan History*, London and Harvard 1932.

85 A similar story comes from the fifth-century Christian historian Socrates Scholasticus, who says that when the Serapium was finally destroyed after Christianity

became the state religion of the Roman Empire the faithful were 'amazed' to discover that Christian crosses adorned the inside of the pagan shrine – i.e. the ankh.

86 The point is already made by Celsus of Rome (c.140 CE) when he identifies 'the Harpocratians of Salome' as a well-known sect from the city. Many have connected this community to the supposed 'heresiarch' Carpocrates, who is also from Alexandria. His adherents are the first to be identified as 'Gnostics'.

87 It is very unfortunate that this term is typically translated as 'word'. This is mostly due to the Latin translation, which is completely off the mark. As Erwin R Goodenough says of the Vulgate's use of *verbum*, 'Of all the scores of nuances in the Greek term, that is one of the few meanings which *Logos* never has.'

88 *On Dreams* 1:227–300.

89 The presence of the term *Memra* in the Targumic literature in no way proves that all Jews acknowledged the existence of a 'Creative Word'.

90 There are numerous parallels between the mysticism of Philo and the kabbala.

91 'He has power over the Holy Spirit and causes his adherents to receive grace and prophecies.' Of Marcus' followers he suggests: 'They proclaim themselves as being "perfect", so that no one can be compared to them with respect to the immensity of their knowledge … They assert that they themselves know more than all others, and that they alone have imbibed the greatness of the knowledge of that power which is unspeakable.

92 *Irenaeus*, Haer, 14:1.

93 Clearly this means he is the 'Christ' to his many followers, but Irenaeus makes it plain that he is seen as the 'antichrist' to Christians of the Roman tradition.

94 Clement makes it plain that even he will not reveal everything he knows, saying: '*Not all true things are to be said to all men.*' Clement himself was eventually removed from office and forced to flee Alexandria.

95 The same story appears in various other forms in the rabbinic tradition. The Mekhilta de Rabbi Shimon, Yitro, to *Exodus* 20:5 which preserves it as: 'The elder Agrippa asked Rabbi Gamaliel: There is no jealousy unless there are rivals, as it is said, "Know this day and consider it good in your heart that he is God [… and there is no other]" (*Deut* 4:39). [Gamaliel] replied: "There is no jealousy not for a superior and not for a peer but for an inferior."'

96 This is how pages of books are numbered, how chapters are numbered, and so on. 954 would be TT (400+400) Q (100) N (50) D (4). Psalm 134 is QLD (100+30+4). Imagine Roman numbers using the whole alphabet, and with no subtractions.

97 Anatolê does NOT mean the direction of east unless the context suggests it. It means the newly risen sun, or otherwise the first appearance of anything. It only

means the east in the phrase *anatolê hêliou*, literally 'the appearance of the sun', and even then only with the right preposition in front. The word can mean the time or point of rising of a constellation over the horizon; the Ascendant (as an astrological term); the first half of the morning; teeth coming through; the first sprouting of new grass above ground; the first appearance of the headwaters of a river above ground.

98 It means the place where someone is before any movement. It would be used to speak of a cat pouncing from a waiting position. Jastrow gives the example of someone saying that money from the treasury is to be counted in his presence here in the treasury, rather than being taken out and then counted in his presence. These words in Zechariah, combined with the concept of the return of Moses, lie behind the words in John 7:27, 'When the Messiah comes, no-one will know where he comes from'.

99 Even this is still slightly paraphrastic. It is literally 'he will rise from under himself'.

100 It has long been noted by scholars of Philo of Alexandria that he refuses to explain Isaac's symbolism in the story of the *Akedah*. Could it be that he doesn't want to reveal the contemporary connection to his cousin Marcus?

BIBLIOGRAPHY

Bargès, J, 'Dissertation sur l'inscription hebraïque de la chaire de saint Marc à Venise', *Annales de philosophie chrétienne*, 3e série, t III, 1880, p 222 ff

Bauer, Walter, *Orthodoxy and Heresy in Earliest Christianity*, translated by a team from the Philadelphia Seminar on Christian Origins and edited by Robert A Kraft and Gerhard Krodel, Fortress Press, Philadelphia, 1971.

Ben Hayyim, Ze'ev. *Tibat Marqe: A Collection of Samaritan Midrashim*, Jerusalem, Israel Academy of Sciences and Humanities, 1988 (Hebrew). (See review in *The Jewish Quarterly Review* LXXXII, Nos 3–4, January–April, 1992, pp 515–18

Ben-Hayyim, Ze'ev, *The Literary and Oral Tradition of Hebrew and Aramaic amongst the Samaritans*, vols 1–2: *The Grammatical, Masoretical, and Lexicographical Writings of the Samaritans*, critically edited with Hebrew translation, commentary and introduction, Jerusalem, 1957

Ben-Hayyim, Ze'ev, *The Literary and Oral Tradition of Hebrew and Aramaic amongst the Samaritans*, vol 3 part 1, p 195: *Recitation of the Law*, Jerusalem, 1961

Boid, I R M *Principles of Samaritan Halachah*, Leiden, 1989, Or. cloth. XIV

Boid, I R M 'Use, Authority and Exegesis of Mikra in the Samaritan Tradition', M J Mulder, ed, *Mikra*, Assen, 1988, pp 595–633

Blocker, Wade, *Hegesippus*, translated from Latin into English (online). Project on Ancient Cultural Engagement, 2005

Boismard, M E, *Le Diatesseron: De Tatien à Justin*, Gabalda, Paris, 1992

Brown, S, 'Critical edition and translation of the ancient Samaritan Defter (i.e. liturgy) and a comparison of it with early Jewish liturgy', 1954–1955, unpublished PhD thesis, Leeds

Bundy, David, 'Marcion and the Marcionites in early Syraic apologetics', *Muséon* 101 (1988), pp 21–32

Bundy, David, 'The Anti-Marcionite Commentary on the Lucan Parables (Pseudo-Ephrem A)', *Muséon* 103, 1990, pp 111–23

Burmester, O H E *The Egyptian or Coptic Church: A Detailed Description of Her Liturgical Services and the Rites and Ceremonies Observed in the Administration of Her Sacraments*, Cairo (no publisher), 1967.

Butcher, E L, *The Story of the Church of Egypt*, 2 vols, London, 1897, reprint AMS

Chaillot, C, *The Coptic Orthodox Church, A brief introduction to its life and spirituality*, Inter-Orthodox Dialogue, Paris, 2005

Cohen, Shaye J D, *Josephus in Galilee and Rome: his vita and development as a historian*, Brill, Leiden, 1979

Cowley, Arthur E, *The Samaritan Liturgy*, Oxford University Press, 1909

Crown, Alan D, *A Bibliography of the Samaritans*, Scarecrow Press, 2nd edition, 1993

Crown, Alan D, Reinhard Pummer and Abraham Tal (eds) *A Companion to Samaritan Studies*, J C B Mohr (Paul Siebeck), Tübingen, 1993. Includes article by Purvis: 'Pseudipigrapha – OT, and the Samaritans', pp 194–96

Crum, Walter E, *A Coptic Dictionary*, Clarendon, Oxford, 1939

Davis, S, *The Early Coptic Papacy, the Egyptian Church and its leadership in Late Antiquity*, American University in Cairo Press, Cairo, 2004

Detering, Hermann, *Der Gefaelschte Paulus (Paul Falsified): Das Urchristentum Zwielicht*, Patmos, Dusseldorf, 1995

Detering, Hermann, 'The Synoptic Apocalypse (Mark 13/par): A Document from the Time of Bar Kochba', *JHC* 7/2, Fall, 2000, pp 161–210

Detering, Hermann, 'The Dutch Radical Approach to the Pauline Epistles', *JHC* 3/2, Fall, 1996, pp 163–93

Dorigo, Wladimiro, 'La cosidetta cattedra di San Marco', *Venezia Arti*, 1989, no 3, pp 5–13

Drijvers, H J W, 'Marcionism in Syria: Principles, Problems and Polemics', Special edn of *The Second Century*, vol 6, 1987/88, pp 129–91

Epstein, Rabbi Dr Isidore (ed), *The Babylonian Talmud*, translated into English with notes, glossary and indices, Soncino Press, London, 1935–48

Gaborit-Chopin, G, 'Throne-reliquary (the Sedia di San Marco)', *The Treasury of San Marco*, Venice (catalogue), Milan, 1984, pp 98–105

Gardner, Iain *The Kephalaia of the Teacher: The Edited Coptic Manichaean Texts in Translation with Commentary*, E J Brill, Leiden, 1995

Grabar, André, 'La Sedia di San Marco à Venise', *Cahiers Archéologiques* VII, 1954, pp 19–34

Grabar, André, 'Trono-reliquario di albastro calcareo detto "sedia di S. Marco"', Hahnloser, H R *Il Tesoro di San Marco*, vol 2 *Il Tesoro e il Museo*, pp 19–34, Florence, 1971

Grant, Robert M, 'Rival Theologies: Gnosticism, Marcion, Origen,' Arnold Joseph Toynbee, (ed), *The Crucible of Christianity*, London, 1969, pp 316–30

Greenlees, Duncan *The Gospel of the Gnostics*, Theosophical Publishing House, Adyar, Madras, India, 1958

Greenlees, Duncan *The Gospel of the Prophet Mani*, Theosophical Publishing House, Adyar, Madras, India, 1958

Harrington, Daniel J, 'The Reception of Walter Bauer's Orthodoxy and Heresy in Earliest Christianity During the Last Decade', *Harvard Theological Review* 73, 1980, pp 289–98

Hengel, Martin, *The 'Hellenization' of Judaea in the First Century after Christ*, CSM Press, London; Trinity Press International, Philadelphia, 1989

Hengel, Martin, *The Pre-Christian Paul*, Trinity Press International, 1991

Hoffmann, R Joseph, *Marcion, On the Restitution of Christianity: An Essay on Radical Paulinist Theology in the Second Century*, Scholars Press, 1984

Isaac, Benjamin, *The Limits of Empire: The Roman Army in the East*, Oxford University Press, 1990.

Isser, Stanley, *Abu'l Fath*, Vilmar edition, p 82f: 'The Dustan Sect'

Jastrow, M, *Dictionary of the Targumim, The Talmud Babli and Yerushalmi*, Pardes Publishing House, Inc, 1950

Josephus, Flavius: Complete Works, translated by William Whiston, Kregel Publications, Grand Rapids, 1960

Kamil, J, *Christianity in the Land of the Pharaohs, The Coptic Orthodox Church*, Routledge, London and New York 2002

Klimkeit, Hans-Joachim, *Gnosis on the Silk Road: Gnostic Texts from Central Asia*, Harper, San Francisco, 1993

Kokkinos, Nikos, 'The Herodian Dynasty: Origins, Role in Society and Eclipse', *Journal for the Study of the Pseudepigrapha* Supplement Series 30, Sheffield Academic Press, Sheffield, 1998

Kokkinos, Nikos, 'Justus, Josephus, Agrippa II and his Coins', *Scripta Classica Israelica* 22, 2003, pp 163–80

Knox, John, *Marcion and the New Testament*, University of Chicago Press, 1942; reprinted 1980

Landau, Tamar, 'Out-Heroding Herod: Josephus, Rhetoric, and the Herod Narratives', *Ancient Judaism and Early Christianity* 63, Brill, Leiden, 2006

Landman, Rabbi Isaac (ed), *The Universal Jewish Encyclopedia*, The Universal Jewish Encyclopedia, Inc, New York, 1939–43

Le Hir, André, 'La Chaire de saint Marc', *Etudes religieuses d'histoire et de littérature*, 1870, 4e série, t V, p 672 ff

Leiman, Sid, *The Canonization of Hebrew Scripture: The Talmudic and Midrashic Evidence*, 2nd ed, Connecticut Academy of Arts & Sciences, New Haven, 1991

Lewis, Lionel S, *St Joseph of Arimathea at Glastonbury*, James Clarke, London, 1955

Lieu, Samuel N C *Manichaeism in Mesopotamia & the Roman East*, E J Brill, Leiden, 1994

MacDonald, John, *Memar Marqah*, 2 vols, Topelmann, Berlin, 1963

MacDonald, John, *The Theology of the Samaritans*, London/Philadelphia, 1964

MacDonald, John, 'The Beginnings of Christianity According to the Samaritans', *New Testament Studies* 18, 1971–72, pp 54–80, introduction, text, translation and notes by John Macdonald, commentary by A J B Higgins

MacDonald, John, 'The Theological Hymns of Amran Darah', *The Annual of the Leeds University Oriental Society* 2, 1959–61, pp 54–73

Mead, G R S, *Fragments of a Faith Forgotten*, London and Benares, 1900; 3rd ed 1931

Meeks, Wayne, 'The Prophet-King: Moses Traditions and the Johannine Christology', Supplement to *Novum Testamentum*, Brill, Leiden, 1967

Meinardus, Otto, *Two Thousand Years of Coptic Christianity*, AUC Press, Cairo, 2002

Meinardus, Otto, *Monks and Monasteries of the Egyptian Deserts*, American University in Cairo Press, Cairo, 1992

Mitchell, C W S, *Ephraim's Prose Refutations of Mani, Marcion, and Bardaisan*, volumes I and II, completed by A A Bevan and F C Burkitt, Williams & Norgate, 1921

Montgomery, James A, *A Critical and Exegetical Commentary on the Book of Daniel. International Critical Commentary*, T and T Clark, Edinburgh, 1973.

Montgomery, James, *The Samaritans, the Earliest Jewish Sect: their history, theology and literature*, Philadelphia, 1907; reprinted New York, 1968, with a new introduction by Abraham S Halkin

Netzer, E and Weiss, Z, 'Byzantine Mosaics at Sepphoris: New Finds', *Israel Museum Journal*, 10, 1992

Neusner, Jacob, 'Oral Tradition and Oral Torah: Defining the Problematic', J Neusner (ed), *Method and Meaning in Ancient Judaism*, Scholars Press, Missoula, 1979, pp 59–78

Neusner, Jacob, *The Oral Torah: the sacred books of Judaism: An Introduction*, Harper & Row, San Francisco, 1986

Neusner, Jacob, *Introduction to Rabbinic Literature*, Doubleday, New York, 1994

Neusner, Jacob, *The Midrash: An Introduction*, J Aronson, Northvale, NJ, 1990

Neusner, Jacob, *The Mishnah: An Introduction*, J Aronson, Northvale, NJ, 1989

Pagels, Elaine H, *The Gnostic Paul: Gnostic Exegesis of the Pauline Letters*, Trinity Press International, Philadelphia, 1975

Partrick, Theodore Hall, *Traditional Egyptian Christianity: A History of the Coptic Orthodox Church*, Fisher Park Press, Greensboro, NC, 1996

Pearson, B and J E Goehring, *The Roots of the Egyptian Christianity*, Philadelphia Press, 1986

Petrement, Simone, *A Separate God: The Christian Origins of Gnosticism*, Harper, San Francisco, 1990

Price, Robert M, *Deconstructing Jesus*, Prometheus Books, Amherst, NY, 2000

Pryke, E J, *Redactional Style in the Marcan Gospel: a Study of Syntax and Vocabulary as Guides to Redaction in Mark*, Cambridge University Press, Cambridge; New York, 1978

Pucci Ben Zeev, Miriam, 'Josephus' Ambiguities: His Comments on Cited Documents', *Journal of Jewish Studies* 57/1, 2006, pp 1–10

Quispel, Gilles, *Diatessaron and the Gospel of Thomas*, EJ Brill, Leiden, 1975

Quispel, Gilles, 'Marcion and the text of the New Testament', *Vigiliae Christianae* 52.4 (1998), pp 349–60

Räisänen, Heikki, *Marcion, Muhammad and the Mahatma: Exegetical Perspectives on the Encounter of Cultures and Faiths*, The Edward Cadbury Lectures at the University of Birmingham, 1995/96

Ratzinger, Cardinal Joseph, *Many Religions, One Covenant: Israel, the Church, and the World*, Ignatias Press, San Francisco, 1999

Roberts, Colin H, *Manuscript, Society and Belief in Early Christian Egypt*, Oxford University Press for the British Academy, London, 1979

Robinson, James M (ed), *The Nag Hammadi Library in English*, Harper & Row, New York, 1977; revised edition, Harper, San Francisco, 1988

Rodkinson, Rabbi Michael L, *History of the Talmud*, revised and corrected under the editorship of The Rev Dr Isaac M Wise, New Talmud Publishing Company, New York, 1903

Rodkinson, Rabbi Michael L, *New Edition of the Babylonian Talmud*, revised and corrected under the editorship of The Rev Dr Isaac M Wise, New Talmud Publishing Company, New York, 1896–1903; 2nd ed 1918

'The Samaritan Chronicle of Abu'l Fath', the Arabic text from the manuscript in the Bodeleian Library with a literal English translation by R Payne Smith, *Deutsche vierteljahrsschrift für Englisch-theologische Forschung und Kritik*, 1863, pp 303–33, 431–59

Sandmel, Samuel, *Philo of Alexandria: An Introduction*, Oxford University Press, New York, 1979

Schaff, P *et al*, *The Ante-Nicene, Nicene and Post-Nicene Fathers*, 32 vols, Edinburgh, 1884

Schiffman, Lawrence H, 'The Dead Sea Scrolls and Rabbinic Judaism: Perspectives and Desiderata', *Henoch* 27/1–2, 2005, pp 27–33

Schur, Nathan, *History of the Samaritans (Beitrage Zur Erforschung Des Alten Testaments Und Des Antiken Judentums)*, Peter Lang Pub Inc, 2nd Rev/English edition, 1992

Schur, Nathan, *The Karaite Encyclopedia (Beitrage Zur Erforschung Des Alten Testaments Und Des Antiken Judentums, 38)*, Peter Lang Pub Inc, 1995

Schwartz, Daniel, 'Agrippa I: The Last King of Judaea' (Zalman Shazar Center, Jerusalem, 1987), *Texte und Studien zum Antiken Judentum*, vol 23, Mohr (Siebeck), Tübingen, 1990

Schwartz, Daniel, 'KATA TOUTON TON KAIRON: Josephus' Source on Agrippa II', *Jewish Quarterly Review* 72, 1981/82, pp 241–68

Schwartz, Daniel, 'Pontius Pilate's Suspension from Office: Chronology and Sources', *Tarbiz* 51, 1981/82, pp 383–98 (in Hebrew; English version in no 67)

Schwartz, Daniel, 'Herod in Jewish Sources', 'King Herod and His Period', *Idan* 5, ed M Naor, Jerusalem, 1985, pp 38–42 (in Hebrew)

Secchi, Giampietro, 'La Cattedra Alessandrina di S. Marco', Venice, 1853

Segal, J B, *Edessa, the Blessed City*, Oxford University Press, 1970

Shenouda III, Pope, S*t Mark the Evangelist: A Concise English Translation of the Fourth Edition,* trans Samir F Mikhail MD and Maged S, Mikhail, St Peter and St Paul Coptic Orthodox Church, Santa Monica

Sherman, Phillip, 'Review: Stephen M Wylen, *The Seventy Faces of Torah: The Jewish Way of Reading the Sacred Scriptures*', *Review of Biblical Literature*, 2006

Singer, Dr Isidore (managing editor), *The Jewish Encyclopedia*, Funk and Wagnalls, New York, 1901–06

Smith, Abraham, 'Tyranny Exposed: Mark's Typological Characterization of Herod Antipas (Mark 6:14–29)', *Biblical Interpretation* 14/3, 2006, pp 259–93

Smith, Morton, *Palestinian Parties and Politics*, Columbia, 1971

Smith, Morton, *The Secret Gospel: The Discovery and Interpretation of the Secret Gospel according to Mark*, Harper & Row, New York, 1973

Smith, Morton, *Jesus the Magician*, Harper & Row, New York, 1981

Smith, Morton, *The Cult of Yahweh*, 2 vols; vol 2, ch 34, 'The History of the Term "Gnostikos"', E J Brill, Leiden, 1996

Tal, Abraham, *A Dictionary of Samaritan Aramaic* (Handbook of Oriental Studies/Handbuch Der Orientalistik), Brill Academic Publishers, 2000

Throckmorton, Burton, *Gospel Parallels: A Synopsis of the First Three Gospels*, Thomas Nelson, Nashville, 1992 (fifth ed)

Tov, Emanuel, *Textual criticism of the Hebrew Bible*, Fortress Press, Minneapolis; Van Gorcum, Assen/Maastricht, 1992

Trobisch, David, *Die Entstehung der Paulusbriefsammlung: Studien zu den Anfängen der christlichen Publizistik*, NTOA, 10, Universitätsverlag, Freiburg, Switzerland; Vandenhoeck, Göttingen, 1989

Trobisch, David, *Paul's Collection of Letters: Exploring the Origins*, Fortress Press, Minneapolis, 1994; reprint: Bolivar, Quiet Waters Publications, 2001

Trobisch, David, *The First Edition of the New Testament*, Oxford University Press, New York, 2000. (Translation of the German Endredaktion des Neuen Testaments)

Trotter, R J F, *Did the Samaritans of the Fourth Century Know the Epistle to the Hebrews?* Leeds University Oriental Society, Department of Semitic Languages and Literatures, monograph series, 1, Leeds, 1961

Van Lohuizen-Mulder, Mab, 'The Cathedral of St Mark in Venice', *Babesch Bulletin Antieke Beschaving*, vol 63, 1988, pp 165–79

Von Harnack, Adolf, *History of Dogma*, vol I, trans N Buchanan, Boston, Little, 1901

Von Harnak, Adolf, *Marcion: The Gospel of the Alien God*, trans John E Steely and Lyle D Bierma, Labyrinth Press, Durham, NC, 1990

Walker, William O (Jr), 'The Burden of Proof in Identifying Interpolations in the Pauline Letters', *NTS* 33, 1987, pp 610–18

Welburn, Andrew, *Mani, the Angel and the Column of Glory: An Anthology of Manichean Texts*, Floris Books, Edinburgh, 1998

Williams, David Salter, 'Reconsidering Marcion's Gospel', *Journal of Biblical Literature* 108, 1989, pp 477–796

Wilson, J, *Banias, the Lost City of Pan*, London, 2004

Yonge, C D, *The Works of Philo: New Updated Edition*, Hendrickson, Peabody, Mass, 1993

Zahn, T *Tatian's Diatessaron (Forschungen zur Geschichte des neutestamentlichen Kanons 1)*, Erlangen, 1881

Zarrow, Edward M, 'Imposing Romanisation: Flavian Coins and Jewish Identity', *Journal of Jewish Studies* 57/1, 2006, pp 45–55

INDEX

Note: MJA refers to Marcus Julius
Agrippa

Abodah Zarah 155
'abomination of desolations' 114–15, 116,
    239
Abraham 54–6, 196, 210
    and Isaac 54–5, 56, 173–4
Acts of Pilate 230, 233
Acts of the Apostles 142, 205
Adler, William 234, 235, 238
Agrippa, Berenice, wife and sister of MJA
    3–4, 23, 65, 71, 75–85
    'House of Berenice' 81–3
    identified with St Veronica/St Berenice
        80
    love affair with Titus 4, 74, 82, 84–5, 93
    and MJA
        betrothal 160
        'incestuous' marriage 76, 129
        post-marital relationship 78
    survival of memory 118
Agrippa, Marcus Julius 1, 3–4, 13, 14–15,
    20–1
    Alexandria visit (38 CE) 3, 38, 41–8,
        52–4, 111, 131, 132, 139, 140, 158, 184,
        189, 191, 202, 220, 225
    apostolos 120
    arrest 56, 130
    attitude to Torah 118, 155–6, 162–3

authorship of Gospel of Mark 95, 113,
    115–120, 161
and Berenice
    betrothal 160
    'incestuous' marriage 76, 129
    post-marital relationship 78
birth 22
and Caligula 36, 38–9, 59, 86, 130, 131,
    225
childhood in Rome 22–3
childhood influences 138–9
as Christ 38, 47, 112–13
Christian tradition (two Agrippas)
    19–20
and Claudius 61–2, 62–3
contemporary neglect 94
controls Temple in Jerusalem 63
creates proto-monasteries 144
creative instincts 64
Davidic bloodline 53, 126
founds Catechetic School 141–2, 145
in gospels 76
heresy 150
historical setting 157–65
identified with Barabbas 30, 33, 112, 191
identified with Marqe 124, 143–4
identified with St Mark 38, 111, 118, 119,
    141–2, 154, 163
imprisonment in Jerusalem 23, 40, 56,
    57, 130

Isaac connection 55–6, 57–8
Jewish antipathy 68, 121, 116, 160–1
Jewish tradition (one Agrippa) 19
and Jewish War 64–6, 70–1, 73, 74, 81,
    91–2, 116–17, 162
Jewishness 89
kingdom expanded 63, 64
leaves Alexandria 59
lifespan 86
marginalization 4, 94, 163, 216–17
as Messiah 1, 3, 4, 21, 29, 33–4, 35, 47–8,
    53–4, 58, 88–90, 130–1, 158–9, 191
    acclamation by disciples 206
    crowning 46, 125
    of Daniel 108, 114–15, 116, 237–9
    enthronement 3, 46, 159, 182, 197,
    222, 225
    Jesus acknowledges 3, 90, 130
    'sprout' (child) 188–9, 191, 193, 194–5,
    198
    self-belief 3, 54, 86–7, 90, 113, 121, 221
    sun god 189–90, 198–200
as mystagogue 160
and Nero 64
new covenant 3, 89–90, 92–3, 157, 161,
    162–3
    failure 94, 220–1
as paraclete 205
parentage 20, 22
and the Passion 3, 29–36, 55, 56, 57–8,
    200
Pharisee opposition 19, 68–9
and Philo
    first Alexandria visit 132, 139, 158
    kinship 42, 125–6
    Messiah status 158–9, 160
as Platonic Gnostic 151, 156, 160, 161
post-kingship prevarication 40–1, 222,
    225
release from imprisonment 19, 35–6, 44,
    86, 130
resurrection date 233
rise post-37 CE 40, 159
role in Christianity 1, 89, 94, 156, 163,
    220–1
and Rome 20, 53, 74, 86, 89, 91–2, 94,

160, 202, 216–17
    scholarship 64, 89
    'St Berenice' statue 84
    Syria kingship 40
    and Throne of St Mark 21, 38, 48, 58,
    187, 191, 192–202
Agrippa Code 2, 4, 192–202
Agrippina 42, 63
Akedah ('binding' of Isaac) 54–5, 57, 187,
    191, 196
Alexander 'the Albarch' 133
Alexander the Great 16, 41, 90, 126, 133
Alexandria
    anti-Jewish revolt (38 CE) 42–6, 131,
    159, 222
    Caligula, and MJA's synagogue statues
    164
    cultural suffusion 125, 126
    Gnosticism in 154–5
    Horus-Harpocrates cult 128
    importance to Rome 41, 42, 59
    importance to world development 140
    MJA visits (38 CE) 38, 41–8, 52–4, 111,
    131, 132, 139, 140, 158, 184, 189, 191,
    202, 220, 225
    proto-monasteries 144
    Salome's origins 125–6
    Serapis cult 128–9
    St Mark's relics removed 6
    Therapeutæ 144–5
    Throne of St Mark manufactured 166,
    197
    Throne of St Mark removed 5
    see also Coptic Church; Greeks of
    Alexandria; Jews of Alexandria;
    Samaritans of Alexandria
Alexandrian Christianity
    commencement 146, 203
    cube symbolism 182
    and date of Passion 228–9, 231–6
    division with Rome 109
    Gematria 195–6
    headquarters 5
    and Irenaeus' innovations 208
    MJA forms Church 102
    MJA as Messiah 108, 116

persecution 109
reluctance to accept 'throne revelation'
    of St John 178–9
and secret Gospel of Mark 108–9
and Throne of St Mark 185
see also Coptic Church/Copts; Markan
    tradition
Alpha and Omega 177–8, 179, 180, 187
Amun 127
Andros 48
Annanius of Alexandra 234–6
Anthony, St 144
Antiochus IV Epiphanes 16–7, 114
Apis 198
'apostles' 120
Aquarius 193
Aquila 189
Aquileia 166–7
Arabs 54
Aramaic 34, 45, 55, 153, 187, 189
Archelaus, bishop of Osorhone 204–5
Aristobulus, father of MJA 20, 22, 126
    murder 22, 127
Aristotle 134
Ark of the Covenant 67
Assyrians 16
Augustan History 129
Augustus (Octavian), Emperor 18, 60

Babylonians 16, 136–7
Barabbas 30, 32, 33, 34, 57, 112
    'bar Abbas' (son of Abraham) 55–6, 191
    Carabas insult 45
    identified with MJA 30, 33, 112, 191
Benedict, St 145
Berenice, St 79–80, 83
Berenice, wife of St mark 141
Beth Horon, Battle 71–2
Biancini, Dr 8
'binding' of Isaac see Akedah
Boid, Rory 6, 12, 171–3, 181–2, 187, 191,
    192
Book of Revelation see Revelation of John
Borgian Diatessaron 105–6
Broadie, Alexander 143
Bronze Age 15

Buddhism 159
Butler, Alan 27, 192, 225
Byzantine Empire 5, 7, 168
Byzantium 53

Caesarea 71, 110
Caesarea Maritima 72
Caesarea Philippi 79, 81
Caligula 14, 64, 97, 111, 134
    accession (37 CE) 19, 27, 40, 130
    and Alexandrian synagogue idols 48,
        164
    assassination 60
    early popularity 19, 40
    extortion 59–60
    and Flaccus 42, 46–7, 48
    and MJA 20, 36, 38–9, 59, 86, 130, 131,
        159, 202, 222, 225
    perversions 39
    and Tiberius murder plots 23
    upbringing 38–9
Canaan 54
Canaanites 15
Capri 14, 23, 39, 130
Catechetic School 110, 141, 142, 144, 145,
    146, 174
Catholicism/Catholic
    accepted gospels 100
    claim Therapeutæ 146
    dominance in Europe 96
    Holy Spirit as paraclete 205
    Jubilee tradition expunged 232
    radicalism shunned 89
    twelve apostles 120
Catholic Church see Church
Cerinthus of Alexandria 179, 180
Chalcis 22
Children of Israel 48–51, 134, 137, 162
Christ
    as Alpha and Omega 177–8, 179
    MJA as 38, 47, 112–13
    throne creature symbolism 209
Christianity/Christians
    and 'abomination of desolations' 114
    Alexandrian/Roman divide 152
    of Aquileia 167

belief over proof 98
Berenice's place 78–9
central concepts 96
conformity 216
controversies 176–7
early sects 10
foretold by Daniel 114
Gnostic 150
Ireneaus' restructuring 205–6
Jesus' experience basic 57
Jewish curse 121
Messiah concept 29, 52
MJA's role 1, 89, 94, 156, 163, 220–1
modification 216, 200, 221, 225
oral traditions 149
origins 4, 9, 78, 140, 220, 226
Samaritan conversion to 11
secret at the heart 2–3
Serapis association 128–9, 131
thirteen, unlucky 236
Throne of God 210
as tool of oppression 217
true story 13
see also Alexandrian Christianity
Church (Roman, Catholic)
    assault on MJA's memory 20
    Book of Revelation accepted 179
    building of Jesus 100
    Chrestos title shunned 57
    controversies 176–7
    crucifixion details suppressed 37
    cult of St Veronica 77–8
    divorced from reality of Jesus 6
    early heresies 138
    establishment from gospels 96
    formation of power base 149
    fractured 215
    Gnostics in 151–2
    and gospels 101, 103, 104, 206
    hatred of heresy 148, 149
    Irenaeus' influence 208
    orthodoxy imposed 110
    persecutions of Eastern Church Fathers
        109–10, 174, 177
    Samaritans excluded 11

St Mark hagiography 102
true origins of Christianity suppressed
    2, 163, 226
two Agrippas tradition 19–20
and Throne of St Mark 10, 215, 226
Church Fathers 2, 12, 13, 216
    and Daniel's prophecies 115
    and date of resurrection 228, 229
    and Gospel of Mark 113, 117–18
    and gospels 97, 99–100, 105
    as heretics 156
    and 'messianic secret' 240
    need to survive 164, 216
    notion of truth 98
    perverted testimony 205
    and proto-monasteries 144, 145
    and St Berenice 77, 79, 83
    see also Eastern Church Fathers;
        Irenaeus of Lyons; Jerome; Origen
Claudius, Emperor 61–3, 64, 133, 234
Clement of Alexandria 238
    on cube symbolism 182
    excommunication 154
    Gematria knowledge 195–6
    Gnosticism 151–2, 163
    on Jesus' age at crucifixion 234
    on Mark's attitude to Messiah's timing
        119
    and Revelation of John 177, 178, 185
    on secret Gospel of Mark 108–9, 110–11
    vilification by Rome 153
Cleopatra 75–6, 126
Collins, Adela Yarbro 55–6
Commodius, Emperor 108, 206, 216
Constantine, Emperor 101, 122, 220
Constantinople 5
Coptic Church/Copts 164
    alleged Hebrew Throne inscription 170
    Chrestos 57
    current ignorance of Throne of St Mark
        185
    'Doxology of St Mark' 200
    and Mani 204–5
    Mark as Beholder of God 107, 120
    Mark as Jesus' eyewitness 106–7

Mark/MJA connection 141–2, 154
'throne' as heavenly female figure
    179–80
cosmology 24–7, 225
Council of Nicaea 101
Cyrus 16

Da Vinci Code, The 2, 219–20
Dalai Lama 159
Daniel 108, 113–15, 187, 237–9
David, House of 29, 49, 52, 85, 126
David, King 51, 53, 54
Davies, S L 30
Demetrius of Alexandria 109, 110
'demiurge' 150
Derrida, Jacques 118
Deuteronomy 87, 88–9, 119, 123, 202
diatessaron (Gospel harmonization) 100–1,
    104–5, 107–8
Diocletian, Emperor 236
Diogenes Laertes 142
Dionysius of Alexandria 174, 175, 177,
    178–9, 180, 185
Dionysus 128, 216
Dorigo, Wladimiro 180–1, 223
Duat 224

Easter 228, 229, 236
Eastern Church Fathers
    persecution 153, 177
    and super gospel 108–9
    see also Clement of Alexandria;
        Dionysius of Alexandria; Philo of
        Alexandria
Eastern Orthodox Church 154
Edomites 17
Egypt 112
    alabaster 166
    Coptic Church 107
    Hebrews in 15, 49–50
    political transformations 5–6
    religious confusion 129
    Roman prefecture 41
    St Anthony's retreat 144
    see also Alexandria
Egyptian culture 223–4

360-day calendar 223, 235, 236
    importance of Sirius 224
Egyptian Ptolemies 16
Egyptian religion
    influence on Berenice Agrippa 127–8,
        129
    marriage with Judaism 129–30
    and Throne of St Mark 179–80, 197–8,
        199–200, 201
Eleazar 196
Eliezer ben Hannania 71
Elizabeth I of England 159
Emeth 178, 187
epagomenes 223
Epiphanius, bishop of Salamis 227
Era of Martyrs 235, 236
Euschius 79
Eusebius of Caesarea 79–80, 83, 145
evangelists 96, 221
    and four creatures 168–9, 209, 211
    see also John; Luke; Mark; Matthew
Exodus 123, 158
Ezekiel 167–8, 169, 209, 211, 214

Février, Professor 169
Finnegan, Jack 227
Flaccus, Aulus Avilius 132
    and Alexandrian riots 42, 43–5, 46, 159,
        222
    arrest 46–7
    torture and execution 48, 53
    transformation into Jew-hater 41
Florus, Gessius 65

Galilee 23, 63, 65, 71, 91, 130
    cultural suffusion 127
    Herodian rule 17, 18, 69–70
    Jesus in 30
    Jewish War epicentre 69
    MJA's unpopularity 68–9
Galileo 177
Gallus, Cestius 71–2
Gematria 136–8, 195–6, 203–4
Genesis 123
    ninth vision 187, 191, 196, 201–2
Gentiles 3, 113

Gerizim, Mount 31, 32, 54–5, 56
Gethsemane 31
gnosike techne 151
gnosis 150–1, 161
Gnosticism/Gnostics 115, 131, 150–6, 163, 240
    Cerinthus 179
    Clement 110, 151–2, 163
    MJA 151, 156, 160, 161
    and Throne of St Mark 181, 196
Goliath 54
Goria clan 69
Gospel of John 101, 107, 177, 174–5, 178–9, 230
    and length of Jesus' ministry 231, 232, 234
Gospel of Luke 97, 98, 101, 107
Gospel of Mark
    abrupt ending 35, 206, 207
    date of composition 113
    and Daniel's Messiah 113–14, 116
    diatessaron parallels 105
    earliest interpretations 57
    first canonical 98–9, 104
    hidden meaning 146–7, 161
    Irenaeus' alternative ending 206, 207–8
    and Logos 134
    MJA's authorship 95, 113, 115–20, 161
    objective study 98
    original (secret) 9, 101, 103, 104–11, 112, 113–14, 135–6, 200, 204, 206–7
    parallels Matthew and Luke 97
Gospel of Matthew 97, 98, 110
gospels 95–103
    alterations 99–100, 103
    diatessarons 100–1, 104–5, 105–6, 107–8
    Irenaeus creates fourfold 105, 108, 109, 149, 176, 206
    Ireneaus' proof of fourfold 208–9
    see also individual gospels
Grabar, André 168–9
Grado 167
Greek (language) 102, 133, 148, 179, 188
Greek philosophy
    in Alexandria 140
    gnosis in 151

    as heresy 149
    and Judaism 90, 131, 133, 138, 158
    Logos 134
    MJA's understanding 131
    paralleled in scripture 143
Greeks
    Claudius' trust in freedmen 63
    provoke Jewish War 71
Greeks of Alexandria
    and anti-Jewish riots 41, 44, 45, 222
    Egyptian and Jewish hostility to 53, 158
    Egyptianization 126
    Harpocrates cult 128
    understanding of Judaism 133

Hades 198
Hadrian, Emperor 122, 129
Hagar 54
Harpocrates 128, 129
Hasidim 90
Hasmoneans 15, 17, 53, 125–6
Hebrew (language) 90, 138, 178, 179, 186–7, 188, 195
    Throne of St Mark inscription 7–8, 9, 10–11, 12, 169, 170–1, 181–2
Hebrew calendar 235
Hebrews 49–51, 137, 209
    in Egypt 15, 49–50
Heraclitus, Emperor 5, 167
heresy/heretics 148–9
    Irenaeus' attacks 149–50, 217
    Markan doctrine 150, 217, 226
Herod Agrippa 70
Herod Antipas 18–19, 22, 127
    deposition 19, 40, 130
Herod Antipater 17
Herod the Great 17–18, 46, 72, 91
Herodians 1, 65, 118, 125
    Josephus' criticism 69–70
Heschel, Abraham 118, 119
Holocaust 55
Holy Spirit 96, 205
Horsley, Richard 70
Horus 127–8, 129, 160, 199–200, 214, 216
Idumæans 17–18
Inquisition 148

Irenaeus of Lyons 163, 240
  alternative ending for Gospel of Mark
    207–8
  attacks on heretics and Gnostics 148,
    149–54, 155, 217
  creates fourfold gospel 105, 108, 109,
    149, 176, 206, 217
  and date of Passion 228, 231–2, 233, 234
  on Markan tradition 27–8, 177–8, 180,
    196
  as propagandist 218
  restructures Christianity 205–6
  and Throne of St Mark 200, 207–16
Isaac 54–5, 173–4, 190–1
  'binding' (Akedah) 54–5, 57, 187, 191,
    196
  connection with MJA 55–6, 57–8
Isaiah 52, 168, 211, 214
Ishmael 54
Isis 127, 160, 179–80, 224
Islam 107
  Jesus as herald 240
  Middle Eastern conquests 5–6
Israel 52
  founding 49, 239
  Isaac symbol of 54
  promise of redemption 196
  Samaritans 7, 9, 10
  single deity (Yahweh) 16, 138
Israeli nationalism 88

Jerome 55, 142
Jerusalem
  attack on Roman garrison 71
  civil war 72–3
  destruction (66 CE) 73–4, 162
  Jesus' arrival 30–1
  MJA's imprisonment 23, 40, 57
  return of Babylonian captives 16
  siege 73, 92
  St Mark's House 205
  tax riot deaths 65
  see also Temple of Jerusalem
Jesus
  acknowledges MJA as Messiah 90, 130
  arrest 31, 56

  arrival in Jerusalem 30–1
  built by Church 100
  in canonical gospels 96, 151
  Chrestos 57
  crucifixion 9, 12, 34, 130, 198
    date (March 23rd 37 CE) 37, 40
    Mark/MJA witnesses 3, 107, 112, 200
  in Gospel of Nicodemus 201
  as herald of Messiah 29, 56–7, 114, 203,
    240, 242–3
  as Lamb of God 58
  as Logos 134
  Mark's presence alongside 106–7, 112–13
  and Mary Magdalene 2
  as Messiah 164, 205, 208
    own denial 3, 27–9, 33, 203, 237,
    240–1
  in original gospel 9, 156
  Passion date (March 23rd–25th 37 CE)
    31, 227–36
  and Pharisees 69
  resurrection date (March 25th, 37 CE)
    40, 227–30, 231
  as sacrifice 29–30, 56, 57–8, 182, 197
  'Son of Man' 115
  and St Berenice 83
  star billing 4, 94, 163, 216–17
  Temple destruction prophecy 68, 113
  and Throne of St Mark 172–73, 182,
    192–3, 207, 208, 210, 211
  and Torah 118–19
  and Veronica's veil 77–8
Jewish insurrection (4 BCE) 18
Jewish law, and 'incestuous' marriage 76
Jewish mysticism 135, 153, 161, 178, 179
Jewish nationalism 89–90, 91
Jewish priesthood 196
Jewish synagogue mosaics 196
Jewish uprising (169 BCE) 17
Jewish War (66-73 CE) 12, 64–6, 69–74,
    81, 86, 91–2, 116–17, 133, 162
Jews
  Abrahamic descent 54, 56
  annoyed by 'Logos' 134
  antipathy to Herod the Great 17–18, 19
  antipathy to Herod Antipas 18–19

antipathy to MJA 1, 68, 116, 121, 160–1
Babylonian captivity 16, 26, 137
Birchat ha-Minim 121
centrality of Temple 68
cultural influences in Galilee 127
early history 15–16
and Gematria 136–7
Holocaust survivors (Isaacs) 55
interest in numbers 23–4, 123–4
liberate 'Barabbas' 29–30, 33–4
and 'Messiah Agrippa' 88–9, 237–9
Messiah concept 24, 29, 51–2, 87–8, 89
mistrust of Samaritans 10–11
nationalism 87–8
and Sun–Venus association 25–7
see also Pharisees
Jews of Alexandria 134
anti-Jewish riots 42–7, 132, 222
autonomy 41–2
conversion drive 53
cultural surroundings 126
delegations to Claudius 62
dependence on Rome 139
lack of power 158
MJA as Messiah 47–8, 49, 53–4, 58, 158–9, 162
Platonic/Judaic synthesis 158
Jews of Aquileia 167
'John', author of Revelation 171–3, 177, 221
identity 174–5, 178–9
knowledge of Throne of St Mark 172–3, 182–3
'John', beloved disciple 118
John, St 221
and four creatures (lion) 169, 209, 211
Jordan 196
Josephus 237
and 'abomination of desolations' 114
on 'Barabbas' release 29–30, 33
Goria clan membership 69
identifies MJA with Messiah 116–17
on MJA's age at Alexandria visit 184
on Pilate's removal from office 40, 232
part in Jewish War 65, 69–70, 72, 73
Pharisee and Zealot 91
on Titus 82–3

two Agrippas theory 19–20
on Vespasian at Caesarea Philippi 81
Jubilees 12, 24, 32, 182, 231, 232, 237
38 CE 12, 32, 46, 47, 158, 189
Judah 16, 17–18
Judaism 3, 219, 225
and 'abomination of desolations' 114
antipathy to effigies 164
and Greek philosophy 90, 131, 133, 138, 158
'hidden truths' 134–5, 146
Idumæan conversion 17–18
Jubilee cycle 12
MJA reorders 157
Roman philosophers' attacks 155
suffusion of Egyptian paganism 129–30
and ten *mitzvoth* 50
Torah interpretations 51
Judas Maccabaeus 17, 71
Judea 41, 138, 139, 219
cosmological portents 27
cultural suffusion 125
Hasmonean rule 17
Jewish uprisings 64–6, 71–3, 92, 133
Pharisees and Zealots 90–1
Ptolemaic rule 16
Roman rule 15, 17, 18, 23, 133, 161
Salome in 126
Seleucid rule 16–17
turmoil 22, 23, 216
Julius Caesar 17, 18, 75
Justin 121
Justus, Agrippa's secretary 141–2, 145

Kennedy, John F 94–5
Knight, Christopher 25, 26, 27

Lactantius 229, 230
Last Judgement 168
Last Supper 227, 230
Laws of Moses *see* Torah
Leo 193, 199
Levant 15, 16
Leviticus 123
Lion of Judah 199
Logos 134–5

Lohuizen-Mulder, Mav van 169–71
Lomas, Robert 25, 26, 27
Luke, St 221
  and four creatures (calf) 169, 209, 211

Macarius Magnes 80
Malachi 202
Malalas, John 80, 230
Mani 204–5, 206–7
Marcionites ('followers of Mark') 27–9, 31,
  33, 35 see also Markan tradition
Marcus the Gnostic (the Magician) 152–3,
  155
Mark, St 221
  absence in history 101–2, 104
  Alexandria visit (43 CE) 234
  Aquileian veneration 167
  'Beholder of God' 107
  Church 'hagiography' 102
  connection with Philo 141–2
  Egyptian monasteries 145, 146
  'enthronement' 11–12
  founds Coptic Church 107
  and four creatures (eagle) 169, 209, 211,
    213
  identified with MJA 38, 111, 118, 119,
    141–2, 154, 163
  Jewishness 113
  lifespan 12
  as light of the Sun 200
  presence alongside Jesus 106–7, 112–13
  relics 5, 6, 10, 168
  Samaritan connection 8–9, 10
Mark Anthony 75
Markan tradition
  centrality of Throne of St Mark 147, 201
  Chrestos 57
  codes and ciphers 146–7, 196
  Irenaeus on 27–8, 177–8, 180, 196
  and later heresies 226
  'monks and nuns' 146
  in Osorhone 204–5
  rejection of Revelations 174, 177
  secret flourishing 154
  unacceptable to Rome 153, 163–4
  see also Marcionites

Marque, son of Titua 121–4, 162
  identified with MJA 124, 143–4
  similarity to Philo 143–4
Marriage at Cana 106–7, 112
Mary, at empty tomb 35, 206
Mary, mother of Jesus 78
Mary, mother of John Mark 35, 102
Mary Magdalene 2
Mary Salome see Salome
Masada 74
mashiach 237, 238
Matthew, St 221
  and four creatures (man) 169, 209, 211
Maximin, Emperor 233
menachem 204
Mesopotamia 54
Messiah
  astronomical portents 26–7
  Christian conception 29, 52
  Jesus as see Jesus
  Jesus as herald 29, 56–7, 114, 203, 242–3
  Jewish conception 24, 29, 51–2, 87–8, 89
  MJA as see Agrippa, Marcus Julius
  timing of arrival 119
  tsemah and menachem 204
Mishnah 88, 120
Mithras 206, 216
Montgomery, James 122
Moses 49–50, 67, 87, 88, 134, 158, 162, 239
  as Apostle 120
  numerological equivalence to Marqe
    124
  and ten Commandments 50
  see also Torah
mystery religions 128

Nag Hammadi texts 99, 112
Nebuchadnezzar 16
Nero 63–4, 72
  and MJA 64
  suicide 73
Netzer, E 196
new covenant 3, 51, 203
  failure 94, 220–1
  MJA's 3, 89–90, 92–3, 157, 161, 162–3
New Testament 56, 69 see also gospels

Newton, Isaac 137–8
Nicetas, bishop of Aquileia 167
Nicodemus, Goria patriarch 69
Nicodemus, Gospel 34, 201
Nile, River 223–4
nomina sacra 100
nous 161, 189
Numbers 123

Old Testament 15, 36, 137–8, 151, 159, 210
 prophets and prophecies 24, 29, 38,
  51–2, 87, 157, 202
 see also individual prophets
Origen of Alexandria 110, 116, 122, 174,
 185, 238, 240
Osiris 127, 198, 199, 224
Osiris–Dionysus cults 128
Osorhone 204–5

Pachomius 145
Palestine 3, 4, 64, 110
 Children of Israel 50
 cult of St Berenice 79
 cultural environment 119–20
 'historic' 15
 Jewish nationalism 87–8
 Jewish vested interest 69
 MJA's rule 63
 synagogue mosaics 196
Paneas (Banyas) 66, 79, 81, 83
Panodorus, monk 235, 236
paraclete (comforter) 203–5
Pascal, Blaise 136
Passion
 Berenice's presence 78, 118
 date (March 23rd–25th 37 CE) 31,
  227–36
 Mark's presence 107
 Mary Salome's presence 78
 MJA and 29–36, 55, 56, 57–8
 Throne of St Mark 'picture book' 201
Passover 32, 56, 232, 234, 236
 and date of Resurrection 227–30
Patriarchs of Grado 167
Paul, St 102
Pentateuch 143

Pentecost 205
Peræa 18, 64
Persians 5, 16
Peter, St 102, 113
Pharisees 69, 90–1, 118–19, 139
 downfall 92, 162
 opposition to MJA 69, 91, 161
Philip, Uncle of MJA 40, 63
Philo of Alexandria 52, 132–9, 203
 acquaintance with St Mark 140–1
 on Alexandrian uprising 41, 42–6, 47,
  222
 Christianization 145
 creates proto-monasteries 144
 Gematria knowledge 137, 195, 204
 heresy 150
 influence on first gospel 135–6
 interest in Greek philosophy 131, 133,
  134, 138, 150
 and Judaism 134, 138, 146
 and 'Logos' 134–5
 and MJA
  first Alexandria visit 132, 139, 158
  kinship 42, 125–6
  as Messiah 158–9, 160
 solar allegory 190–1
 similarity to Marqe 142–4
 on Therapeutæ 144–5
Philostorgius 79
Pilate, Pontius 27, 30, 32, 33, 34
 removal from office 40, 232–3
Plato 134, 138, 142, 148
 gnosis and Gnosticism 150–1, 152, 155,
  156, 160, 189
Platonism 131, 150
Polycarp 105
Pompey the Great 17
Praetorian Guard 60, 61, 93
priesthoods 25
Primigenio, Patriarch 166
Promised Land 12, 51
proto-monasteries 144
Ptolemy I 16, 126, 133, 138

'Q' gospel 98–9
Qumran scrolls 99, 112, 120, 170

Reformation 97
reliquaries 168
resurrection date (March 25th, 37 CE) 40,
    227–30, 231
Revelation of John 209, 211, 213, 214
    disputes over 174–5, 177–9
    and Throne of St Mark 168, 169, 171–4,
        175, 182–3, 186, 191, 210, 215
Roman Empire 10, 22, 82, 85, 107
    absorbs Judea 15, 18
    Christianity adopted 217
    under Claudius 62, 63
    disintegration 216
    Mithras cult 206
    Tiberius' disinterest 14
Rome (city) 4
    appearance of gospels 100
    Caligula's assassination 60
    Irenaeus in 105
    MJA in 22–3, 62
    Philo in 132
    rabbinic authorities summoned 155
    Salome in 130
    St Mark in 102
    Triumph parodies 46
Rome (power)/Romans
    arrest of Flaccus 46–7
    cosmological knowledge 27
    distrust of Berenice 75–6
    in Egypt 5
    and Herod the Great 17, 18
    importance of Alexandria 41, 42, 59
    and Jewish War 66, 70, 71–4, 91–2
    MJA and 20, 53, 74, 86, 89, 91–2, 94,
        160, 202, 216
    rule in Alexandria 53, 62, 133, 139
    rule in Judea 15, 18, 216
    significance of the eagle 202
Ronen, Avraham 170–1

Salome (Mary Salome, mother of MJA)
    20, 22, 23, 39, 118, 138
    Alexandrian upbringing 125–6
    ambition for MJA 44, 130, 131, 138,
        159–60
    cultural influences 126–7

Horus cult 159–60
    presence alongside Jesus 77, 78
    reverence for Isis and Horus 127–8, 129,
        131, 159–60
Samaria 121
Samaritan Jubilee (38 CE) 44, 46, 47, 189
Samaritan script 8, 11, 12, 182
Samaritanism 219
Samaritans 7–8, 9–10, 38
    accept MJA as Messiah 58, 121–2, 162
    Abrahamic descent 56
    calendar 23–4
    Christian converts 10, 31
    contempt for Temple 68
    exclusion from Church 11
    Jewish mistrust 11–12
    and Marque 106, 121–4, 142–3, 162
    Messiah conception 51
    Mount Gerizim heartland 55
Samaritans of Alexandria 10, 41, 47, 90
    accept MJA as Messiah 58, 162
    anti-Jewish riots 44
    conversion drive 53
Sarah, wife of Abraham 54
Sargon II 136
Schwartz, Daniel 19, 232
Scorpio 193
Seleucids 16–17, 71
Sepphoris 196
Serapis cult 128
    link with Christianity 128–9, 131
Sermon on the Mount 112
Set 127
seven, significance of 24
Severus, Septimius, Emperor 152
Severus, St 179
Severus of Al'Ashmunein 204–5
Shabbath Tractate 120
Shakespeare, William 76
Shenouda III 141–2, 154
Sicarii 72
Siegel, George 98
Simon, Great High Priest 17
Simon bar Goria 72
Sinai 50
Sirius 224, 225

Smith, Morton 151, 152, 189
Socrates 151
Solomon 16, 68
'Son of Man' 115
Sopdet 224
Sozomen 79
St Mark's Basilica, Venice 6, 166, 219
St Mark's Church, Alexandria 5
Stations of the Cross 77
Suetonius 93
Sun
    solar allegory 196, 189–90, 198–200, 201
    and Sirius 224
    Sun–Venus association 25–7, 159
Symmachus 189
Syncellus, George 233–4, 235
Synoptic Gospels 98, 118
Syria 15, 40, 63

Tabernacles (*Succot*) 47–8
Tacitus 14
Talmud 120–1, 155–6
Tatian 101
Taurus 193, 195, 198
Teachings of Marque, The 123
Temple in Jerusalem
    'abomination of desolations' 114, 116,
      239
    destruction (586 BCE) 16
    destruction (70 CE) 3, 4, 19, 29, 73–4,
      92, 120, 122, 162, 237
    Edomite looting 17
    effects of completion 65
    First (Solomon's) 16, 17, 138
    Herod's rebuilding 17
    Holy of Holies 67
    Jesus' prophecies 113
    MJA controls 63
    polarized opinion 67–8
Temple Mount 73
Ten Commandments 50–1, 118, 119, 121,
  162
Theodore (Clement's correspondee) 109,
  110
Therapeutæ/Therapeutrides 144–6
Third Mithridatic War 15

Throne of God 52, 167–8, 169, 210, 211
Throne of St Mark 2, 5–13, 46, 47, 48, 157,
    165, 221, 225–6
    Agrippa Code 192–202
    antiquity 6, 10
    bush (fruit /leaves) 171–5, 185–91, 192,
      197
    and Cerinthus 179–80
    dimensions 167, 180–1, 223–5
    fifty stars 182
    four creatures 167–8, 168–9, 193,
      197–200, 209–16
      astrological associations 193
      bull 195, 212–13, 193, 197–8, 211
      eagle 193, 195, 199–200, 201–2, 211,
       213–16
      as evangelists 168–9, 209, 211
      lion 193, 198–9, 211–12
      man 193, 198, 213
      symbolizing MJA 197–200, 211
    four rivers of Paradise 182
    Hebrew/Samaritan inscription 7–8, 9,
      10–11, 12, 169, 170–1, 181–2
    history 5–6, 166–7
    importance 10, 13, 147, 226
    Irenaeus and 200, 207–16
    Mani and 204–5, 207
    'medallion' 168, 181, 199
    and MJA 21, 38, 48, 58, 187, 191,
      192–202
    palm trees 194–6, 198
    ram 56, 58, 173–4, 182, 190–1, 196–7
    reliquary theory 184
    and Revelation of John 168, 169, 171–4,
      175, 182–3, 186, 191, 210, 215
    revelation of secret 219–20
    as smoking gun 203
    studies 168–71
Tiberias 18, 64, 68
Tiberius, Emperor 14, 18, 41, 42, 130, 230
    death 14, 19, 23, 26, 27, 40, 130, 159
    'minnows' 39
    and St Veronica 77
Tiberius, Procurator of Judea 133
Titus, Emperor 81, 124, 133, 238, 239
    accession 84–5

change of character 93
Josephus on 82–3
love affair with Berenice 4, 74, 82, 84–5, 93
storms Jerusalem 73
Torah (Laws of Moses) 3, 24, 47, 51, 54, 118, 120, 121, 196
    Greek translation 133
    Marqe's interpretation 123
    MJA's attitude 118, 155–6, 162–3
    Philo and 134, 138
Trajan, Emperor 86
tribes of Israel 12
Trobisch, David 99, 100, 105
Tsedaka, Benny 8
tsemah 188–9, 194–5, 204
Tulida 124
Tyre 82

Vatican 10
Venice 2, 3, 6, 10, 47, 166, 167, 219, 226

Veniti 166
Venus–Sun association 25–7, 159
Veronica, St 77–8, 80
Vespasian, Emperor 72, 73, 81, 84, 133
Vitellius 232

Weiss, Z 196
Wendland, Paul 30
Wilson, John Francis 80, 82, 83–4
'Wisdom' 135
Works of the Anti-Nicene Fathers 101

Yahweh 138
Yosippon 238–9

Zealots 65–6, 72, 74, 91, 92, 161, 162
Zechariah 87, 187, 190, 213
    ninth vision 188–9, 191, 192–3, 195, 197, 202, 204
Zeus 114
Zodiac 25, 193, 195